Auschwitz and After

Auschwitz and After

Charlotte Delbo

Translated by Rosette C. Lamont
With an introduction by Lawrence L. Langer

Yale University Press
New Haven and London

Published with assistance from the Charles A. Coffin Fund.
Frontispiece and jacket photograph by Eric Schwab.

Designed by Deborah Dutton.
Set in Bembo type by Marathon Typography Service, Inc., Durham, North
Carolina.
Printed in the United States of America by Vail-Ballou Press, Binghamton, New
York.

Library of Congress Cataloging-in-Publication Data
Delbo, Charlotte.
    [Auschwitz et après. English]
    Auschwitz and after / Charlotte Delbo ; translated by Rosette C. Lamont ; with
an introduction by Lawrence A. Langer.
        p.   cm.
    ISBN 0-300-06208-7 (cloth)
            0-300-07057-8 (pbk.)
    1. Delbo, Charlotte.   2. Auschwitz (Poland : Concentration camp)   3. World
War, 1939–1945—Personal narratives, French.   4. Political prisoners—France—
Biography.   I. Title.
D805.P7D41613   1995
940.53'174386—dc20   94-38669
                                                                            CIP

A catalogue record for this book is available from the British Library.

The paper in this book meets the guidelines for permanence and durability of the
Committee on Production Guidelines for Book Longevity of the Council on
Library Resources.

10   9   8   7   6

Contents

Translator's Preface

Translating Charlotte Delbo's trilogy proved to be a sublime duty. As I was working I recalled her impassioned tone as she explained that she had to transmit the knowledge she acquired in *l'univers concentrationnaire*. "Je veux donner à voir!" she kept on repeating. She was referring to the moral obligation she felt to raise the past from its ashes, to carry the word (the title of one of her plays). One might call her entire *œuvre* "a literature of conscience." In French *conscience* would signify both conscience and consciousness. It is Delbo's acute consciousness which makes her a privileged witness. However, to bring the word back requires a great deal of restraint. In order to bear and bare the unbearable, Charlotte struggled to render her style unobtrusive, almost transparent. Because she wrote from the extreme edge of being, she sought never to attract attention to the manner in which she expressed herself. How she said was important only because of what she had to say. The Holocaust experience, which she described as "the greatest tragedy of the twentieth century," spoke through her as its messenger.

I would like to take this opportunity to express my profound gratitude to two friends who made this work possible. My former student, Dr. Cynthia Haft, who wrote her Ph.D. dissertation under my direction at the CUNY Graduate School, introduced me to Charlotte in Paris. I recall thinking as soon as I saw this tall, proud, beautiful woman: "She looks the way I envision Electra." Later I was to find out how important Jean Giraudoux's *Electra*, staged by her great master and friend, Louis Jouvet, was to her. In fact, the final poem of the trilogy, the one she entitles "Envoi," refers directly to this play.

Charlotte's close friend, the actress Claudine Riera Collet, Delbo's literary executrix, facilitated all the transactions that led to this publication. She also provided the photograph for the frontispiece and showed me some important papers and documents. Although Claudine did not share the camp experience with Charlotte, they became close, loving friends. After Charlotte's death from cancer, Claudine and I grieved together, and we also made plans to ensure that our friend's message would reach future generations so that, as Charlotte kept on saying, "such a horror would not happen again."

Introduction by Lawrence L. Langer

Charlotte Delbo is still little known in this country, and not very well known in her own, even though her memoir about her experience in Auschwitz and Ravensbrück and her return to France after her liberation shows the pen and imagination of the genuine artist. She writes not as a heroine but as a victim. Her language is exquisite, but the pain of her memories is not, and this may help to explain why her audience has never been very large.

She was born in Vigneux-sur-Seine, near Paris, in 1913. As a young woman, she worked as assistant to the theater impresario Louis Jouvet and was on tour in South America with his theatrical company when the Germans occupied her country in 1940. After learning that the Gestapo had executed an acquaintance, she decided to return home, and in November 1941, in spite of Jouvet's strong opposition, she made her way back to Paris via Portugal and Spain and the unoccupied zone of France to rejoin her husband, Georges Dudach, who was working with the resistance.

In March 1942 French police arrested them in their apartment, where they were editing and producing anti-German leaflets. Delbo believed that the police had followed the courier who had come to deliver the leaflets. The French turned Delbo and her husband over to the Gestapo, who imprisoned them. Georges was executed by firing squad in May, after Charlotte was permitted to visit him in his cell (a scene she returned to often in her writing, most notably in a brief dramatic piece, *Une Scène jouie dans la mémoire*). Delbo remained in prisons in France until the end of 1942, then in January 1943 she was sent to Auschwitz from Romainville in a convoy of 230 French-women, most of whom were not Jewish but were involved in underground or anti-German political activity. Only forty-nine returned. She offers an account of this journey, together with brief biographies of all but one of the deportees and some interesting statistical appendices on the relationship between survival and age, profession, education, and political affiliation, in a fascinating work called *Le convoi du 24 Janvier* (1965).

Delbo stayed in Auschwitz and a satellite camp called Raisko until January 1944, when she was sent with a small group of her compatriots to Ravensbrück. Near the end of the war, she was released to the Red Cross, who moved her to Sweden to recuperate from the severe malnutrition and ill-health that resulted from her camp experiences. Although she has written numerous plays and essays, Delbo's masterpiece is the trilogy *Auschwitz and After* (*Auschwitz et après*). She finished the first volume, *None of Us Will Return* (*Aucun de nous ne reviendra*) in 1946 but put it away in a drawer and did not let it be published until 1965, when, as she said, it had stood the test of time. The second volume, *Useless Knowledge* (*Une connaissance inutile*), sections of which were also written in 1946 and 1947, appeared in 1970 and was followed soon after by its sequel, *The Measure of Our Days* (*Mesure de nos jours*). Delbo's last work, *La mémoire et les jours*, translated as *Days and Memory*—it contains some of her most subtle reflections on her Auschwitz experience—appeared in 1985, the year of her death.

Delbo's ambition as a writer about the Nazi concentration camps is enshrined in one of her favorite expressions, which became the ruling principle of her art: *Il faut donner à voir,* which we might translate as "they must be made to see." In *None of Us Will Return* she says about the new arrivals in Auschwitz, "They expect the worst [*le pire*]—not the unthinkable [*l'inconcevable*]." She then resolves to reveal to her readers "the way it really was," so that when later generations in France remember the ordeal of the Nazi years they not only will focus on the charitable behavior toward Jews of the villagers of Le Chambon, celebrated by Pierre Sauvage in his film *Weapons of the Spirit*, but also will recall the daily struggle of Delbo and her friends to stay alive while besieged by hunger, thirst, abuse, fatigue, and despair. Each of these, at one point or another during her time in Auschwitz, had nearly driven Delbo to surrender to death.

Delbo must have realized, as she was writing *Days and Memory* toward the end of her life, that the challenge to future readers would be how to remember those years whose "unthinkable" incidents no one really wished to reawaken from the slumber of forgetfulness. She began that volume with the words *Expliquer l'inexplicable*, "Explain the inexplicable," and like Primo Levi, she was still trying to do it forty years after the event, even though, again like Levi, she had made the attempt in other works many times before. She spoke of two selves, her Auschwitz self and her post-Auschwitz self, and used the image of a snake shedding its skin to conjure up a sense of her "new" nature emerging after the camp years. Unfortunately, unlike the snake's skin, which shrivels, disintegrates, and disappears, what Delbo called the skin of Auschwitz memory remained. "Auschwitz is so deeply etched on my memory," she wrote, "that I cannot forget one moment of it. So you are living with Auschwitz? No, I live next to it [*à coté de*]. Auschwitz is there, unalterable, precise, but enveloped in the skin of memory, an impermeable skin that isolates it from my present self. Unlike the snake's skin, the skin of memory does not renew itself . . . . Thinking about it makes me tremble with apprehension."

Delbo foresaw that because of this, those who came after her might prefer not to think about it at all. She developed a crucial distinction to help us discriminate between two operations of memory, speaking of the "me" of now, living under the control of what she called *mémoire ordinaire*, what I translate as "common memory," and the "me" of then, the Auschwitz "me," living under the dominion of *mémoire profonde*, or "deep memory." Common memory urges us to regard the Auschwitz ordeal as part of a chronology, a dismal event in the past that the very fact of survival helps to redeem. It frees us from the pain of remembering the unthinkable. "I am very fortunate," Delbo writes, "in not recognizing myself in the self that was in Auschwitz. . . . I feel that the one who was in the camp is not me, is not the person who is here, facing you." Deep memory, on the other hand, reminds us that the Auschwitz past is not really past and never will be, although on occasion Delbo seems to believe that the two kinds of memory can remain insulated from each other. But her own experience, as well as that of countless other survivors, violates her theory.

One of the most interesting—and exasperating—examples of this comes from a story Delbo once told me. After she returned from the camps and regained her strength, she resolved to track down the two French policemen who had arrested her and her husband, and were therefore indirectly responsible for his execution and her deportation. And she succeeded. She found them living in the south of France, assembled the evidence, and reported them. The authorities checked their wartime activities and discovered that about a year after they had arrested Delbo and her husband, they had switched allegiance and joined the resistance and had fought with it bravely until the end of the war. Under the circumstances, the authorities informed Delbo, they could not be prosecuted. So she lived with her frustrated appeal for justice until her death.

Such paradoxes are not that rare, and they create a problem for those of us trying to decide how to remember this past. The same Poles who hid Jews in their attic or cellar sometimes denounced others to the Gestapo. I know of at least one Polish policeman whose job was to help the Germans round up Jews for deportation and death during the day, while at night he returned to a home where he and his wife were hiding a Jewish girl in their bedroom. Were they hedging their bets, so to speak, building a moral nest egg for the future in case the Germans lost, or were they genuinely courageous? How shall we assess and then remember them? And what of the two French policemen, who divided their war years between doing the dirty work of the Vichy regime and risking their lives in underground activity? It would be convenient if the one were to cancel out the other, the "good" time redeeming the bad one. Indeed, the chronological view of experience tempts and encourages us to adopt this attitude, transforming even survivors into heroes and heroines by the very fact of their survival.

Deep memory teaches us otherwise. It tells us that the Nazi interlude is one abyss that we cannot pass over with equanimity into the future. The Holocaust experience is the gadfly of the modern imagination, chafing memory to pursue the true meaning of *voir*, "see." *Essayez de regarder, essayez pour voir*—"Try to look, try to see"—is one of the recurrent refrains of *None of Us Will Return*. The language of moral victory and the triumph of the human spirit belong to a genre of discourse that nurtures Delbo's common memory, the traditional sense that the past can be remembered in a constructive and hopeful way. But as Delbo admits, we pay a price for sailing toward this haven; an inner turbulence threatens our journey. "The skin enfolding the memory of Auschwitz," she writes in *Days and Memory*, "is tough":

> Even so it gives way at times, revealing all it contains. Over dreams the conscious will has no power. And in those dreams I see myself, yes, my own self such as I know I was: hardly able to stand on my feet, my throat tight, my heart beating wildly, frozen to the marrow, filthy, skin and bones; the suffering I feel is so unbearable, so identical to the pain endured, that I feel it physically, I feel it throughout my whole body which becomes a mass of suffering; and I feel death fasten on me, I feel that I am dying.

In spite of her insistence that she is describing a nightmare, Delbo has found a genre of discourse to pierce the skin of memory, to expose the naked self divested of its heroic garments, a self cold, filthy, gaunt, the victim of unbearable pain. It is no wonder that common memory does not enjoy dwelling on such images. But if we are to pursue the effects of the Nazi past on the lives of individual men and women— in this case, of a particular Frenchwoman—we cannot do so without the help of Delbo's deep memory.

Refining the opposition between common and deep memory, Delbo develops a parallel distinction between *mémoire externe*, "external memory" or what we might call "thinking memory," and *mémoire des sens*, "sense memory." "Because when I talk to you about Auschwitz," she says, "it is not from deep memory my words issue. They come from external memory, the memory connected with the thinking process." Such memory, I would add, may allow us to imagine the worst, but only sense memory, which preserves and tries to transmit the *physical* imprint of the ordeal, enables us to approach the unthinkable. *External* memory gives us access to the heroic exploits of a man such as Jean Moulin, the legendary leader of the French resistance, who was captured, tortured, and executed by Klaus Barbie; but only sense memory can give us a glimpse of the unimaginable anguish leading to his death.

Fortunately, Delbo does not rely on external memory to convey her experience of Auschwitz. The first volume of *Auschwitz and After* shuns the narrative impulse, with its dependence on reflection, and forges instead a remarkable style of direct confrontation that lures us into the maelstrom of atrocity while simultaneously drowning all intellectual defenses. In *None of Us Will Return* Delbo describes the death of one of her fellow Frenchwomen, who against orders has broken from ranks to run to a ditch for some clean snow to quench her thirst. Delbo's sense memory evokes her face: "Her prominent cheekbones are violet, accentuated, her swollen mouth a black violet, her eye sockets filled with dark shadows. Her face reflects naked despair." She sucks the snow, then in agonizing slow motion tries to crawl out of the ditch. But the SS will not tolerate such violation of their rules, and Delbo's verbal and visual portrait of her fate combines deep memory with sense memory to challenge our ability and our willingness to see—*Il faut donner à voir:*

> The woman moves forward. She seems to be obeying an order. She stops in front of the SS. Shudders runs down her curved back with shoulder blades protruding from under the yellow coat. The SS has his dog on a leash. Did he give an order, make a sign? The dog pounces on the woman—without growling, panting, barking. All is silent as in a dream. The dog leaps on the woman, sinks its fangs in her neck. And we do not stir, stuck in some kind of viscous substance which keeps us from making the slightest gesture—as in a dream. The woman lets out a cry. A wrenched-out

scream. A single scream tearing through the immobility of the plain. We do not know if the scream had been uttered by her or by us, whether it issued from her punctured throat, or from ours. I feel the dog's fangs in my throat. I scream. I howl. Not a sound comes out of me. The silence of a dream.

The plain. The snow. The plain.

The woman collapses. One last palpitation and that's all. Something snaps. The head in muddy snow is nothing but a stump. The eyes dirty wounds.

Il faut donner à voir. Delbo's Auschwitz experience, like all of the Holocaust, is a story of dirty wounds, and if common or external memory sometimes tempts us to disinfect them, to soothe them with the salves and lotions of personal valor—as if such wounds could ever be healed—we need to understand that this is both a natural and an evasive impulse. Memory must serve a seeing truth as well as a thinking truth, the *profonde* as well as the *ordinaire*, and perhaps more than any other writer on this subject Delbo clarified the options that still lie before us when we remember this event.

Near the end of the second volume of her Auschwitz trilogy, *Useless Knowledge*, Delbo includes a poem that offers a distilled variant on this dilemma:

As far as I'm concerned
I'm still there
dying there
a little more each day
dying over again
the death of those who died

That last doom-laden line stretches the circle of its recruits to include its audience as well. Delbo knows that no one returns from an encounter with Auschwitz unmarked. But she also acknowledges the necessary burden of adjustment. When she admits, "I have returned from beyond knowledge / and now must unlearn / for otherwise I

clearly see a world / I can no longer live," she intends not to slight
her past but to invite us to share with her the twin vision that a
journey through Auschwitz has etched on our memory. We pay a
price for learning how to imagine what happened, to "see"; then we
add to our debt by feigning that beyond those mounds of corpses and
heaps of ashes a chaste future is still feasible, "because it would be too
senseless / after all-" as Delbo affirms, "for so many to have died /
while you live / doing nothing with your life." But she frames this
with a more somber paradox, one that echoes hollowly through the
Holocaust universe, leaving us little but a bleak query to kindle hope:

> I've spoken with death
> and so
> I know
> the futility of things we learn
> a discovery I made at the cost
> of a suffering
> so intense I keep on wondering
> whether it was worth it.

The passage I have cited from Delbo's trilogy should give the
reader a glimpse of her unique blend of poetry and prose, resulting in
a lyrical rendering of atrocity that is alarmingly beautiful, an aesthetics
of agitation. Her feat threatens Theodor Adorno's early conviction
that to write poetry after Auschwitz would be barbaric. Of course,
Adorno later retracted that statement, faced as he was with the body
of artistic work we now label Holocaust literature. Delbo might well
be called one of the founders of that literature. She understood that
before one could speak of the renewal of the human image after
Auschwitz, one had to crystallize its disfigured form and the horror
that had defaced it. She invented a style to freeze that horror, first in
its original guise, then as it was prolonged in the memory of its victims. As Delbo subtracts epithets in an effort to reach the physical
essence of anguish, she profanes the very energy of art by shrinking
space into the narrow stage of barrack and camp, converting motion

to immobility and reducing expression to silence. Her language approaches the status of music, with its melodic repetitions that often resemble incantations, though she seeks visual images equivalent to the rhythmic phrases of sound.

The secret of how she achieves this is locked in the mystery of artistic vision. Delbo writes as if one faculty were not enough to respond to the experience of Auschwitz. The blending of senses is a hallmark of her art. How does one hear terror, or see anguish? How does one describe the feelings of women on the way to the gas chamber, or of the temporarily reprieved who must watch them? As witness to the panic of the human condition when atrocity rules, Delbo attempts the impossible:

> We watch with eyes that cry out, eyes full of disbelief.
>
> Each face is inscribed with such precision over the icy light, the blue of the sky, that it remains marked there for eternity.
>
> For eternity, these shaven heads, squeezed against one another, bursting with shouts, mouths twisted by cries we do not hear, hands waving in a mute cry.
>
> The cries remain inscribed upon the blue of the sky.

They are also etched on the imagination of the reader, who depends on Delbo's prose sculptures to gain access to this inconceivable reality. Her penchant for naming bodily parts reflects not a gruesome obsession with dismembering but a human and artistic concern with the painful process of re-membering her violated fellow victims as a first step in remembering them, both those who did not and those who were not meant to return.

None of Us Will Return invites us to "see" the unthinkable as a basis for all that follows. The subsequent volumes, *Useless Knowledge* and *The Measure of Our Days*, warn us that Delbo is not imitating the model of Dante's *Commedia*, in which contract with evil leads through penance to purification. Delbo's survivors do not transcend but learn to endure their harsh past. Dante's pilgrim may be bathed in the flames of Hell, but he escapes that realm of death and looks for-

ward to the blinding light of Divine Love at the end of his journey.
Delbo's survivors never escape their realm of death; their journey
through the underworld does not lead to a myth of renewal but to the
haunting legacy that was best expressed by one of Delbo's fellow
deportees when she interviewed her years after their return: "I died in
Auschwitz, and no one knows it." This paradoxical refrain, which
emerges as a subterranean theme in so many survivors testimonies, is
one of the most disturbing motifs in the verse and prose sequences of
Delbo's trilogy. It challenges us to grasp the impact that mass murder
has had on our efforts to reaffirm a reverence for life in the post-
Holocaust era.

Charlotte Delbo told me that several years after the war the government held a commemorative ceremony for some of the French
men and women who died in the Nazi camps. While sitting in the
audience, she was stunned to hear from the podium her own name
being read. It seemed a bizarre perversion of her discovery that one
could die in Auschwitz and still be alive. Her paralysis lasted only an
instant; then she modestly raised her hand and murmured, "Non,
Monsieur: présente." The presence of "presence" is not too hard to
understand. When memory imprints on us the meaning of the presence of "absence" and animates the ghost that such a burden has
imposed on our lives, then the heritage of the Holocaust will have
begun to acquire some authenticity in our postwar culture. Charlotte
Delbo's art is in the vanguard of that summons.

Auschwitz and After

1

None of Us Will Return

Today, I am not sure that what I wrote is true.
I am certain it is truthful.

Arrivals, Departures

People arrive. They look through the crowd of those who are waiting, those who await them. They kiss them and say the trip exhausted them.

People leave. They say good-bye to those who are not leaving and hug the children.

There is a street for people who arrive and a street for people who leave.

There is a café called "Arrivals" and a café called "Departures."

There are people who arrive and people who leave.

But there is a station where those who arrive are those who are leaving

a station where those who arrive have never arrived, where those who have left never came back.

It is the largest station in the world.

This is the station they reach, from wherever they came.

They get here after days and nights

having crossed many countries

they reach it together with their children, even the little ones who were not to be part of this journey.

They took the children because for this kind of trip you do not leave without them.

Those who had some took gold because they believed gold might come in handy.

All of them took what they loved most because you do not leave your dearest possessions when

you set out for far-distant lands.

Each one brought his life along, since what you must take with you, above all, is your life.

And when they have gotten there

they think they've arrived in Hell
maybe. And yet they did not believe in it.

They had no idea you could take a train to Hell but since they
were there they took their courage in their hands ready to face what's
coming

together with their children, their wives and their aged parents
with family mementoes and family papers.

They do not know there is no arriving in this station.

They expect the worst—not the unthinkable.

And when the guards shout to line up five by five, the men on
one side, women and children on the other, in a language they do not
understand, the truncheon blows convey the message so they line up
by fives ready for anything.

Mothers keep a tight hold on their children—trembling at the
thought they might be taken away—because the children are hungry
and thirsty and disheveled by lack of sleep after crossing so many
countries. At last they have reached their destination, they will be able
to take care of them now.

And when the guards shout to leave their bundles, comforters and
keepsakes on the platform, they do so since they are ready for the
worst and do not wish to be taken aback by anything. They say: "We
shall see." They have already seen so much and they are weary from
the journey.

The station is not a railroad station. It is the end of the line. They
stare, distressed by the surrounding desolation.

In the morning, the mist veils the marshes.

In the evening floodlights reveal the white barbed wire with the
sharpness of astrophotography. They believe this is where they are
being taken, and are filled with fear.

At night they wait for the day with the small children heavy in
their mothers' arms. They wait and wonder.

With the coming of daylight there is no more waiting. The

columns start out at once. Women and children first, they are the most exhausted. After that the men. They are weary too but relieved that their women and children should go first.

For women and children are made to go first.

In the winter they are chilled to the bone. Particularly those who come from Herakleion, snow is new to them.

In the summer the sun blinds them when they step out of the cattle cars locked tight on departure.

Departure from France and Ukraine Albania Belgium Slovakia Italy Hungary Peloponnesos Holland Macedonia Austria Herzegovina from the shores of the Black Sea the shores of the Mediterranean the banks of the Vistula.

They would like to know where they are. They have no idea that this is the center of Europe. They look for the station's name. This is a station that has no name.

A station that will remain nameless for them.

Some of them are traveling for the first time in their lives.

Some of them have traveled in all the countries in the world, businessmen. They were familiar with all manner of landscape, but they do not recognize this one.

They look. Later on they will be able to describe how it was.

All wish to remember the impression they had and how they felt they would never return.

This is a feeling one might have had earlier in one's life. They know you should not trust feelings.

Some came from Warsaw wearing large shawls and with tied-up bundles
    some from Zagreb, the women their heads covered by scarves
    some from the Danube wearing multicolored woolen sweaters knitted through long night hours
    some from Greece, they took with them black olives and loukoums
    some came from Monte Carlo
    they were in the casino

they are still wearing tails and stiff shirt fronts mangled from the
trip
    paunchy and bald
    fat bankers who played keep the bank
    there are married couples who stepped out of the synagogue the
bride all in white wrapped in her veil wrinkled from having slept on
the floor of the cattle car
    the bridegroom in black wearing a top hat his gloves soiled
    parents and guests, women holding pearl-embroidered handbags
    all of them regretting they could not have stopped home to
change into something less dainty
    The rabbi holds himself straight, heading the line. He has always
been a model for the rest.
    There are boarding-school girls wearing identical pleated skirts,
their hats trailing blue ribbons. They pull up their knee socks carefully
as they clamber down, and walk neatly five by five, holding hands,
unaware, as though on a regular Thursday school outing. After all,
what can they do to boarding-school girls shepherded by their
teacher? She tells them, "Be good, children!" They don't have the
slightest desire not to be good.
    There are old people who used to get letters from their children
in America. Their idea of foreign lands comes from postcards.
Nothing ever looked like what they see here. Their children will
never believe it.
    There are intellectuals: doctors, architects, composers, poets. You
can tell them by the way they walk, by their glasses. They too have
seen a great deal in their lifetimes, studied much. Many made use of
their imagination to write books, yet nothing they imagined ever
came close to what they see now.
    All the furriers of large cities are gathered here, as well as the
men's and women's tailors and the manufacturers of ready-to-wear
who had moved to western Europe. They do not recognize in this
place the land of their forebears.
    There is the inexhaustible crowd of those who live in cities where

each one occupies his own cell in the beehive. Looking at the endless lines you wonder how they ever fit into the stacked-up cubicles of a metropolis.

There is a mother who's boxing her five-year-old's ears because he won't hold her by the hand and she expects him to stay quietly by her side. You run the risk of getting lost if you're separated in a strange, crowded place. She hits her child, and we who know cannot forgive her for it. Yet, were she to smother him with kisses, it would all be the same in the end.

There are those who having journeyed for eighteen days lost their minds, murdering one another inside the boxcars and

those who suffocated during the trip when they were tightly packed together

they will not step out.

There's a little girl who hugs her doll against her chest, dolls can be smothered too.

There are two sisters wearing white coats. They went out for a stroll and never got back for dinner. Their parents still await their return anxiously.

Five by five they walk down the street of arrivals. It is actually the street of departures but no one knows it. This is a one-way street.

They proceed in orderly fashion so as not to be faulted for anything.

They reach a building and heave a sigh. They have reached their destination at last.

And when the soldiers bark their orders, shouting for the women to strip, they undress the children first, cautiously, not to wake them all at once. After days and nights of travel the little ones are edgy and cranky

then the women shed their own clothing in front of their children, nothing to be done

and when each is handed a towel they worry whether the shower will be warm because the children could catch cold and when the men enter the shower room through another door, stark naked, the women hide the children against their bodies.

Perhaps at that moment all of them understand.

But understanding doesn't do any good since they cannot tell those waiting on the railway platform

those riding in the dark boxcars across many countries only to end up here

those held in detention camps who fear leaving, wondering about the climate, the working conditions, or being parted from their few possessions

those hiding in the mountains and forests who have grown weary of concealment. Come what may they'll head home. Why should anyone come looking for them who have harmed no one

those who imagined they found a safe place for their children in a Catholic convent school where the sisters are so kind.

A band will be dressed in the girls' pleated skirts. The camp commandant wishes Viennese waltzes to be played every Sunday morning.

A blockhova will cut homey curtains from the holy vestments worn by the rabbi to celebrate the sabbath no matter what, in whatever place.

A kapo will masquerade by donning the bridegroom's morning coat and top hat, with her girlfriend wrapped in the bride's veil. They'll play "wedding" all night while the prisoners, dead tired, lie in their bunks. Kapos can have fun since they're not exhausted at the end of the day.

Black Calamata olives and Turkish delight cubes will be sent to ailing German hausfrauen who couldn't care less for Calamata olives, nor olives of any kind.

All day all night

every day every night the chimneys smoke, fed by this fuel dispatched from every part of Europe

standing at the mouth of the crematoria men sift through ashes to find gold melted from gold teeth. All those Jews have mouths full of gold, and since there are so many of them it all adds up to tons and tons.

In the spring men and women sprinkle ashes on drained marshland plowed for the first time. They fertilize the soil with human phosphates.

From bags tied round their bellies they draw human bone meal which they sow upon the furrows. By the end of the day their faces are covered with white dust blown back up by the wind. Sweat trickling down their faces over the white powder traces their wrinkles.

They need not fear running short of fertilizer since train after train gets here every day and every night, every hour of every day and every night.

This is the largest station in the world for arrivals and for departures.

Only those who enter the camp find out what happened to the others. They cry at the thought of having parted from them at the station the day an officer ordered the young prisoners to line up separately

people are needed to drain the marshes and cover them with the others' ashes.

They tell themselves it would have been far better never to have entered, never to have found out.

You who have wept two thousand years
for one who agonized for three days and three nights

what tears will you have left
for those who agonized
far more than three hundred nights and far more than three hun-
    dred days
how hard
shall you weep
for those who agonized through so many agonies
and they were countless

They did not believe in resurrection to eternal life
and knew you would not weep.

O you who know
did you know that hunger makes the eyes sparkle that thirst dims
    them
O you who know
did you know that you can see your mother dead
and not shed a tear
O you who know
did you know that in the morning you wish for death
and in the evening you fear it
O you who know
did you know that a day is longer than a year
a minute longer than a lifetime
O you who know
did you know that legs are more vulnerable than eyes
nerves harder than bones
the heart firmer than steel
Did you know that the stones of the road do not weep
that there is one word only for dread
one for anguish
Did you know that suffering is limitless
that horror cannot be circumscribed
Did you know this
You who know.

My mother
she was hands, a face
They made our mothers strip in front of us

Here mothers are no longer mothers to their children.

All were marked on their arm with an indelible number
All were destined to die naked

The tattoos identified the dead men the dead women

It was a desolate plain
on the edge of town

The plain was covered with ice
and the town
was nameless.

Dialogue

"You're French?"

"Yes."

"So am I."

She has no F on her chest. A star.

"From where?"

"Paris."

"You've been here a long time?"

"Five weeks."

"I've been here sixteen days."

"That's already a long time, I know."

"Five weeks . . . How can it be?"

"Just like this."

"And you think we can survive this?"

She is begging.

"We've got to try."

"For you perhaps there's hope, but for us . . ."

She points to my striped jacket and then to her coat, a coat much too big, much too dirty, much too tattered.

"Oh, come on, it's the same odds for both of us."

"For us, there's no hope."

She gestures with her hand, mimics rising smoke.

"We've got to keep up our courage."

"Why bother . . . Why keep on struggling when all of us are to . . ."

The gesture of her hand completes her sentence. Rising smoke.

"No, we've got to keep on struggling."

"How can we hope to get out of here. How will anyone ever get out of here. It would be better to throw ourselves on the barbed wire immediately."

What can one say to her? She's small, frail. And I can't even convince myself. All argument is senseless. I'm struggling against my reason. One struggles against all reason.

The chimney smokes. The sky is low. Smoke sweeps across the camp weighing upon us and enveloping us with the odor of burning flesh.

The Dummies

"Look. Look."

We were crouching on our tier, on the boards which were used by us as bed, table, floor. The roof was very low. You could only fit there sitting down, head lowered. There were eight of us, perched on a narrow platform, a group of friends death would separate. Soup had been dealt out. We had waited a long time outside to file one by one past the bucket steaming into the face of the stubhova. Her right sleeve rolled up, she dipped the ladle into the bucket to dish out the gruel. She was yelling from behind the cloud of steam. The vapor dampened her voice. She was yelling because of the shoving and talking. Sluggish, we waited, our numb hands holding our tin cups. Now we ate, our soup in our laps. The soup was murky, but it had the taste of hot.

"Look, did you see, in the yard . . ."

"Oh!" Yvonne P. drops her spoon. She's not hungry any more.

The barred window looks out on the yard of block 25, a courtyard enclosed by walls. There is a door that leads into the camp, but if it opens when you're passing by, you run fast, you take off, you don't try to look at the door, or see what's on the other side. But we can see, right through the window. However, we never turn our heads in that direction.

"Look. Look."

At first, we doubt that we've seen what we've seen. It's hard to tell them from the snow. The yard is full of them. Naked. Stacked side by side. White, a bluish whiteness against the snow. Heads shaved, pubic hair straight and stiff. The corpses are frozen. White with brown toenails. There is something ridiculous about these cocked-up toes. Horrifyingly laughable.

Boulevard de Courtais in Montluçon. I was waiting for my father at the Nouvelles Galeries. It was summer, the sun was hot on the asphalt. A parked truck was being unloaded. They were delivering dummies for the display window. Each man grabbed a dummy in his arms and set it down in front of the store's entrance. The dummies were bare, their joints clearly visible. The men carried them carefully, laying them down near the wall on the hot sidewalk.

I couldn't take my eyes off them, embarrassed by the nakedness of these dummies. I had often seen dummies in the store windows, wearing a dress, shoes, a wig, their arms folded in affected gestures. I had never thought of them as naked, without hair. I had never imagined them outside the display window, without electricity to highlight their poses. To discover them thus made me as uneasy as seeing a dead person for the first time.

Now the dummies are lying in the snow, bathed in a winter light which reminds me of the sunlight on the asphalt.

The women lying there in the snow are yesterday's companions. Yesterday they were lined up for the roll call. They stood in ranks of five, on each side of the Lagerstrasse. They were setting out to work, dragging themselves toward the marshes. Yesterday they were hungry. They were lice-infested and scratched themselves. Yesterday they gulped the murky gruel. They had diarrhea and were beaten. Yesterday they suffered. Yesterday they wished to die.

Now they are there, nude corpses in the snow. They died in block 25. Death in block 25 has none of the serenity one associated with it, even here.

One morning, because they fainted at roll call, because they were more ashen than the others, an SS beckoned to them. He formed them into a column which magnified the sum total of all the degradations, all the infirmities which until then, lost in the human mass, had escaped notice. And the column, commanded by the SS, was driven toward block 25.

Some went alone, willingly. As if to commit suicide. They awaited the inspection of an SS for the door to open—and stepped in.

There were also those who failed to run fast enough on a day on which they should have.

There were also those whose companions had to abandon them at the door, and who shouted, "Don't leave me. Don't leave me."

For days on end they had been hungry and thirsty above all. They had been cold, lying almost naked on boards without straw or blankets. Locked up with dying or crazy women, they awaited their turn to die or go mad. In the morning, they stepped outside. They were driven out by cudgel blows. Blows imparted to the dying and the insane. The living had to pull out into the yard those who died during the night, because the dead had to be counted also. The SS walked by. He enjoyed setting his dog on them. This was the howling heard at night. Then silence. The roll call was over. It was the daytime silence. The women still alive went back. The dead women remained in the snow. They had been stripped naked. Their clothes would be used by others.

Every two or three days, trucks arrived to take the living to the gas chamber, the dead to the crematorium. Madness must have been the final hope of those who entered there. Some, made canny by their stubborn desire to survive, escaped at the outset. Sometimes they would last several weeks, never more than three in block 25. They could be seen at the barred windows begging: "Something to drink. Something to drink." There are ghosts that talk.

"Look. I'm sure she moved. That one, next to the last. Her hand . . . her fingers are opening, I'm sure of it."

The fingers open slowly, the snow blooms like a discolored sea anemone.

"Don't stare! Why are you staring?" Yvonne P. pleads, her eyes wide open, riveted to a living corpse.

"Eat your soup," says Cecile. These women no longer need anything.

I look too. I look at this corpse that moves but does not move me. I'm a big girl now. I can look at naked dummies without being afraid.

The Men

In the morning and in the evening, on the way to the marshes, we
walked by columns of men. The Jews wore civilian clothes. Tattered
clothing with a red lead cross smeared on their backs. It was also the
case for the Jewish women. They fastened these shapeless clothes
about their persons. The others wore striped uniforms that floated
upon their thin backs.

We pitied them because they had to march in step. As for us, we
walked as best we could. The kapo, at the head, was fat, warmly dressed
and booted. He called cadence: Links, Zwei, Drei, Vier. Links. The
men found it hard to keep up. They were wearing canvas foot-wraps
with wooden soles that did not stay on. We couldn't imagine how they
kept on walking. When there was snow or ice, they carried them in
their hands.

They had the special gait we all had over there. Head thrust forward, neck forward. The head and neck propelled the rest of the body.
The head and neck pulled the feet. Deeply circled eyes with dilated
pupils burned within their gaunt faces. Their swollen lips were either
black or bright red and when they parted one caught a glimpse of
bleeding gums.

They walked past us. We whispered, "We're French, French
women," just to find out whether there might be fellow countrymen
among them. We hadn't met any yet.

Intent on marching, they did not look in our direction. However,
we looked at them. We stared. Our hands were wrung with pity. The
thought of them, of their gait, their eyes haunted us.

There were so many sick women among us unable to eat that we
had a lot of bread. We tried to talk them into eating, to overcome
their disgust for the food we were given. They had to eat in order to
survive. But our words failed to arouse their willpower. They had
given up on arrival.

One morning, we carried bread under our jackets. For the men. We failed to meet a men's column. We awaited the evening impatiently. On our way back, we heard their tread behind us. Drei. Vier. Links. They walked faster than us. We stepped aside to make way for them. Poles? Russians? Pitiful men, oozing misery like all men here.

As soon as they were abreast with us, we took out our bread and tossed it to them. There was a mad scramble. They caught the bread, fighting over it, snatching pieces from one another. They had wolves' eyes. Two of them rolled into the ditch with the bread that had escaped from their grasp.

We watched them fight, and wept.

The SS shouted, setting his dog on them. The column reformed, resuming its march. Links. Zwei. Drei.

They did not even turn their heads in our direction.

Roll Call

SS in black capes have walked past. They made a count. We are waiting still.

We are waiting.

For days, the next day.

Since the day before, the following day.

Since the middle of the night, today.

We wait.

Day is breaking.

We await the day because one must wait for something.

One does not live in expectation of death. One expects it.

We have no expectations.

We expect only what happens. Night because it follows day. Day because it follows night.

We await the end of the roll call.

The end of the roll call is a whistle blast which makes each woman turn about-face towards the gate. Motionless ranks become ranks ready to be set in motion, in the direction of the marshes, the bricks, the ditches.

Today we are waiting longer than usual. The sky grows paler than usual. We are waiting.

What are we waiting for?

An SS appears at the end of the Lagerstrasse, walking towards us. He stops in front of our ranks. Judging by the caduceus on his cap he must be the doctor. He scrutinizes us. Slowly. He begins to speak. He does not scream. He is actually speaking. He calls: "A translator." Marie-Claude steps forward. The SS repeats his question, translated by Marie-Claude: "He's asking whether there are among us women who cannot endure the roll call." The SS looks at us. Magda, our blockhova, standing by his side, looks at us and, taking a step to one side, blinks ever so slightly.

Indeed, who can endure the roll call? Who can remain motionless for hours? In the middle of the night. In the snow. Without having eaten or slept. Who can endure this cold for hours on end?

A few of us raise their hands.

The SS makes them step out of the ranks. Counts them. Too few. Softly he utters another sentence and Marie-Claude translates again. "He asks whether there might not be others, aged or sick, who find roll call too hard in the morning." Other hands are raised. Then Magda elbows Marie-Claude who says without shifting her inflection, "But it's better not to say so." The raised hands are lowered. Except one. A tiny old lady gets up on her toes, stretching and waving her arm as high as she can for fear of not being noticed. The SS is walking away. The little old lady grows bold: "Here I am, sir. I'm sixty-seven years old." The SS has heard her, turns round: "Komm." She joins the group just formed, which the SS doctor escorts to block 25.

One Day

She was clinging to the other side of the slope, her hands and feet grasping the snow-covered embankment. Her whole body was taut, her jaws tight, her neck with its dislocated cartilage straining, as were her muscles—what was left of them on her bones.

Yet she strained in vain—the exertion of one pulling on an imaginary rope.

She was arched from her index finger to her big toe, but every time she raised her hand to grip something higher in order to scale the sharp slope she'd fall back. Her limp body was pathetic. When she raised her head one could read upon her face the mental processes going on within as she mustered all her energy for a final effort. With her teeth clenched her chin grew sharp, her ribs protruded like staves under her skin-tight garment, the civilian coat of a Jewess. From under that coat her ankles dangled stiffly. Once more she tried to hoist herself up the snow-covered bank.

Each of her movements was so slow and awkward, revealing her weakened condition, that one wondered how she was still able to move. At the same time, it was difficult to grasp why she needed to work so hard, quite out of proportion to her enterprise, her weightless body.

Now her hands were grasping a crust of hardened snow, while her feet, deprived of support, sought some crag or rung. They dangled in the void. Her legs were bound with rags. They were so thin that despite these tatters they looked like swinging bean poles, scarecrow legs. Even more so when they were kicking in the air. Finally the woman fell to the bottom of the ditch.

She turns her head as if to measure the distance, looks upward. One can observe a growing bewilderment in her eyes, her hands, her convulsed face.

"Why are all these women looking at me like this? Why are they here, lined up in close ranks, standing immobile? They look at me yet do not seem to see me. They cannot possibly see me, or they wouldn't stand there gaping. They'd help me climb up. Why don't you help me, you standing so close? Help me. Pull me up. Lean in my direction. Stretch out your hand. Oh, they don't make a move."

And her hand writhed toward us in a desperate call for help. The hand falls back—a faded mauve star upon the snow. Once fallen, it lost its fleshless look, grew soft, became once again a living, pitiful thing. The elbow props itself up, slips. The whole body collapses.

Back there, beyond the barbed wire, a plain, snow, a plain.

All of us were there, several thousand of us, standing in the snow since morning—this is what we call night, since morning starts at three A.M. Dawn illumined the snow which, until then, was the night's sole light—the cold grew bitter.

Standing motionless since the middle of the night, we had grown so heavy on our legs that we sank into the earth, the ice, unable to fight off numbness. The cold bruised our temples, our jaws, making us feel that our bones were about to break, our craniums to burst. We had given up hopping from one foot to the other, tapping our heels, rubbing our palms together. Exhausting exercises.

We did not move. The will to struggle and endure, life itself, had taken refuge in a shrunken part of our bodies, somewhere in the immediate periphery of our hearts.

We stood there motionless, several thousand women speaking a variety of languages from all over, huddled together, heads bowed under the snow's stinging blasts.

We stood there motionless, reduced to our heartbeats.

Where is she going, the one who has stepped out of the rank? She walks like a cripple, or a blind woman, a blind woman who is looking. She walks towards the ditch on wooden legs. She is at the edge, crouching, ready to go down. She falls. Her foot slipped on the crumbling snow. Why does she want to go down into the ditch? She broke rank without hesitation, without hiding from the SS standing stiff in her black cape, her black boots, keeping close watch. She took off as though she were somewhere else, on a street where she might cross from one sidewalk to the other, or in a garden. To mention a garden here may make you laugh. Could she be one of those crazy crones who scare little children in public parks? No, this is a young woman, still a girl. Such frail shoulders.

There she is in the hollow of the ditch with her hands scratching the ground, her feet looking for support, straining to lift her heavy head. Her face is now turned toward us. Her prominent cheekbones are violet, her swollen mouth a black violet, her eye sockets filled with dark shadows. Her face reflects naked despair.

For a while she struggles against her limbs' intractability in order to right herself. She thrashes like someone drowning. Then she stretches out her hands to hoist herself onto the other bank. Her hands seek to take hold of something, her nails claw at the snow, her whole body stretches spasmodically. Then she grows limp, drained.

I no longer look at her. I no longer wish to look. If only I could change my place in order not to see her. Not to see the dark holes of these eye sockets, these staring holes. What does she want to do? Reach the electrified barbed-wire fence? Why does she stare at us? Isn't she pointing at me? Imploring me? I turn away to look elsewhere. Elsewhere.

Elsewhere—ahead of us—is the gate of block 25.

Standing, wrapped in a blanket, a child, a little boy. A tiny, shaven head, a face with jutting jaws and a salient superciliary arch. Barefoot, he jumps up and down ceaselessly with a frenzy like that of some barbaric dance. He also waves his arms to keep warm. The blanket slips open. It's a woman. A female skeleton. She is naked. Her ribs and pelvic bones are clearly visible. She pulls the blanket up to her shoulders while continuing to dance. The dance of an automaton. A dancing female skeleton. Her feet are small, gaunt, bare in the snow. There are living skeletons that dance.

Presently I am writing this story in a café—it is turning into a story.

A break in the clouds. Is it afternoon? We have lost all notion of time. The sky appears. Very blue. A forgotten blue. Hours have passed since I succeeded in not looking at the woman in the ditch. Is she still there? She has reached the top of the slope—how was she able to do this?—and stopped there. Her hands are drawn by the glittering snow. She takes a handful of it, bringing it up to her lips in exasperating slow motion which must require infinite effort. She sucks the snow. Now we understand why she broke rank, the resolute expression of her face. She wanted clean snow for her swollen lips. Since the break of day she was fascinated by this clean snow she hoped to reach. On this side of the ditch, the snow we trampled is black. She sucks her snow, yet seems to have lost interest in it. Snow does not quench thirst when you have fever. All that exertion for a handful of snow which turns in her mouth into a handful of salt. Her hand drops, her neck bends. A fragile stalk that must break. Her back hunches, shoulder blades protruding through the worn fabric of her coat. It's a yellow coat, like that of our dog Flac which had grown thin after being ill, and whose whole body curved, just before he died, looking like the skeleton of a bird in the Museum of Natural History. This woman is going to die.

She no longer looks at us. She is huddling in the snow. His backbone arched, Flac is going to die—the first creature I ever saw die. Mama, Flac is at the garden gate, all hunched up. He's trembling. André says he's going to die.

"I've got to get up on my feet, to rise. I've got to walk. I've got to struggle still. Won't they help me? Why don't you help me all of you standing there with nothing to do."

Mama, come quick, Flac is going to die.

"I don't understand why they won't help me. They're dead, dead. They look alive because they're standing up, leaning one against the other. They're dead. As for me, I don't want to die."

Her hand flutters once more, like a shout—yet she is not shouting. In what language would she shout if she were to shout?

Here comes a dead woman who moves toward her. A dummy in a striped uniform. A matter of two steps and the dead woman has reached her. She pulls her by the arm, drags her over to our side so that she may assume her place within the ranks. The black cape of the SS has come close. The dead woman is dragging nothing more in our direction than a dirty yellow sack which just lies there. Hours and hours. What can we do? She's going to die. Flac, you know, our scrawny yellow dog, is going to die. Still many hours to go.

Suddenly a shudder runs through this heap of a yellow coat lying in muddy snow. The woman attempts to rise. Her every act falls apart in unbearable slow-motion sequences. She kneels, looks at us. Not one of us will make a move. She puts her hands palms down on the ground—her body is scrawny and arched like that of the dying Flac. She manages to stand up. She reels, tries to regain her balance. The void all around. She takes a few steps. She is walking in the void. She is so bent down you wonder how she manages not to fall again. No. She is walking, staggers yet keeps on. And the bones of her face convey a frightful kind of willfulness. We watch her make her way across the empty void before our ranks. Where is she heading now?

"Why are you amazed that I am walking? Haven't you heard the SS standing in front of the gate with his dog call out to me? You cannot hear because you're dead."

The woman SS in the black cape has left. Now an SS officer, wearing a green uniform, is standing at the gate.

The woman moves forward. She seems to be obeying an order. She stops in front of the SS. Shudders runs down her curved back with shoulder blades protruding from under the yellow coat. The SS has his dog on a leash. Did he give an order, make a sign? The dog pounces on the woman—without growling, panting, barking. All is silent as in a dream. The dog leaps on the woman, sinks its fangs in her neck. And we do not stir, stuck in some kind of viscous substance which keeps us from making the slightest gesture—as in a dream. The woman lets out a cry. A wrenched-out scream. A single scream tearing through the immobility of the plain. We do not know if the scream has been uttered by her or by us, whether it issued from her punctured throat, or from ours. I feel the dog's fangs in my throat. I scream. I howl. Not a sound comes out of me. The silence of a dream.

The plain. The snow. The plain.

The woman collapses. One last palpitation and that's all. Something snaps. The head in the muddy snow is nothing but a stump. The eyes dirty wounds.

"All these dead women who no longer look at me." Mama, Flac is dead. He was a long time dying. Then he dragged himself up to the steps. A death rattle stuck in his throat and he died. It is as if someone had strangled him.

The SS pulls on his leash. The dog lets go. There is some blood on his muzzle. The SS whistles softly under his breath as he leaves.

In front of the door of block 25, the blanket with its bare feet, shaven head, has not stopped jumping up and down. Night is falling.

And we remain standing in the snow. Motionless amid the motionless plain.

And now I am sitting in a café, writing this text.

Marie

Her father, her mother, her brothers and sisters were all gassed on
arrival.

Her parents were too old, the children too young.

She says: "She was beautiful, my little sister.

You can't imagine how beautiful she was.

They mustn't have looked at her.

If they had, they would never have killed her.

They couldn't have."

The Next Day

The roll call began when it was night and now it's daylight. The night
was clear and cold, crackling with frost—the flowing of ice flowing
down from the stars. The day was clear and cold, clear and cold to the
point of being unbearable. The blow of a whistle. The columns start
out. The motion undulates till it reaches us. Without being aware of it
we have faced about. Without being aware of it we are moving also.
Moving forward. So numb that we seem to be nothing but a chunk of
cold moving in one piece. Our legs move forward as though they did
not belong to us. The first columns file through the gate. On each
side the SS and their dogs. They are bundled in their overcoats, bala-
clava helmets, woolen mufflers. Their dogs too, in their dog coats,
sporting the two SS letters black on a white circle. Coats cut from
flags. The columns stretch out. We've got to dress ranks before passing
through the gate, to space ourselves. Once past the gate, we huddle
close together as animals do but the cold is so intense we no longer
feel it. Before us the plain sparkles: the sea. We follow. The ranks cross
the road, walk straight toward the sea. In silence. Slowly. Where are
we going? Onward into the sparkling plain. Into congealed light. The
SS shout. We do not understand what they are shouting. The columns
sink into the sea, farther and farther into icy light. The SS repeat their
commands over our heads. We continue to move forward, dazzled by
the snow. And all at once we are gripped by fear, vertigo, at the edge
of this blinding plain. What do they want? What are they going to do
with us? They shout. They run and their weapons jingle. What are
they going to do with us?

Then the columns form into squares. Ten by ten, in ranks of ten.
One square after the other. A gray checkerboard on the dazzling
snow. The last column. The last square comes to a halt. Shouts to
straighten out the edges of the checkerboard profiled against the snow.
The SS supervise the corners. What are they planning to do? An

officer on horseback canters by. He examines the perfect squares formed by fifteen thousand women standing on the snow. He reins in the horse, wheels around, satisfied. The shouts stop. Sentries begin to pace around the squares. We become conscious of ourselves, we are still breathing. We are breathing in the cold. Beyond us lies the plain.

The snow sparkles in refracted light. There are no beams, only light, hard and glacial, where everything is etched in sharp outline. The sky is blue, hard and glacial. One thinks of plants caught in ice. It must happen in the Arctic region, when the ice freezes even under-water vegetation. We are frozen in a block of hard, cutting ice, transparent like a block of pure crystal. And this crystal is pierced by light, as if the light were frozen within the ice, as though ice were light. It takes a long time to realize that we are able to move within the block of ice which encloses us. We wiggle our toes within our shoes, stamp our feet. Fifteen thousand women stamp their feet yet no noise is heard. The silence is solidified into cold. We are in a place where time is abolished. We do not know whether we exist, only ice, light, dazzling snow, and us, in this ice, this light, this silence.

We remain motionless. The morning leaks out—time outside of time. And the edges of the checkerboard are not as sharp as they were. The ranks are disintegrating. Some of the women take a couple of steps, regain their place. The snow sparkles, immense, upon a stretch where nothing casts a shadow. The electric poles, the roofs of the barracks buried under snow, stand out groined, as do the barbed-wire enclosures, traced in ink. What are they going to do with us?

Time oozes without the light's changing. It remains hard, frozen, solid, and the sky is just as blue, as hard. The ice draws tight on our shoulders, weighs hard on us, crushes us. Not that we feel colder, we have grown increasingly inert, increasingly sensitive. We are caught within a block of crystal through which we see the living, far back in our memories. Viva says, "I won't ever like winter sports again." Strange that snow might evoke something other than a mortal, hostile element, unnatural and until now unfamiliar.

A woman sits down awkwardly in the snow, at our feet. We hold

back from saying to her, "Not in the snow. You'll catch cold." It is still
a reflex action of memory, former notions. She sits in the snow, digs
out a place for herself. A childhood recollection, animals digging out
a hole to die in. The woman busies herself with precise, minute gestures, lies down. Her face in the snow, she moans gently. Her hands
unclench themselves. She is silent.

We looked without comprehending.

The light is still motionless, wounding, cold. It is the light of a
dead planet. And the frozen immensity, with its dazzling infinity, is
also that of a dead star.

Immobile in the ice wherein we are caught, inert, unfeeling, we
have lost all living senses. Not one of us utters, "I'm hungry. I'm
thirsty. I'm cold." Ferried over to another world, we are subject to
drawing breath in another life, we the living dead caught in ice, light,
silence.

All of a sudden, on the road running along the barbed-wire
fences, a truck appears. It rides noiselessly over the snow. It is an open
truck which ought to be used to carry gravel. It is full of women.
They are standing in it, bareheaded. Small, shaven, boy-like, narrow
heads. They are tightly squeezed against one another. The truck moves
silently with all these heads sharply profiled against the blue of the
day. A silent truck sliding along the barbed wire like some careful
ghost. A frieze of faces against the sky.

The women pass by near us. They are shouting. They shout and
we do not hear anything. This cold, dry air should be conductive in
an ordinary human environment. They shout in our direction without
a sound reaching us. Their mouths shout, their arms stretched out
toward us shout, everything about them is shouting. Each body is a
shout. All of them torches flaming with cries of terror, cries that have
assumed female bodies. Each one is a materialized cry, a howl—
unheard. The truck moves in silence over the snow, passes under a
portico, disappears. It carries off the cries.

Another truck just like the other one, similarly full of women
who cry out and remain unheard, comes sliding by and disappears in

turn under the portico. Then a third. This time it is our turn to shout, a shout which the ice in which we are frozen fails to transmit—or could it be that we have been struck by lightning?

In each truckload dead women are mingled with the living. The dead women are naked, their bodies piled up. And the living are doing all they can to avoid contact with the dead. But with each bump, each jolt, they hang on to a stiff arm or leg sticking over the rail. The living are shrinking with dread. With dread and disgust. They are howling. We hear nothing. The truck slides in silence on the snow.

We watch with eyes that cry out, eyes full of disbelief.

Each face is inscribed with such precision over the icy light, the blue of the sky, that it remains marked there for eternity.

For eternity, these shaven heads, squeezed against one another, bursting with shouts, mouths twisted by cries we do not hear, hands waving in a mute cry.

The cries remain inscribed upon the blue of the sky.

It was the day they were emptying block 25. The condemned women were loaded in trucks going up to the gas chamber. The last ones in were ordered to load the corpses to be incinerated, then climb up.

Since the dead were cast at once into the crematorium, we wondered, "Those of the last truck, the living mingled with the dead, would they go through the gas chamber or be poured out by the dump truck directly into the flames?"

They were howling because they knew, but their vocal cords had snapped in their throats.

And as for us, we were walled in the ice, the light, the silence.

The Same Day

We had been turned into statues by the cold, on a pedestal of ice formed by our legs welded to the ice on the ground. All gestures had abolished themselves. To scratch one's nose or blow on one's hands belonged to the realm of the fantastic, as though a ghost were scratching its nose or warming its hands with its breath. Someone says, "I think we're being ordered back." But within us nothing replies. We have lost consciousness and feeling. We had died to ourselves. "They're bringing us back in. The first squares are forming ranks." The command reached all the squares. The ranks reformed by fives. The walls of ice widened. The first column was on its way to the road.

We were leaning on one another so as not to fall. Yet, we were not aware of making any effort. Our bodies walked outside of us. Possessed, dispossessed. Abstract. We were unfeeling. We were taking shrunken steps, only what our frozen joints would allow. Without speaking. The return to camp. We had not counted on the end of this immobility which had lasted since the previous night.

We were returning. The light grew less implacable. That's what must be meant by twilight. Perhaps also everything was getting mixed up in our heads, the barbed wire so distinct a while back, the dazzling snow now spotted with diarrhea. Dirty puddles. The end of the day. Dead women strewn about on the snow, in the puddles. Sometimes we had to step over them. They were just ordinary obstacles so far as we were concerned. It was no longer possible for us to feel anything at all. We were walking. Walking automatons. Walking ice statues. Exhausted women were walking.

We were on our way when Josée, in the preceding rank, turned toward us to say, "When you get to the gate you'll have to run. Tell the others." She believes I can't hear her and repeats, "We'll have to run." The order was passed on without awakening in us the slightest wish to carry it out, no picture of our running. It was as if someone had said, "If it starts to rain, open your umbrellas." Pure nonsense.

When there is a stampede ahead of us, we know we have reached the gate. All the women start to run. They are running. Clogs, ill-fastened clodhoppers fly every which way with no one caring a whit. They are running. In the kind of disorder that would be grotesque for a statue made of ice, yet they run. When our turn comes, when we reach the gate, we start running too, straight ahead, determined to run till we are out of breath, without purpose or judgment. And this no longer strikes us as grotesque. We run. Toward what? Why? We just run.

I do not know if I understood that we had to run because on each side of the gate, and all along the Lagerstrasse, a double row of the camp's female personnel, SS women, female prisoners wearing armbands and blouses of every color and every rank, stood there, armed with walking sticks, clubs, straps, belts, lashes, whips, ready to flail and scourge whatever passed between the two rows. To elude the blow of a club meant to walk smack into a whip lash. Blows came raining down upon our heads, the napes of our necks. And the furies kept on screaming, Schneller! Schneller! Faster, faster, while flailing faster and faster this grain that flowed, ran, ran. I do not know if I had understood that running was a life-and-death matter. I was running. And no one ever thought of not conforming to the absurd. We ran. We ran.

I have no idea whether I reconstituted this whole scene after the fact or if I had an overall concept from the start. I always thought I was endowed with keen, attentive faculties so that I could see and grasp everything, as well as ward off the dangers. I ran.

It was an insane race which should have been observed from some familiar promontory in order to gauge its senselessness. Nor was it possible for anyone of us to imagine that we were watching these happenings objectively. We were running. Schneller. Schneller. Running.

Back inside the camp and out of breath, I hear someone say, "To

the block now. Quick. Go back to the block." The first human voice
you hear on awakening. I get a grip on myself and look around me. I
had lost my buddies. Others were flocking in, recognizing one another.
"So you're here? And Marie? And Gilberte?"

I am emerging from the hallucination whence arose grimacing
heads, the congested, disheveled heads of the furies. Schneller.
Schneller. And the Drexler woman hooking one of the women near
me with the crook of her stick. Who? Which one was it? Impossible
to remember and yet I saw her face, her expression set once and for
all as she was being strangled from behind. Drexler pulled on her
cane, tripping the woman up, and casting her to the side. Who was it
then? And this frantic flight, where only an outsider would detect
insanity, since we had gotten used to the fantastic, forgetting the
reflexes of the normal human being face to face with the preposterous.

"Go back to the block. Here. This way." The first women to get a
grip on themselves guided the others. I step into the darkness where
voices direct me: "This way. There. That's it. Climb up." And I grab
hold of the planks to scramble up to our square.

"Where were you? You were the only one missing from our
group. We were beginning to be frightened." Hands hoist me up.
"Who were you with?" "With me, we were together," says Yvonne
B. She had never stopped being by my side, I had not seen her.

"Did you see Hélène?"

"Hélène?"

"Yes, she was down on the ground. She let Alice Viterbo lean on
her arm and they both fell."

"Alice was caught."

"Hélène wanted to draw her along, but Alice was no longer able
to get up."

"So did Hélène leave her there?"

Hélène was coming. "You were able to escape?"

"Someone extricated me from under and pulled me, shouting,
'Leave her alone. Leave her.' I started running again. I had to abandon
Alice. Can't we go get her?"

"No, we musn't step out of the block."

One by one the women are coming back. Dazed. Drained. Each time we are making a count.

"Viva, you're all here, your whole group?"

"Yes, all eight of us."

"What about the next square? Are you all there?"

"No, Madame Brabander is missing."

"Who else is missing?"

"Madame Van der Lee."

"Marie is here."

"And what about Grandma Yvonne?"

We inquire about the aged, the sick, the weak.

"Here I am," answers the almost imperceptible voice of Grandma Yvonne.

We make another count. Fourteen are missing.

I saw Madame Brabander when the Drexler woman stopped her with her cane. She said to her daughter, "Take off. Run. Leave me."

I had run, run without seeing anything. I had run, run without thinking of anything, unaware of the danger, having only some vague notion of it, yet somehow close. Schneller. Schneller. Once I had glanced down at my shoe, seen the lace undone, without stopping running. I had run without feeling the blows of the bludgeon, of the belts that stunned me. And then I felt like laughing. Or rather, I saw my double who wanted to laugh. A cousin of mine used to insist that a duck could walk even with its head off. And this duck would run and run, with his head on the ground behind him so he couldn't see it. This duck ran as a duck never runs, looking at its shoe and not caring a hoot about the rest now that, with its head off, it ran no risk.

We are waiting, hoping still to see the women who are missing. They're not coming back. One can hardly speak of worrying during this waiting. This has become second nature to us. And we are able to piece together what happened.

"You see, they allowed only the young ones to squeak through. Those who were good runners. All the others were caught."

"I wanted so much to drag off Alice. I held on to her as long as I could."

"Madame Brabander was a very good runner."

And a sister was saying to her sister, "If something like this were to happen again, don't bother about me. Run along. Think only of yourself. Please promise me, won't you? You swear?"

"Listen, Hélène, Alice with her leg would not have lasted long."

"They also caught a lot of Polish women."

"With her face all wrinkled, Madame Brabander used to look like an old woman."

They already speak of the others in the past tense.

The Brabander girl, in her bunk, has the look of those who can no longer be affected by anything.

I am wondering how a duck is able to run without a head. My legs were paralyzed by the cold.

What do they intend to do with the women they caught?

The chief of the block, Magda, a Slovak, asks us to keep silent and says something translated by Marie-Claude: "They need volunteers. It won't be long. The youngest in the group." It seemed impossible to expect even a bit of effort from our arms, our legs. For our group, it is Cécile who gets up: "I'm off," and she puts on her shoes. "We've got to go, just to find out what's going on."

When she returns her teeth are chattering. Literally, making the sound of castanets. She was frozen and she cried. We rubbed her in order to warm her up, to stop this shuddering which communicated itself to us. We questioned her as one questions a child, with silly words: "It was to pick up the dead women who were left in the field. We had to carry them in front of block 25. One was still alive, she was begging, hanging on to us. We wanted to carry her off, when someone shouted: 'Take off. Run. Don't linger in front of block 25. Taube will come and throw you in there. Run for your life.' Our companions are there already, those who were caught a while back.

So we left them there and ran off. The dying woman was holding on to my ankles."

All fourteen are dead. They say Antoinette was gassed. Some lasted a long time. It seems that Madame Van der Lee lost her mind. The one who took the longest time to die was Alice.

Alice's Leg

One morning before roll call, little Simone, who had gone to the latrines behind block 25, returned all shaken. "Alice's leg is over there. Come see."

Behind block 25 was the morgue, a wooden hut where they piled up the dead hauled from the charnel house. Stacked one on top of the other, the corpses awaited the truck that would carry them to the crematorium. The rats were devouring them. Through the doorless opening one could see the heap of naked corpses and the glittering eyes of the rats darting to and fro. When there were too many of them, they were piled up outside.

It is a haystack of carefully piled corpses, as with a real haystack under the moonlight and snow, at night. But we look at them without fear. We know that here one is on the borderline of the bearable and we struggle against letting go.

Lying in the snow, Alice's leg is alive and sentient. It must have detached itself from the dead Alice.

We kept on going there to see if it was still there, and each time it was intolerable. Alice abandoned, dying in the snow. Alice we could not approach because weakness nailed us to the spot. Alice dying alone, not calling anyone.

Alice had been dead for weeks yet her artificial leg was still resting in the snow. Then it snowed again. The leg was covered over. It reappeared in the mud. This leg in the mud. Alice's leg—severed alive—in the mud.

We saw it a long time. One day it was not there any more. Someone must have filched it to make a fire. A gypsy woman surely, no one else would have dared.

Stenia

No one can fall asleep tonight.

The wind blows and whistles and groans. It is a moan mounting from the marshes, a sob swelling, swelling and bursting, then subsiding into shivering silence, another sob swells, swells and bursts and dies down.

No one is able to fall asleep.

And amid the silence, between the sobbing of the wind, death rattles. First stifled, then distinct, then strong, so strong that the ear wanting to locate them hears them still as the wind dies down.

No one is able to fall asleep.

Stenia, the blockhova, cannot fall asleep. She comes out of her room, a small hovel at the entrance to the block. Her candle burrows through the dark passage between the tiers where we are recumbent, stacked in rows. Stenia awaits the tornado's abatement, and in the silence where the death rattle rises she shouts, "Who's making that racket? Silence!" The death rattle continues. Stenia shouts, "Silence!" but the dying does not hear her. "Silence!" The death rattle fills the silence between the wind's waves, fills all the blackness of the night.

Stenia holds up her candle, walking in the direction of the rattles, identifies the dying woman and orders that she be brought down. The dying woman's companions, under Stenia's blows, carry her out. They lay her down, as gently as possible, close to the wall, and then go back to lie down again.

Stenia's light moves off, disappears. Squalls of wind and rain beat down upon the roofing threatening to break it.

In the barracks, no one is able to fall asleep.

A plain
covered with marshes
with tipcarts
with gravel for the tipcarts
with shovels and spades for the marshes
a plain
covered with men and women
for the spades the tipcarts and the marshes
a plain
of cold and fever
for men and women
who struggle
and die.

Daytime

The marshes. A plain covered with marshes. Marshes as far as the eye can see. An infinite expanse of icy plain.

We pay attention only to our feet. To walk in rank formation creates a sort of obsession. You tend to look at feet moving in front of you. You have these feet going forward, heavily, walking before you, these feet you are avoiding and you'll never catch up with, feet preceding yours, always, even at night in a nightmare of trampling, these feet so fascinating that you would see them even if you were in the front rank, feet that drag or stumble yet keep on going. They move forward with their uneven sound, their uncoordinated step. You happen to be behind a woman walking barefoot because her shoes were stolen, feet bare on the ice, in the mud, bare feet, bare in the snow, tortured feet you would prefer not to see, pitiful feet you fear to tread on and the sight of which torments you, makes you ill. Occasionally a clog falls off a foot, lands in front of you, and bothers you like a summer fly. You do not stop for this clog which the other bends down to pick up. You have to keep on walking. You walk. And you pass by the laggard who is cast out of the ranks on the shoulder of the road, and who runs to retrieve her place, unable to identify her companions now swallowed in the stream of the others, and seeks out their feet, since she knows she will recognize their clodhoppers. You walk on. You go toward the marshes drowned in fog. You walk without seeing anything, eyes riveted to the feet ahead of you. You go on. You walk through the plain covered by marshes. Marshes reaching to the line of the horizon. In the limitless plain, the frozen plain. You walk.

We were walking since daybreak.

There is always a moment when the cold clings more humidly to your bones, a raw cold. The sky grows lighter. It is daytime. They call it day.

We waited till daybreak to set out. Each day we waited for daybreak to set out. We were not allowed to set forth before it was light, before the sentries posted in the watchtowers could shoot at the runaways. The thought of running away did not cross anyone's mind. You must be strong to wish to escape. You must be able to count on all your muscles, all your senses. No one dreamt of escaping. It was daytime. The columns were being formed. We let ourselves be assigned to any one of them. Our only concern was in not being separated, so we clung to one another.

Once the columns were formed, there was still a long wait. Thousands of women take time going out, five by five, counted as they pass. Passing through the gate made us tighten. Passing under the eyes of the Drexler woman, of Taube, under the eyes of so many scrutinizers, all drawn to an improperly fastened collar, an open button, hands hanging limply, a number not readily legible. In front of the control barracks, a woman SS touched with her stick the first woman of each rank and counted: fünfzehn, zwanzig, up to one hundred, up to two hundred, according to the commando's size. When that one had passed through, two SS, each holding a dog on a leash, closed the line of march. Coil by coil, the camp cast out into daylight the entrails of the night.

We turned either to the right or to the left. To the right were the marshes. To the left the houses to be demolished, the tipcarts to fill and push. For weeks I was hoping we would turn right because then we would walk across a small stream where I might get some water to drink. Most of the time we were taken to the marshes.

We would set out upon the road. The discipline loosened. We could walk arm in arm, leaning on a companion, straighten our collar, stick our hands up our sleeves. The column stretched out along the road.

Today the road is iced over, polished like a mirror. We slide on this icy surface, fall. The column keeps on going. There are those we must carry because their legs are so swollen they are unable to take a step. The column keeps on going. We reach another turn in the road, apprehensive because there the wind shifts. It blows straight into our

faces, cutting, icy. We know we are drawing close to the marshes
because of the fog. We walk in the fog where we see nothing. There is
nothing to see. An infinite expanse of marshy land, the plain drowned
in fog. The plain wrapped in icy cotton.

We are on our way. We keep on walking, intent on feet alone. We
have been walking since early daybreak.

We walk.

When we slow down, the SS who bring up the rear incite their
dogs.

We keep on walking.

We walk through the icy plain.

At the marsh's edge, the column stops. Each of the female non-
commissioned officers in charge of a detail proceeds to a head count:
Fünfzehn. Zwanzig. Vierzig. We must not make a move. They are still
counting. Dreissig. Fünfzig. No one must move. They recount. Then
they lead us to a pile of tools shining dimly in the fog. We pick up the
spades. There are handbarrows next to them, piled up with bricks.
Too bad for those who were not quick enough to grab a spade.

Tool in hand, we go down into the marsh. We sink into the denser
fog over the marshes. We see nothing ahead of us. We slip into holes,
ditches. The SS yell. Stepping firmly in their boots, they come and
go, and make us run. They measure the square to be worked on. We
have to pick up where the spadework stopped the day before. Like
miserable, defenseless insects dimly outlined in the mist, the women
take their places, bending down along a line lost in the fog at both
ends. Everything screams. The SS, the anweiserins, the kapos. We must
drive our spades into the ice, grapple with the earth underneath, pull
up clods of it, pile up these clods on the handbarrows placed by two
of us next to the furrow dug out by the spades. Once the handbarrow
is full, they carry it off. They walk painfully, their shoulders wrenched
by the load. They are to empty the handbarrow on top of a pile of
earth which they scale stumbling, falling. The carriers form an uninterrupted circle which tips, rights itself, bends under the weight,
empties the handbarrow on top of the pile and returns to assume its

place in front of a digger. All along their way, clubs on the nape of the neck, switches on the temples, lashes on the lower backs. Screams. Screams. Screams screaming to the invisible confines of the marsh. Those who scream are not the insects. Insects are mute.

For the diggers, the blows come from behind. Three furies come and go hitting everything on their way, without a moment's respite, screaming, yelling always the same words, the same curses repeated in an incomprehensible foreign tongue, taking turns flaying with all their might the same victims, those they have singled out, this one because she is tiny and is struggling with her spade, that one because she is tall and her height seems a defiance, the other because her chapped hands are bleeding. Standing off to the side, the SS have made a fire with some sticks. They are warming themselves. Their dogs warm themselves too next to their masters. When the screams reach a peak, they get into action, screaming and hitting also. Without thinking. Without reason. Kicking. Hitting with their fists. Then silence falls over the marsh, as if the mist were growing thicker, muffling the sounds. Soon screams shatter the silence once again.

So this is why we were waiting for daybreak.

We waited for daybreak to start the day.

What is closer to eternity than a day? What is longer than one day? How can we tell that it is passing? Clods of earth follow clods of earth, the furrow lengthens, the carriers continue their rounds. And the screams, the screams, the screams.

What is longer than a day? We know that time is passing because the fog slowly lifts. Our hands are less numb. Vaguely, far off, a bit of sunlight. It tears off tatters of fog. The ice softens, softens and melts. Then our feet sink in the mud, our clods are covered by icy slime which rises to our ankles. We remain motionless in murky water, motionless in icy water. For the carriers of handbarrows, the pile of earth grows increasingly hard to scale, wet, slippery.

Daylight has come.

The marsh grows pale with a hazy, cold radiance as the yellow rays of the sun pierce the mist.

The marsh has turned liquid again under the sunlight which has now dispelled all of the fog.

It is broad daylight.

Daylight on the marshland where tall, golden reeds shine.

Daylight on the marsh where insects with eyes full of terror labor to the point of exhaustion.

The spade grows increasingly heavier.

The carriers bear the handbarrow lower and lower.

It is day on the marsh where insects in human form die.

The barrow has become impossible to lift.

It is day till the end of the day.

Hunger. Fever. Thirst.

It is day until evening.

The small of the back is a solid block of pain.

It is day until night.

Frozen hands, frozen feet.

It is day over the marsh where the sun makes the distant shapes of the trees gleam in their icy shrouds.

It is day for a whole eternity.

The Farewell

At noon they made them step out. As they passed her, the blockhova tore off their scarves and coats. Tattered scarves, tattered coats.

It was a dry, cold winter day. One of those wintry days when people say: "It would be nice to take a walk." People. Somewhere else.

The ground was covered with frozen snow.

Stripped of their coats, many of the women were bare-armed. They folded their arms and rubbed their thin hands. Others protected their heads. None had more than a centimeter of hair, none had been there long. All shivered spasmodically.

The courtyard was too small to hold them, but they huddled in the sunny part, pushing toward the shade those who were close to death. Seated in the snow, they waited. One could tell by the look in their faces that they saw nothing, nothing of their surroundings, nothing of the courtyard, nothing of the dying and the dead, nothing of themselves. They were there, on the snow, unable to control their fitful shivering.

All at once, as though heeding some kind of signal, they would start to howl. A swelling howl that rose, rose and spread above the walls. They were nothing but howling mouths, howling at the heavens. A pitful of twisted mouths.

When the howling subsided you heard some lone sobs in the silence. They sagged. Disheartened, resigned perhaps. They were nothing but hollow eyes. A pitful of hollow eyes.

Soon they could no longer endure accepting, being resigned. A howl rose, wilder than the ones before, rose and snapped, as silence fell again with its sobs and the hollow eyes of despair.

Amid the motley tatters and the crowd of faces, those who neither cried nor howled had stopped shivering.

And the howling resumed.

Nothing heard these cries from the edge of dread. The world stopped far from here. The world that says, "It would be lovely to take a walk." Only our own ears heard and we were no longer living beings. We were awaiting our turn.

The most recent silence lasts a long time. Are they all dead? No. They are here. Defeated, yet their conscious minds still refuse, keep on denying, steeling themselves, wishing to protest, to keep on struggling. The howling rises anew, rises and swells, ever widening. Again these are nothing but mouths howling in the direction of the sky above.

The silences and the howls streaked the passing hours.

The sun was beginning to withdraw. Lengthening shadows spread over the whole yard. Nothing was left but one illuminated row of heads touched by the last rays of the dying day that revealed their bony outlines, twisted by their cries.

Then you hear the rumbling of trucks immediately covered by the howling. And when the gate swings open, the yard becomes too large. All the women have risen to their feet, huddling against the opposite wall. Strewn on the foul snow of the vacated space lie more corpses than had been counted.

Two prisoners enter. At this sight, the cries grow twice as loud. This is the death squad, the "heaven commando."

Armed with clubs, they try to push the women in the direction of the gate. They do not move. Inert. Then they give in. Almost without being pushed, they draw near.

The first truck is parked smack against the gate.

A prisoner is standing on the truck, a giant wearing a jacket with an upturned fur collar and an astrakhan cap pulled down over his ears.

(Those who serve in the "heaven commando" enjoy special privileges. They are well dressed, eat their fill, at least for a space of three months. Once their time runs out, others take over, sending them off in turn. Off to heaven. Off to the crematorium. That's how it goes every three months. They are the ones who keep the gas chambers and smokestacks working.)

On the back of the prisoner's jacket a cross is traced in red lead. The women have the same red cross; there are more and more of them now on striped dresses.

The two other prisoners push the women toward him. He loosens his belt, grasps it strongly at both ends, passing it under the arms of each woman in turn as he pulls them up. He throws them onto the floor of the truck. When they come to, they get up. Some reflexes can never be altered.

Hep. Hep. One more, one more. Hep. Hep. One more.

He works fast, like someone who is good at his work, but he wants to do a little better every time. The truck is full. Not full enough yet. With a hard shove he packs and packs them, then goes on loading. The women are crushed against one another. They do not cry out any longer, do not shiver.

When he can no longer add anything more, he jumps to the ground, pulls up the back, attaches the chains. He casts a last glance at his work, inspecting the job. Grabbing a few more around the waist, he throws them over the others who feel them come down on their heads, their shoulders. They do not shout, do not tremble. Once he has finished loading, he sits down next to the driver. Let's go! The SS starts the car.

The Drexler woman observes the departure. Her fists on her hips, she supervises, like a foreman who oversees a job and is satisfied.

The women in the truck do not shout. Pressed tightly together they try to release their arms from their torsos. It is incomprehensible that one would still try to work an arm free, that one could wish to lean on something.

One of the women thrusts her chest far over the side panel. Straight. Stiff. Her eyes shine. She looks at Drexler with hate, scorn, a scorn that should kill. She did not shout with the others, her face is ravaged only by illness.

The truck starts up. Drexler follows it with her eyes.

As the truck pulls away, she waves a farewell and laughs. She is laughing. And for a long time she keeps on waving good-bye.

This is the first time we have seen her laugh.

Another truck pulls up in front of the door of block 25.

I no longer look.

Roll Call

When it lasts too long a time it means there is something wrong. An error in the count or danger. What kind of danger? One never knows. Danger.

An SS approaches, whom we recognize at once. The doctor. Immediately, the stronger women slip to the front, the bluest ones pinch their cheeks. He draws near, looks us over. Is he aware of the gripping anxiety that fills us under his stare?

He passes by.

We can draw breath again.

Further on, he halts at the ranks of the Greek women and asks: "Which are the women between twenty and thirty who have given birth to a living child?"

They must renew their supply of guinea pigs in the medical-experiment block.

The Greek women have just arrived.

As for us, we have been here much too long. A few weeks. We are too thin or weak for them to cut open our bellies.

Night

The octopi strangled us with their viscous muscles, and if we succeeded in freeing an arm it was only to be strangled by a tentacle
coiling itself around our necks, tightening round our vertebrae,
squeezing them until they cracked, the vertebrae, the trachea, the
esophagus, the larynx, the pharynx, and all the canals in the throat,
squeezing them to the breaking point. In order to free our throats and
save ourselves from strangulation, we had to yield our arms, legs, waist
to the grasping, invading tentacles which multiplied endlessly,
appeared from everywhere, so numerous that we were tempted to
give up the struggle and this exhausting vigilance. The tentacles
uncoiled, uncoiling their threat. The threat hung deferred for a long
time while we stayed there, hypnotized, unable to risk a dodge for
fear that the beast would fall upon us, winding itself about our flesh,
glued to it, crushing our bones. We were about to succumb when, all
of a sudden, we felt we were waking up. These are not octopi, it is
mud. We swim in mud, a viscous slime with the inexhaustible tentacles of waves. It is a sea of mud in which we must swim, swim
strongly, to the point of exhaustion, running out of breath as we keep
our heads above eddies of mire. We shrink with disgust, slime enters
our eyes, nose, mouth, chokes us and we flap our arms in order to
steady ourselves in this ooze which envelops us in its octopus arms.
Swimming in the mud would not be so bad if we did not have to
carry handbarrows loaded with clods of earth, so heavy that the
weight irremediably pulls you down to the very bottom so that the
slime oozes into your throat, your ears, sticky and ice cold. To keep
these barrows above our heads entails a superhuman effort, and our
comrade ahead sinks, disappears, is swallowed up by the mud. We
must pull her out, set her on course in the slime, yet we cannot let go
of the barrow, impossible to get rid of it, it is chained fast to our
wrists, so securely that both of us sink in a mortal embrace, tied to

each other by the barrow spilling its clods which get mixed up with
the mud we churn in an ultimate attempt to free ourselves and the
barrow is now full of eyes and teeth, eyes that gleam, teeth that
snicker and light up the mud as do phosphorescent madrepores in the
deep, and all these eyes and teeth flare up and vociferate, flashing,
biting, stinging and biting from every direction, and shrieking:
Schneller, schneller, weiter, weiter, and when we punch these maws
all teeth and eyes, our fists hit nothing but soft leucomas, rotting
sponges. We wish we might run away, swim away from this sludge.
The slough is full, like a pool in the summer at noon, and we go
knocking against fleeing, oily masses that block all retreat, shoulders
roll, turn around, bump other shoulders. It is a tangle of bodies, a
melee of arms and legs and, when at last we believe we grasped something solid, it is because we knocked our heads against the planks we
sleep on and everything vanishes in the shadowy dark where Lulu's
leg is moving, or Yvonne's arm, and the head resting heavily on my
chest is that of Viva so that awakened by the feeling that I am on the
edge of the void, on the edge of our tier, about to go tumbling down
into our passageway, I plunge into another nightmare, for this
shadowy cavern breathes and puffs, stirred in every one of its innermost recesses by a thousand pain-filled nightmares and fitful sleep. A
shadow glides from the shadows, stands out and slides onto the
muddy ground as it runs to the door of the cavern. This shadow
awakens others who also glide, run, and in the night find their way
with difficulty. They move gropingly, hesitate, brush against one
another, exchange senseless words: "where are my shoes? Is that you?
Dysentery, I'm going out for the third time tonight." Other shadows
return, grope for their place, the place for their head which they can
tell by feeling other heads, and from all the tiers nightmares rise, take
shape in the dark, as groans and moans escape from bodies bruised by
struggling against the mud, against the howling hyena faces. "Weiter,
weiter," they shout, and the only escape is to nestle within oneself and
try to summon up a bearable nightmare, perhaps the one in which
you see yourself returning home and saying, "Here I am. I've come

back you see," but all your relatives you assumed tormented by your absence turn their backs on you, grown mute and strange in their indifference. You say again, "It's me, I'm here, and now I know it's really so, that I'm not dreaming, I dreamt so often of returning but waking up from such a dream is frightful. This time it's real, it's true since I'm in the kitchen, I'm touching the sink. You see, mama, it's me, but the cold of the stone sink propels me out of my dream. A brick has come loose from the low wall separating our cell from the next where other larvae sleep, moan and dream under the blankets that cover them—these are shrouds covering them for they are dead, today or tomorrow what does it matter, they are dead when it comes to returning to the kitchen where their mothers await them. We feel that we teeter on the edge of a dark pit, a bottomless void—it is the hole of the night where we struggle furiously, struggle against another nightmare, that of our real death. We must return, return home, return in order to touch with our hands the stone kitchen sink, and we struggle against the vertigo sucking us down into the pit of night and death, for the last time we use all our strength in a desperate effort, holding on to the brick, the cold brick we carry against our chest, the brick we extracted from a pile of bricks held together by ice, detached it by breaking the ice with our nails, quick, quick, as the clubs and whips fly and fall over our backs—faster, faster, with our nails bleeding—and we carry this icy brick, propped against our chest, to another pile, in a dismal procession where each holds a brick against her heart, for this is the way in which bricks are carried here, from morning till evening, and it is not enough to carry bricks all day to the building yard, we continue carrying them throughout the night, for at night everything hounds us at once, the mud of the marshes in which we sink, the cold bricks we must bear against our hearts, the shrieking kapos and the dogs treading the mud as though it were firm ground and leaping to bite us at the least sign of eyes gleaming in the night, and we feel the hot, humid dog breath upon our faces as our temples bead with the sweat of fear. Night is far more exhausting than day, echoing with coughs and death rattles, women dying alone, squeezed against the others who are still in the throes of struggling with the mud, the dogs, the bricks and the shrieks, those whom we will find dead when we awaken, whom we will carry out into the mud in front of our door, leaving them there, wrapped up in the blankets in which they gave up their lives. And each dead woman is as light or as heavy as the shadows of the night, light because her flesh melted away, and heavy with the burden of a pain that no one will ever share.

And when the whistle blows reveille, it is not that night is ending

for night ends only with the stars waning and the sky suffused with color,

it is not that night is ending

for it ends only with the day,

when the whistle blows reveille there are still the straits of eternity to traverse between night and day.

When the whistle blows reveille, a nightmare congeals, another begins

there is only a lucid moment between the two, when we listen to the pounding of our heart wondering whether it has the strength to beat much longer

longer is counted in days because our hearts are unable to count weeks or months, we count day by day and each day is measured by a thousand deaths, a thousand eternities.

The whistle blows in the camp, a voice shouts: "Zell Appell" and we hear, "It's the roll call," and another, "Aufstehen," but it is not the end of night

it is not the end of night for those who are delirious in the charnel house

nor the end of night for the rats devouring lips still alive

it is not the end of night for the stars frozen in a frozen sky

it is not the end of night

it is the hour when shadows slip back into the walls, when other shadows issue into the night

it is not the end of night

only the end of a thousand nights and a thousand nightmares.

Up to Fifty

The man kneels. Crosses his arms. Lowers his head. The kapo steps forward. He has his club. He comes close to the kneeling man and plants his feet firmly.

The SS steps up to them with his dog.

The kapo raises his club, which he holds in both hands, and delivers a blow across the small of the man's back. Eins.

Another. Zwei.

Another. Drei.

It is the man himself who is counting. One can hear him in the intervals between the blows.

Vier.

Fünf. His voice is growing weaker.

Sechs.

Sieben.

Acht. We can no longer hear him, but he is still counting. He is supposed to count up to fifty.

With each blow his body sags a bit more. The kapo is tall, he strikes with all his might, from his great height.

With each blow the dog yelps, wants to leap. Its muzzle follows the club's trajectory.

"Weiter," shouts the anweiserin seeing us motionless, leaning on our spades.

"Weiter." We cannot move.

The sound of the beating is like the beating of a rug.

The man is still counting. The SS listens to make sure he does.

His head is touching the ground. Each blow imparts a tremor to his body, tearing it apart. Each blow makes us jump.

The sound of fifty blows on a man's back is interminable.

If he stopped counting, the blows would stop and start again from zero.

Fifty strokes of a club on a man's back is an endless number. They reverberate.

The Tulip

There is the outline of a house in the distance. Whipped by the squalls it suggests a ship in winter, anchored in a Nordic port. A ship on a gray horizon.

We were walking head down under squalls of melting snow which lashed our faces, stinging like hail. With each blast we lowered our heads even more in anticipation of the next. The squalls came sweeping down, slapping and lacerating our skin. It was as though a handful of coarse kitchen salt was flung smack in our faces. We were moving forward, shoving before us a cliff of wind and snow.

Where were we going?

It was a direction we had never taken before. We had taken a turn before reaching the brook. The embankment ran along a lake. A great frozen lake.

Toward what were we going? What could we possibly have been doing there? This was the question raised by the dawn every dawn. What work awaited us? Marshes, hand trucks, bricks, sand. We could not think of these words without losing heart.

We kept on walking, questioning the landscape. A steely, frozen lake. A landscape that will not answer.

The road swerves off, away from the lake. The wall of wind and snow shifts to one side. This is where a house comes into view. We walk a little more softly. We are walking in the direction of a home.

It is next to the road. Made of red brick. The chimney is smoking. Who could be living in this remote house? It draws nearer. We can see white curtains. Muslin curtains. We utter "muslin" softly in the mouth. And in front of the curtains, in the space between the window and the storm sash, there is a tulip.

Our eyes light up at this apparition. "Did you see? You did see, didn't you? A tulip." All eyes converge on the flower. Here, in a desert of ice and snow, a tulip. Pink between two pale leaves. We look at it. We forget the stinging hail. The column slows down. "Weiter," shouts the SS. Our heads are still turned toward the house that we passed a long time back.

All day we dream of the tulip. The melted snow fell, adhered to the back of our soaked, stiff jackets. The day was long, as long as all our days. Down at the bottom of the ditch we were digging, the tulip's delicate corolla bloomed.

On our way back, long before reaching the lake house, we were on the lookout for it. It was still there, against the white background of the curtains. Pink beaker between pale leaves. During the roll call, we said to our companions who had not accompanied us on this detail, "We saw a tulip."

We were never taken back to this ditch. Others must have completed it. In the morning, at the intersection where the road to the lake began, we experienced a moment of hope.

When we found out that this house belonged to the SS in charge of the fishery, we despised this memory and the tender feeling which had not yet dried up within us.

Morning

From the edge of the dark a voice shouted "Aufstehen." From within
the darkness another echoed "Stavache," and a black stirring followed
with everyone extricating their limbs. All we had to do was to find
our shoes in order to jump down. The whip whistled and lashed those
who did not emerge fast enough from their blankets. Lash in hand,
the stubhova standing in the passageway would fly up to the third tier,
to the center of the cells, whipping faces and legs numb with sleep.
When everything moved and stirred, when everywhere blankets
shook themselves out and folded themselves, we heard the clink of
metal against metal, vapor veiled the candle's flickering at the core of
the dark. They were uncovering the tin cans to dish out tea. Those
who had just come in were leaning against the wall, out of breath,
trying to contain with their hand on their chest the rapid beating of
their heart. They had come back from the kitchens which are far, very
far when you must carry a huge, heavy can by holding on to handles
that cut into the palms of your hands. Far in the snow, on ice-covered
roads or in the mud where you take three steps forward and two back,
moving forward and drawing back, falling and getting up and falling
again under a weight much too heavy for arms devoid of strength.
When they have caught their breath, they say, "It's cold this morning,
colder than last night." They say "this morning." It is the middle of
the night, a little after three.

The tea steams with a nauseating smell. The stubhovas dispense
niggardly portions to our feverish thirsts. They keep the greater part
for their ablutions. It is certainly the best use one can make of this,
and we would also like to have a wash in good hot water. We have not
washed since we arrived, not even our hands in cold water. We drink
the tea from our tin cups still smelling of last night's soup. There is no
water to wash out the cups either. To drink tea means triumphing in a
wild tug-of-war, a melee of club blows, elbowings, fisticuffs, screams.

Consumed by thirst and fever, we whirl and swirl in the melee. We drink our tea standing, jostled by those who fear not being served and those who want to exit, because they must do so at once, as soon as they are up. A last blow of the whistle. Alles raus.

The door swings open on the starry night. Each morning is the coldest it has ever been. Each morning we feel that whatever we had to bear is now unbearable, too much, we can no longer take it. At the stars' sill we halt, hesitating, wanting to draw back. This unleases the clubs, the whips, the shrieks. Those standing at the door are hurled into the cold. From the depths of the block, under a pelting rain of blows, everyone is hurled into the cold.

Outside lies the exposed ground, piles of stones, of earth, obstacles to skirt, ditches to avoid, together with ice, mud or snow and the night's excrement. Outside, the piercing cold penetrates us to our very bones. Icy blades. The night outside is bright with cold. The moon casts blue shadows on the ice and the snow.

It's roll-call time. All the blocks disgorge their shadowy figures. Moving awkwardly from cold and fatigue, a crowd reels toward the Lagerstrasse. It falls into ranks of five in a bedlam of shrieks and blows. It takes a long time for all these shadows to line up, as they lose their footing on the ice, in the mud and the snow, all these shadows looking for each other, huddling together to reduce their exposure to the icy wind.

Then silence reigns.

Neck drawn into her shoulders, chest pulled in, each places her hands under the arms of the one in front of her. Since they cannot do it in the first row, we rotate. Backs to chests, we stand pressed against each other, yet, as we establish a single circulatory system, we remain frozen through and through. Annihilated by the cold. Feet, these remote and separate extremities, cease to exist. Shoes stay wet from yesterday's and all yesterdays' snow and mud. They never dry.

We will have to stay motionless for hours in the cold and the wind. We do not speak. Words freeze on our lips. Masses of women standing immobile are struck with stupor. In the night. In the cold. In the wind.

We remain immobile and the amazing thing is that we remain standing. Why? No one thinks, "What's the good of that?" or no one voices this thought. At the end of our rope, we remain standing.

I am standing amid my comrades and I think to myself that if I ever return and will want to explain the inexplicable, I shall say: "I was saying to myself: you must stay standing through roll call. You must get through one more day. It is because you got through today that you will return one day, if you ever return." This is not so. Actually I did not say anything to myself. I thought of nothing. The will to resist was doubtlessly buried in some deep, hidden spring which is now broken, I will never know. And if the women who died had required those who returned to account for what had taken place, they would be unable to do so. I thought of nothing. I felt nothing. I was a skeleton of cold, with cold blowing through all the crevices in between a skeleton's ribs.

I am standing amid my comrades. I do not look at the stars. They stab with cold. I do not look at the barbed-wire enclosures, white in the night under the lights. They are claws of cold. I see my mother with that mask of hardened will her face has become. My mother. Far. I look at nothing. I think of nothing.

Each breath drawn in is so cold that it strips the whole respiratory system. Skin ceases to be the tight protective covering for the body. The cold strips us nude, down to the bowels. The lungs flap in the icy wind. Wash out on a line. The heart is shrunk from cold, contracted, constricted till it aches, and suddenly I feel something snap there, in my heart. My heart breaks loose from my chest and everything that holds it in its place. I feel a stone falling inside me, dropping with a thud. It is my heart. I am filled with a wonderful sense of well-being. How good one feels, free of this fragile, demanding heart. One sinks into a soft lightness which must be happiness. Everything melts within me, everything assumes the fluidity of joy. I surrender, and it is sweet to surrender to easeful death, sweeter than to love, and to know that it is over, no more suffering and struggling, or requiring the impossible from a heart at the end of its resources. This fit of giddiness lasts less than an instant, but long enough to experience a bliss one did not know existed.

When I come to, it is from the shock of the slaps Viva imprints on my cheeks with all her might, lips tight, eyes averted. Viva is strong. She does not faint at roll call. I do, every morning. It is a moment of indescribable happiness. Viva must never know this.

Again and again she speaks my name which surges, distant, from the bottom of the void—it is my mother's voice I hear. The voice grows hard: "Keep your chin up! On your feet!" And I feel that I cling to Viva as a child to its mother. I am hanging onto her who kept me from falling into the mud, into the snow from which one never rises. And I must struggle to choose between this consciousness which means suffering and this abandon which promised happiness, and I am able to make this choice because Viva tells me, "Keep your chin up! On your feet!" I do not argue with this command, although I long to give in once, once since it will be the only time. It is so easy to die here. All you must do is let go of your heart.

I regain possession of myself, and of my body, as though slipping back into cold and wet clothes. My pulse is returning and beating, my lips seared by the cold are torn at the mouth's corners. I regain possession of the anguish that permanently fills me, and of the hope to which I did such violence.

Viva no longer uses her hard voice and asks, "D'you feel better?" and her voice is so comfortingly tender that I answer, "Yes, Viva. I'm better." It is my lips that answer, and in so doing tear a little more where they are chapped by fever and cold.

I am surrounded by my comrades. I take my place once more in the poor communal warmth created by our contact, and since we must return completely, I return to the roll call and think: It's the morning roll call—what a poetic title it would be—the call of the morning. I no longer knew the difference between morning and evening.

This is the morning roll call. The sky gradually brightens in the east. A flaming spray spills there, frozen flames, and the shadows drowning our own dissolve little by little, letting our faces emerge from the dark. All these purplish, deathly livid faces grow more so as the light spreads in the sky. Now you can tell who was grazed by death last night, who will be taken away this evening. For death is imprinted on the face, clings implacably to it, and our eyes do not need to meet for all of us to realize as we look at Suzanne Rose that she is going to die, that Mounette is going to die. Death is imprinted on the skin drawn tight over the cheekbones, the skin stuck to the eye sockets, stuck to the jawbones. And we know that it is no use now to call forth their home, or their son, their mother. It is too late. There is nothing we can do for them.

Darkness dissolves a bit more. The dogs' barking is coming closer. They mark the arrival of the SS. The blockhovas shout "Quiet!" in their impossible tongues. The cold nips our hands emerging from below our comrades' arms. Fifteen thousand women stand at attention.

The SS women officers stride by—tall in their black capes, boots, high black hoods. They count us as they pass. And it lasts a long time.

When they have passed by, each one of us places her hands back in another woman's armpits. Coughs repressed until then burst forth and the blockhovas shout "Quiet!" at the coughs in their impossible languages. We must still wait, await the break of day.

The dark dissolves. The sky is aglow. We can now see hallucinating processions passing by. Little Rolande asks, "Let me through to the first row. I want to see." Later she will explain, "I was sure of recognizing her. She had deformed feet. I was sure to know her by her feet." Her mother had been taken to the charnel house a few days earlier. She kept watch each day to know when her mother died.

Hallucinating processions pass by. These are the women who died in the night, taken from the charnel houses to the morgue. They are naked on stretchers fashioned roughly from branches, stretchers far too short. The legs—the shinbones—hang over the side with their thin, bare feet at the end. The head hangs over the other side, bony and shaven. A tattered blanket is thrown across the middle. Four prisoners carry the stretchers, one at each handle, and it is true that you go feet first, this was always the direction in which they carried the corpses. They walk with difficulty in the snow or the mud, and fling the body on the pile near block 25. They return with an empty stretcher, hardly less heavy, and pass by again with a new corpse. It is their work every day, their everyday work.

I watch them go by and brace myself. A while back I was surrendering to death. Each dawn I experience the same temptation. When the stretcher passes by, I brace myself. I wish to die but not to be carried on the small stretcher. Not to be carried by on the short stretcher with hanging legs and head, naked under a tattered blanket. I do not wish to be carried on the small stretcher.

Death is reassuring. I would not feel it. "You're not afraid of the crematorium, so what is there to fear?" How fraternal death can be. Those who depicted it as hideous never saw it. However, revulsion wins out. I do not wish to pass by, carried on the small stretcher.

I know then that all those who pass by are passing for me, that all those who died died for me. I watch them passing and I say no. To slide into death, here, in the snow. Let yourself slide. No, because there is the little stretcher. I do not wish to pass by carried on the small stretcher.

The dark is completely dissolved. It is colder now. I hear my heart beating and I speak to it just as Arnolphe spoke to his. I talk to my heart.

When will the time come when I will no longer have to be in charge of my heart, my lungs, my muscles? When will this enforced solidarity between the brain, the nerves, the bones and all the organs we have in our belly cease? When will the time come when we will no longer know one another, my heart and me?

The red of the sky fades and the sky grows pale. Far off, in the livid sky, black crows appear, swooping down over the camp in dense flocks. We await the end of roll call.

We await the end of roll call to go off to work.

Weiter

The SS at the four corners stake out limits not to be crossed. It was a large building yard. Everything that haunted us every night was assembled there: rocks to break, a road to pave, sand to excavate, handbarrows to transport the stones and sand, ditches to dig, bricks to carry from one pile to the next. Assigned to various teams together with Polish women, we exchanged sad smiles whenever our paths crossed.

Now that the sun was shining, it was not so cold. At the noon break, we sat down to eat on some building materials. Once we had downed our soup—it only took a few minutes, the longest time was spent waiting for its distribution, waiting in line in front of the canteens—we had a little time left before returning to the stones, sand, road, ditch and bricks. We squashed the lice at the open collars of our dresses. This is where they swarm the most. In view of their numbers, to kill a few hardly made any difference. It was our playtime. Sad. The midday break when we were able to sit down because the weather was fair.

Clustered in little groups of friends, we chatted. Each one spoke of her province, her home, invited the others to visit her. You'll come, won't you? You will come. We promised. We made so many trips.

"Weiter." The shout shatters the lull of our daydreams.

"Weiter." To whom is he speaking?

"Weiter."

A woman is walking towards the stream, her tin cup in hand, probably to rinse it out. She stops, hesitating.

"Weiter." Does he mean her?

"Weiter." There is a kind of mockery in the tone of the SS.

The woman hesitates. Must she really go farther? Could it be that to lean toward the stream is not allowed at this spot?

"Weiter," orders the SS more imperiously.

The woman draws back, stops again. Standing with the marsh

behind her, everything about her questions: "Is it allowed here?"

"Weiter," shrieks the SS.

Then the woman begins to walk, upstream.

"Weiter."

A shot. The woman crumples.

The SS swings his gun back over his shoulder, calls his dog, walks toward the woman. Leaning over her body, he turns her over as one does game.

The other SS laugh from their posts.

She had gone beyond the limit by less than twenty steps.

We make a count of our group. Are we all here?

When the SS raised his gun and took aim, the woman was walking in the sun.

She was killed instantly.

It was one of the Polish women.

Some had not seen it and were wondering what happened. The others wonder if they had seen right but say nothing.

Thirst

Thirst is an explorer's tale, you know, in the books we read as children. It takes place in the desert. Those who see mirages and walk in the direction of an elusive oasis suffer from thirst for three whole days. This is the pathetic chapter of the book. At the end of that chapter, a caravan bringing provisions appears; it had lost its way on trails erased by sand storms. The explorers pierce the goatskin bottles and they drink. They drink and their thirst is quenched. This is the thirst experienced in the sun, the drying wind. The desert. It is accompanied by the image of a palm tree profiled in filigree against russet sand.

But the thirst of the marsh is more searing than that of the desert. The marsh thirst lasts for weeks. The goatskin gourds never arrive. Reason begins to waver. It is crushed by thirst. Reason is able to overcome most everything, but it succumbs to thirst. No mirages in the marsh, no hope of an oasis. Just mud, slime. Mud and not a drop of water.

There is the thirst of the morning and the thirst of the evening, the thirst of the day and the thirst of the night.

Upon awakening in the morning, lips move but no sound comes out. Anguish fills your whole being, an anguish as gripping as that of dreams. Is this what it means to be dead? Lips try to speak but the mouth is paralyzed. A mouth cannot form words when it is dry, with no saliva. And the gaze drifts off, it is an insane gaze. The others say, "She's mad. She's gone mad during the night." They summon words capable of recalling reason. An explanation is owed them, but lips decline to move. The muscles of the mouth want to attempt articulation and do not articulate. Such is the despair of the powerlessness that grips me, the full awareness of the state of being dead.

As soon as I hear their clatter, I rush toward the tea canteens. They are a far cry from the goatskin gourds of the caravan. Liters and liters of tea but divided into small portions, one per person, and all are still drinking when I'm already finished. My mouth is not even damp and words still decline to be spoken. Cheeks are glued to teeth, the tongue is hard, stiff, the jaws locked, and what persists is the feeling of being dead, of being dead and knowing it. Dread expands in the eyes. I feel dread growing in my eyes to the point of madness. Everything sinks, slips away. Reason no longer exercises control. Thirst. Am I breathing? I'm thirsty. It is colder, or less cold, I cannot feel it. I'm thirsty, to the point of shouting it. The finger I run along my gums feels my mouth's dryness. My willpower collapses. One obsession remains: to drink.

And when the blockhova orders me to fetch her roll-call ledger from her hovel, where I find the soapy water she used to wash up, my first impulse is to sweep off the surface scum and kneel, ready to lap the water as do dogs with their agile tongues. I recoil. Soapy tea in which they wash their feet. On the edge of insanity, I gauge the full extent of the madness to which thirst has driven me.

I return to roll call. And to my obsession. To drink. Perhaps we will turn to the right of the road. There is a brook running under the small bridge. To drink. My eyes see nothing but the brook, far in the distance, the brook I am severed from by the roll call which takes longer than crossing the Sahara. The column is formed for departure. To drink. I place myself last in rank on the side from which the steep riverbank is more easily accessible.

The brook. Long before reaching it I am ready to leap like an animal. Long before the brook is in sight I have my tin cup ready in my hand. And when the brook is reached, one must break rank, run ahead and down the slippery bank. The water is often frozen, so the ice must be broken quickly, fortunately it is less cold now, the ice is not that thick and can be broken with the edge of the tin cup. The cup filled, the sharp slope must be scaled without losing a precious drop as I rejoin my place, avidly eyeing the water which might spill were I to go too fast. The SS is running toward me, shouting. His dog runs ahead, almost catches me. My comrades grab me and the rank swallows me. Avidly eyeing the water which moves with every step I take, I do not see the anxiety in the faces of my friends, the worry I caused them. For them, my absence was interminable. To drink. I was not afraid. To drink. They tell me, as they do every morning, that it was insane to go down to the brook with the SS and his dog behind me. The other day he had a Polish woman bitten to death. Worse still, this is marsh water, the kind that gives typhoid fever. No, it is not marsh water. I drink. Nothing is more awkward than drinking from a cupped tin can while walking. The water moves from side to side, not reaching the lips. I drink. No, it is not marsh water, it is a brook. I do not answer because I am unable to speak as yet. It is not swampy water, but it tastes of rotting leaves, and I feel this taste in my mouth even today as soon as I think of this water, even when I do not think of it. I drink. I drink and feel better. I have saliva in my mouth again. Words return to my lips but I do not speak. Sight returns to my eyes. Life returns. I rediscover my breathing, my heart. I know I am alive. Slowly I suck my saliva. Lucidity returns, and my sight—and I see little Aurore. She is sick, exhausted by fever, her lips discolored, her eyes haggard. She is thirsty. She does not have the strength to run down to the brook. And no one can go there for her. She must not drink that unhealthy water, she is sick. I see her and think: she might drink this water since she is going to die. She is waiting. Her eyes beg and I do not look at her. I feel upon me her thirsty gaze, the pain in her eyes when I hook my tin cup back on my belt. Life returns to me and I feel shame. And each morning I remain insensitive to the sup-plication of her eyes, her lips discolored by thirst, and each morning I feel ashamed after drinking.

My mouth has become moist. I can speak now. I would like for this saliva to last a long time in my mouth. And what about the obses-sion: when will I drink? Will there be water where we work? There is never any water. Only the marsh. A muddy swamp.

My comrades considered me mad. Lulu would say, "Take care of yourself. You know that here you must stay on your guard. You'll get yourself killed." I paid no attention. My friends never left me alone and they said to each other, "We must look out for C., she's crazy.

She does not see the kapos, the SS, the dogs. She just stands there, looking vague, instead of working. She doesn't understand when they shout, wanders off anywhere. They'll kill her." They were afraid for me, they were afraid to look at me with those crazed eyes I had then. They believed I was mad and probably I was. I can remember nothing about those weeks. And during those weeks which were the hardest, so many of those I loved died and yet I could not recall that I had learned of their death.

On the days when we go the other way, away from the stream, I do not know how I can bear the disappointment.

There is the thirst of the morning and the thirst of the day.

Since morning I can think of nothing else but drinking. When the midday soup is dished out, it is salty, so salty that it strips off the mouth's mucous membrane burning with canker sores. "Eat. You've got to eat." So many had died already because they stopped eating. "Try. It is quite liquid today.—No, it's salty." I spit out the spoonful I tried swallowing. Nothing goes down if you have no saliva in your mouth.

Sometimes we are sent to the tipcarts. A demolition site with meager trees growing in between ruins. The shrubs are covered with frost. With each handbarrow I carry to the carts I graze a shrub from which I tear a small branch. I lick the frost, but it does not yield a drop of water in my mouth. As soon as the SS step aside, I run toward clean snow. There is a bit left, like a sheet spread out to dry. I take a fistful of snow, but the snow does not turn to water in my mouth.

If I pass close to the open cistern on the surface of the ground, I am seized with vertigo, everything swims in my head. It is because I walk with Carmen or Viva that I do not hurl myself in. And each time we go by, they try to skirt it. But I drag them in that direction, they follow so as not to let go of me and, at the edge, pull me back roughly.

During the break, the Polish women crowd around the cistern and scoop up water in a tin cup tied on a wire. The wire is too short. The one who leans over is almost entirely suspended within the cistern, while her comrades hold on to her legs. She brings up a bit of murky water at the bottom of her cup and drinks. Another takes a turn at drawing water. I walk toward them and indicate that I would like some too. The tin cup goes down on its wire, the Polish woman leans far enough to fall in. She is pulled back up again and as she hands me the water asks, "Chleba?" I have no bread. I give all my bread in the evening for a bit of tea. I answer that I have no bread, pleading with my lips. She upsets the tin cup and the water spills. I would fall had not Carmen or Viva rushed to my side.

When we are working in the marsh, I think all day of the way back, of the stream. But the SS remembers what happened in the morning. As soon as we reach the turn in the road from where we glimpse the small bridge, he walks up front. He goes down into the stream and makes his dog wade in it. When we get there, the water is slimy and fetid. I would still take some; impossible—all the anweis-erins are on the alert.

There is the thirst of the day and the thirst of the evening.

In the evening, throughout roll call, I think of the tea they will dish out. I am one of the first served. Thirst has made me bold. I shove everything out of the way to get there ahead of the others. I drink and when I have drunk I am thirstier still. This herb tea does not quench one's thirst.

I now hold my bread ration in my hand, my piece of bread and the few grams of margarine which constitute the evening meal. I hold them out in my hand and offer them from cell to cell in exchange for a portion of tea. I tremble at the thought no one will accept. But there is always one who does. Every evening I exchange my bread for a couple of gulps. I drink at once and am thirstier than ever before. When I return to our cell, Viva tells me, "I kept my tea for you (tea or herb tea, it is neither), keep it to drink before falling asleep." She does not succeed in making me wait till then. I drink and am thirstier still. And I think of the water of the stream, spoiled a while back by the dog, the water with which I might have filled my cup, and I feel thirsty, thirstier still.

There is the thirst of the evening and the thirst of the night, the very worst. Because at night I drink, I drink and the water becomes immediately dry and solid in my mouth. The more I drink, the more my mouth fills with hardening rotting leaves.

Or else it is an orange section. It bursts between my teeth and it is indeed an orange section—amazing that one should encounter oranges here—it is indeed a section of an orange. I have the taste of the orange in my mouth, the juice spreads under my tongue, touches my palate, my gums, flows into my throat. It is a slightly acid, marvelously fresh orange. This orange taste and the sensation of freshness flowing wake me up. The awakening is horrifying. Yet the instant when the skin of the orange splits open between my teeth is so delightful that I would like to bring back this dream. I chase after it, corner it. But once again the paste of rotting leaves petrified into mortar fills my dry mouth. It is not even a bitter taste. When you taste bitterness it is because you have not lost the sense of taste, it means you still have saliva in your mouth.

The House

It was raining. A sheet of rain screened off the plain.

We had walked a long time. The road was nothing but potholes.
When we attempted to skirt them the anweiserins shouted, "Fall in!
Five abreast!" and they pushed into the mud the women who paused
because of their shoes. No description can give an idea of the kind of
puddlejumpers we had to wear.

We had come to a large plowed field. We were supposed to pull
out the scutch-grass roots turned up by the plow. Stooping over, we
pulled the whitish filaments, filling our aprons with them. It made
our bellies cold and wet. Heavy too. At the edge of the field, we
emptied our aprons and started down another furrow. It was raining.
We went on stooped over the furrows, furrow after furrow. Our
clothes were soaking wet. It was like being naked. An icy rivulet gathered between our shoulder blades and ran down the small of our
backs. We no longer paid any attention to it. However, the hand that
pulled out the twitch grass was dead. And clods of wet earth, glued to
our clogs, weighing them down, made it increasingly hard to pull out
our feet. It was raining since early morning.

The anweiserins had taken shelter under a branch lean-to. They
kept on shouting from afar. At the far end of the field we could no
longer hear them. We lingered there a bit. In any case we had to stoop
over the furrows; they could see us. And it hurt too much to straighten
up.

We went two by two, speaking to each other while moving. We
spoke of the past and the past became unreal. We spoke even more of
the future, and the future acquired definition. We were making many
plans. We never stopped making plans.

At noon, the rain was falling twice as hard. We could no longer
see the field transformed into a quagmire.

Farther off stood an abandoned house. This house was not for us.

The SS was already blowing his whistle for us to fall into ranks, after the break. We were resigned to return to the twitch roots, the muddy clods of earth. But the column left the field behind. Genevieve said, "If only they'd let us take shelter in the house . . ." She had voiced the wish all of us harbored. To express it was to show how impossible it was. Yet we were moving in the direction of the house. Now we were close. The column stops. An SS shouts that we are to go in, but that if we make any noise we will have to get out at once. Should we believe this?

We enter the house as though it were a church. It is a farmhouse about to be torn down. They demolish all the farmers' houses, pull up the hedges, rip down the fences, level the small gardens to make one vast public property. This is how they get rid of small, private farming. First they got rid of the farmers. The house was marked with a black, painted "J." Jews had lived there.

We come into a smell of wet plaster. The floorboards and the wallpaper have been torn off. As well as almost all the doors and windows. We settle down on the rubble covering the floor. We feel more keenly the cold of our dresses and jackets. The first ones in have secured a spot against the wall, they lean back. The others huddle wherever they can.

We stare at the house as though we had forgotten what a house is like, and we find a whole unused vocabulary. "This is a nice room"— "Yes, good light."—"The table must have stood there."—"Or the bed."—"No, this is a dining room. Look at the paper. There's still a scrap of wallpaper hanging there. If it were up to me, I'd put a sofa here, near the fireplace."—"Country-style draperies would look good. You know, a nice chintz."

The house bedecks itself with all its comfortable, familiar pieces of furniture, polished by time. Although it is now completely furnished we are still adding small touches. "There should be a radio next to the sofa."—"They use storm windows here. You can grow succulent plants."—"Is this what you like? I prefer hyacinths. You place the bulbs in water and next spring you've got flowers."—"I don't care for the way they smell."

The anweiserins have settled down in the other room. The SS are dozing beside them. We are huddled together. Our heat causes steam to rise from our damp clothing, a mist going up to the holes in the windows. The house has grown warm, lived in. We feel good. We look at the rain, hoping it will last till evening.

Evening

At the sound of the whistle, we must lay down our tools, clean them, arrange them in a neat pile.—Fall in.—Keep quiet.—Stay still.—Anweiserins and kapos make the count. Have they made an error? They go over it a second time.—Screams.—Two short.—Remember. They are the two afternoon ones, the two who collapsed by their spades. At once the furies came swooping down, hitting and lashing. You cannot get used to the sight of your comrades being beaten. The blows were useless. Spades fell from hands drained of the life's blood, life drained from eyes that had stopped imploring. Mute eyes. The furies hammered away at the two women who no longer moved. When people no longer react to blows, there is nothing to be done. Cart them off. We carried them tenderly along the embankment, where the grass is dry, and returned to our spades.

Now they are missing. Not everyone knows, they wonder. Their names pass from lips to lips in a murmur devoid of emotion. We are much too weary. Berthe and Anne-Marie are dead. Which Berthe? Berthe from Bordeaux. They were counted in this morning when we left for work, they must be accounted for when we return. We will have to carry their bodies. Not one of us moves. Involuntarily, each woman lowers her head, hoping to disappear in the crowd, to go unnoticed, give no sign. Each is exhausted, anxiously parceling out what she can still expect from her weary legs. Most can move only by leaning on the others' arms. The anweiserins walk back through the ranks, examining faces and feet. They will select the strongest. The ones leaning on one less weak than they fear to lose their support. How will they make it back if the arm they rely on will be taken away? The anweiserins seek out the tall, well-shod ones. "Du, du, du," calling three out. Then some others volunteer. We step out of the ranks, walk toward the dead women. We look at them, feeling embarrassed. How should we pick them up? The anweiserins direct each of us to grab a limb. On the double.

We lean over our companions' bodies. They are not stiff yet. When we grab the ankles and the wrists the body bends, touches the ground, and it is impossible to keep it high. It would be better to lift from under the knees and shoulders, but we cannot get a good hold that way. At last we manage somehow. We line up at the end of the column. Another count is made. This time they have the right number. The column starts on its way.

How many kilometers to go? We measure distances by the effort they cost us. They are enormous.

The column is on its way.

First, we are carrying Berthe and Anne-Marie. Soon they are nothing but heavy loads that slip out of our grasp with each step. From the start, we are left behind. We ask to let the first row know they should slow down their pace. The column continues to move just as fast. The kapo is leading it. She has good shoes. She is in a hurry to get there.

The SS close the march. They drag their feet since we, the last ones in line, go so slowly. The anweiserin laughs with them. She shows them dance steps, while making foul jokes. They are all having fun.

It is a pale, soft evening. Back home, the trees are budding. An SS pulls a harmonica out from his pocket. He plays and our distress turns to discomfort.

We call for a change in shift. No one hears. No one comes. No one feels strong enough to take our place. This labor grows increasingly hard as we go, bent double, wrenched.

Carmen glimpses pieces of broken boards lying in the ditch. We lay our dead comrades down on the road in order to pick up the boards. The SS halt. The second one takes out his knife to pare the bark from the branch he uses as a bludgeon. The anweiserin sings along with the harmonica, "J'attendrai." It is their favorite song.

We place the bodies across two boards we clutch at both ends and we go on. Carmen says: "Do you remember, Lulu, when our mothers would say, "Don't touch this filthy old wood. You'll get a splinter and a nasty abscess in your finger." Our mothers.

At first it seems to be better, then the bodies begin to slide, fold in the middle, fall. With each step we must rearrange an inert body upon the boards. The SS take turns playing the harmonica, laughing and humming. They laugh loudly, the girl louder still.

The column is way ahead. We try as hard as possible, harder than possible. A truck arrives. The column draws to one side to make room. We take advantage of this halt to catch up a bit. It is the truck that picks up the soup canteens brought to the construction site at noon. There are construction sites all around. All around, far and wide, there are piles of spades and shovels. The driver brakes, speaks to the SS. I am standing close to the one with the harmonica. He is just a boy. He looks seventeen. My younger brother's age. I direct my remarks at him: "Couldn't we place our comrades' bodies in this truck going back to the camp?" He snickers insultingly, then bursts out laughing. He laughs and laughs, finding it very funny. He rocks with laughter, the other one chimes in together with the girl, who slaps me, forcing her laugh. I feel ashamed. How can one make any request? The truck pulls away.

That's enough now. They realize that it has gone on long enough, this languid moseying with frolicking, loosely leashed dogs. They put away their harmonica, nose up their dogs and shout: "Schneller jetzt!" We tense up. With the dogs on our heels we must now catch up with the column.

We must. We have to.

We must . . . Why must we since we would rather die at once, killed by the dogs and the bludgeons, here on the road in the pale evening? No. We have to. Perhaps because of the way they laughed a moment ago. We must.

We succeed in catching up with the column, we are almost there. We beg for someone to relieve us. Two come. They replace the weaker two, fainting with exhaustion. We shift hands without breaking march. The dogs' muzzles are right there, on the back of our legs. One sign, a shake of the leash, and they will bite. We walk with these sliding corpses, which we drag as they keep on slipping. Their feet rake the road, their lolling heads almost touch the ground. We cannot stand seeing these heads any longer, with their eyes rolled back. Berthe. Anne-Marie. We try to lift them for an instant with our free hand. We have to give up, to let go of these heads whose eyelids we dared not close.

We do not look because tears are streaming down our faces, streaming though we are not weeping. These are tears of exhaustion and helplessness. And we suffer for this dead flesh as though it were alive. The board under their thighs scrapes and cuts them to the quick. Berthe. Anne-Marie.

To keep their arms from hanging, we try to fold them over their chests. We would have to keep them there. Their arms hang and brush our legs at every step of our lurching walk.

Behind us, the SS are marching army-style. Enough strolling, they say. They tighten their grip on the leashes of the dogs which follow us closer and closer. We no longer turn back. We try not to feel their muzzles, their hot, short breath, not to hear their four-legged step, their dogstep with its scratching of their claws against the pebbles on the road. We try not to hear the pounding of the bludgeon on our backs. Stripped of its bark, it is moist and white.

We walk, tensed. Our hearts are beating wildly, ready to burst, and we keep on thinking: my heart can't take it, it'll burst. It hasn't yet, it is holding up. For how many more meters? Our anguish breaks up the kilometers into paces, meters, light poles, bends in the road. We are always off by a pole or a bend. This is the plain, covered by marshes as far as the eye can see, with no landmarks, except occasionally a tuft of grass reddened by the frost, ever merging with the rest. We are crushed by despair.

But we must. We must.

We are coming closer. We can tell the camp by the smell. A smell of corpses and diarrhea enveloped by the thicker, suffocating odor of the crematorium. Once we are there, we no longer smell it. When we return in the evening, we wonder how we can breathe this stink.

At this point, the spot where we recognize the smell, there must be two kilometers left.

Past the small bridge, we walk faster. One left.

I do not know how we made it. Before going in, our column stopped to let others in. We set down our load. When we had to pick it up once more, we thought we could not do it again.

At the gate, we held ourselves very straight. We clenched our teeth, and raised our chins. We had made this promise to each other, Viva and I. Head high in front of Drexler, in front of Taube. We had even said, "Head high or feet first." Oh, Viva!

The SS counting us as we file by her points an inquiring cane at the two bodies. "Two French women," the anweiserin explains with disgust.

We carry our comrades' bodies to roll call. It makes two rows which disturb the line up: four carriers and their corpse spread out in front of them.

The Jewish commandos return next. They have two dead women this evening. Like us. They have some every evening. They placed the bodies on doors removed from the houses they are tearing down, and carried them on their shoulders. They are disfigured by the effort. We feel sorry for them. Our pity brings us close to sobbing. Their dead are laid out flat, faces turned toward the sky. We reflect: If only we had had doors.

The roll call was as long as usual, but so far as we were concerned it seemed shorter. Our hearts filled our chests and were beating strongly, so strongly, keeping us company like a clock when you are alone. And we listened to this heartbeat rising above all else, then gradually settling back in its niche, assuming its rightful place there. The heartbeats are less frequent, less frantic. And when we heard only their accustomed rhythm, we grew unsettled, as though standing on the edge of solitude.

At that moment, our hands wiped away our tears.

Roll call lasted till the searchlights illuminated the barbed wire, till night.

Throughout the roll call, we never looked at them.

A corpse. The left eye devoured by a rat. The other open with its fringe of lashes.

Try to look. Just try and see.

A man unable to follow any longer. The dog lunges at his back-side. The man does not stop. He continues walking, followed by the dog walking on its hind legs, its muzzle at the man's rear end.

The man is walking. He has not uttered a sound. Blood stains his trousers' stripes. It seeps from inside, a stain spreading as though upon a blotter.

The man goes on walking with the dog's fangs in his flesh.

Try to look. Just try and see.

A woman dragged by two others, holding on to her arms. A Jewish woman. She does not want to be taken to block 25. She resists. Her knees scrape the ground. Her clothing, pulled up by the tug of her sleeves, is wound round her neck. Her trousers—men's trousers—are undone and drag inside out behind her, fastened to her ankles. A flayed frog. Her loins are exposed, her emaciated buttocks, soiled by blood and pus, are dotted with hollows.

She is howling. Her knees are lacerated by the gravel.

Try to look. Just try and see.

Auschwitz

This city we were passing through
was a strange city.
Women wore hats
perched on curly hair.
They also wore shoes and stockings
as is done in town.
None of the inhabitants of this city
had a face
and in order to hide this
all turned away as we passed
even a child who was carrying in his hand
a milk can as tall as his legs
made of violet enamel
and who fled when he saw us.
We were looking at these faceless beings
and it was we who were amazed.
We were disappointed as well
hoping to see fruits and vegetables in the shops.
Indeed, there were no shops
only display windows
wherein I would have liked to recognize myself
amid the ranks sliding over the glass panes.
I raised an arm
but all the women wished to recognize themselves
all raised an arm
and not one found out which one she was.
The face of the station clock registered the time
we were happy to look at it
it was the real time
and relieved to arrive at the beet silos

where we were taken to work
on the other side of the town
we had walked through like a wave of morning sickness.

The Dummy

On the opposite side of the road lies a piece of land where the SS
train their dogs. You can see them go there, with their dogs on a leash,
tied two by two. The SS at the head of the line is carrying a dummy.
It is a large stuffed doll dressed just like us. A discolored, striped suit,
filthy, too long in the sleeves. The SS holds her by one arm. He lets
the feet drag, raking the gravel. They even tied canvas boots onto her
feet.

Do not look. Do not look at this dummy being dragged on the
ground. Do not look at yourself.

Sunday

On Sunday roll call was not so early. Not so long before dawn. On Sunday, the columns did not step out of the camp. We worked inside the camp. Sunday was the day everyone feared the most.

That Sunday, the weather was fine. The sun rose in a sky free of redness, of flaming streaks. The day was blue from the start, like a spring day. The sun also was springlike. Better not think of home, garden, of the season's first outing. Better not think, not think at all.

Here the good season differed from the bad because there was dust instead of snow or mud, because the stench grew pestilential, the setting more desolate with the sun than under snow, more desperate.

A whistle sounds the end of roll call. We must keep ranks which start out slowly toward block 25. Each Sunday is different. Why block 25? We are afraid. Someone says, "Block 25 is not large enough for all of us. We'd be marched straight to the gas." We pull ourselves together.

What are they going to do? We wait. We wait a long time. Until men arrive carrying shovels. They go toward the ditch. During the week, the ditch inside the camp enclosure, next to the barbed wire, has been deepened. Could there be too many suicides? That must be the shooting we hear at night. When a woman draws too close to the barbed wire, she is shot by the guard in the watchtower before she is able to reach it. Then why the ditch?

Why anything?

The men take their place along the ditch, shovel in hand.

The columns stretch Indian file. Thousands of women in one file. An endless file. We follow. What are the ones ahead of us doing? We see them file past the men, stretch out their aprons. The men dump in two shovelfuls of earth taken from the hollowed ditch. What are they going to do with this earth? We follow. They start to run. We run. Here come blows from clubs and straps falling thick and fast. We try to protect our faces, eyes. The blows come raining down on the back of the neck, on our backs. Schnell. Schnell. Run.

On each side of the file, kapos and anweiserins shout. Schneller. Schneller. They shout and hit.

We have our aprons filled and we run.

We run. We are supposed to keep in line. No stampede.

We run.

The gate.

This is where the furies stand closest together. SS in skirts and britches have joined them. Run.

Past the gate, turn left, step onto a plank precariously balanced between the two sides of a ditch. Cross over at a run. Bludgeon blows before and after.

Run. Empty the apron at the spot indicated by the shrieks.

Others use rakes to spread the fresh earth evenly.

Run. Skirt the electrified barbed wire. Careful not to graze it. The power is turned on.

Pass through the gate again on the way back. The passage is narrow. We must run even faster. Too bad for those who trip and fall there; they will be trampled.

Run. Schneller. Run.

Go back facing the men who fill again our aprons with earth.

They have to hurry, they are being beaten. Heaping shovelfuls, they are beaten, we are beaten.

Once the apron is full, more bludgeonings. Schneller.

Run to the gate, pass under whips and lashes, cross the swaying, sagging plank. Careful of the cane of the chief SS, standing at the outer end of the plank. Empty your apron under a rake, run, pass through the gate along the narrowing passage—the club-wielders press close together at the exit—run to the men to pick up two shovelfuls of earth, run to the gate, in an uninterrupted circuit.

They want to make a garden at the camp entrance.

Two shovelfuls of earth do not weigh very much. Gradually, they grow heavier. The weight is greater, the arms grow numb. We take the risk of not holding the apron's corners tight, letting a bit of soil run out. If a fury were to take notice, she would beat us to death. Still, we do it, it's just too heavy.

Among the men there is a Frenchman. Shrewdly we measure out our run to be served by him. We try to exchange a couple of words. He speaks without moving his lips, or raising his eyes, as one learns to do in jail. Three trips are required for a full sentence.

The loop no longer moves fast enough. The furies shout louder, hit harder. There are bottlenecks because some women collapse and their comrades help them to their feet, while others, behind them, pushed by the blows, want to continue running. And also because the Jewish women, believing they are taking more of a beating, slip in between our striped dresses. We are sorry for them. Sorry on account of their attire. They have no aprons. They have been made to turn their coats backwards, buttoned in the back, so they could hold the earth within the bottom folds held up by the seam. They have something of the scarecrow and the penguin, with their sleeves, wrong side out, hampering their arms. And there are those wearing a man's coat with a vent . . . A terrifying comedy.

They fill us with pity but we do not want to be separated from each other. We protect one another. Each wishes to remain near a companion, some in front of a weaker one, so as to be hit in her stead, some behind one no longer able to run, so as to hold her up if she begins to fall.

The Frenchman is a recent arrival. He is from Charonne. The resistance movement is spreading in France. We would brave anything to speak to him.

Run to the gate—schnell—pass through—weiter—teeter on the plank above the ditch—schneller—empty our aprons—run—watch out for the barbed wire—the gate again—there is always one you step on where the officer stands, armed with his cane—run toward the men—stretch out our aprons—blows—race toward the gate. A maniacal run.

We consider slipping off to hide in one of the blocks. Impossible, all the exits are guarded by the clubs. Those who try to force their way through the cordon are given a hiding.

It is forbidden to go to the latrines. Forbidden to stop for a minute.

In the beginning, it is more painful to slow down than keep on racing. At the least slackening of the pace, the blows come raining down twice as heavy. Later, we would prefer to be beaten rather than run, our legs no longer respond. But the moment we slow down, the blows fall so fast and furious that we resume our running.

Some women fall. The furies drag them from the rank to the door of block 25. Taube is there. The pandemonium mounts. There are more and more Jewish women in our midst. With each loop, our group breaks apart. We succeed in staying together two by two. These pairs do not leave one another, holding on to each other, pulling one another when caught within the narrow passage to the entrance, seized by the panic of those stepped on and those afraid of falling on them. A maniacal run.

Some women fall. The round goes on. Run. Keep running. No slowing down. No stopping. We do not even look at those who fall. We stay two by two and this claims every second of our attention. It is not possible to look after the others.

Some women fall. The round goes on. Schnell. Schnell.

The flower bed grows wider. We must extend our circuit.

Run. Go over the shaking plank that keeps on bending more and more—schnell—pour out the earth—schnell—the gate—schnell—fill our apron—schnell—the gate again—schnell—the plank. A maniacal run.

In order to think about something we count the blows we get. At thirty, it has not been too bad a round. At fifty we stop counting.

The Frenchman is being closely watched. There is a kapo next to him. We can no longer be served by him. Occasionally we exchange glances. He says between his teeth, "The scoundrels. Bastards." He is a novice. There are tears in his eyes. He pities us. His task is less painful. He stays in one spot and is not cold.

Our legs swell. Our features tense up. With each round we grow increasingly wasted.

Run—schnell—the gate—schnell—the plank—empty out the earth—schnell—barbed wire—schnell—the gate—schnell—run—apron—run—run run run schnell schnell schnell schnell schnell. A maniacal run.

Each one stares at the others grown increasingly ugly, and does not see herself.

Near us a Jewish woman leaves the line. She goes up to Taube, says something to him. He opens the gate, slapping her so hard she falls to the ground within the confines of block 25. She has given up. When Taube turns around, he calls out another, flinging her in the same yard. We run as fast as we can. He must not think we are unable to run.

The round goes on. The sun is high in the sky. It is afternoon. The race continues, as do the blows and the shrieks. With each loop others fall. The women who have diarrhea smell foul. Streaks of diarrhea dry on their legs. We are still going round and round. How long will we be going? A maniacal race run by maniacal faces.

As we empty our aprons we gauge the flowerbed's progress. We thought it was finished when the level of the soil was not thick enough. We had to begin once more.

The afternoon grows late. The round goes on. The blows. The shrieks.

When Taube blew his whistle, when the furies shouted, "Back to the block!" we returned, holding one another up. Seated on our tiers, we could not summon the strength to take off our shoes. We did not have the strength to talk. We wondered how we had managed, once more.

The next day, several of our group entered the charnel house. They went out on the stretcher.

The sky was blue, the sun had reappeared. It was a Sunday in March.

The Men

They are waiting in front of the barracks. Silent. Their eyes reflect the struggle between resignation and rebellion. Resignation must win out.

An SS is guarding them. He is bullying them. All of a sudden, without rhyme or reason, he begins jostling them, shouting and hitting them. The men remain silent, straighten out their rank, hold their hands on their sides. Not one of them pays attention to the SS. Each is alone, within himself.

There are boys among them, very young, who do not understand what is going on. They observe the men and imitate their grave demeanor.

Before stepping into the barracks, they undress, fold their clothing, which they keep on their arms. They have been working stripped to the waist since the weather turned fair. Undressed, they look as though they are wearing white, bone-tight long johns.

The wait is a long one. They wait and know.

This is a new barracks, which has been fitted out within the confines of the infirmary. Trucks delivered enameled and nickel-plated machines, an almost incredible excess of cleanliness. They turned the barracks into a laboratory for X rays, and diathermy.

This is the first time that men are being treated in our camp. The men's camp is down there. It has a better charnel house than ours, they say. Perhaps slightly less awful. Why are they being sent here? Are people treated here now?

The men continue waiting. Silent. Their gaze far-off and colorless.

One by one, the first ones step out. They dress on the threshold. Their eyes are averted from those who are still waiting. And when you see their faces you know why.

How can one relate the distress of their gestures? The humiliation in their eyes?

Women are sterilized in the surgical ward.

What difference does it make since none of them will return, since none of us will return.

Dialogue

"Oh! Sally, did you remember my request?"

Sally is hurrying down the Lagerstrasse. The way she is put together betrays the fact she works in Effekts. It is the commando that does the sorting, the inventory, puts away the contents of the Jews' luggage, the luggage that the newly arrived leave on the platform. Those who work in Effekts are never short of anything.

"Yes, my sweet, I thought of it, but at this moment there isn't any. There have been no convoys for the past week. We expect one tonight. From Hungary. Just in time, we were short of everything. So long. See you tomorrow. You'll get your cake of soap."

They have just introduced plumbing in the camp.

The Commanding Officer

Two blond boys, their hair standing up like the awns of ripe wheat, legs bare, chests bare. Two little boys. Eleven and seven. Two brothers. Both blond, blue-eyed, tanned. The nape of the neck a little more so.

The older boy hustles the little one. The kid is in a bad mood. He grumbles and finally bursts out:

"No. No. It's always you."

"Of course, I'm the eldest."

"No. That's not fair. I never get to do it."

Regretfully, since something has to be decided, the senior of the two suggests:

"All right, listen. We'll play it like that once more, and then we'll switch. After that we'll take turns. Agreed?"

The little one sniffles, steps away reluctantly from the wall he was leaning on, stubborn, squinting in the bright sunlight, then, dragging his feet, joins his brother. The other shakes him: "Come on! Let's play." He is beginning to turn into the part he wants to play. At the same time he keeps a close watch on his brother to make sure the little one is following the rules of the game. Junior tarries. He has not yet entered in the game. He is waiting for his brother to be quite ready.

The big boy is getting there. He buttons up a jacket, buckles an imaginary belt, slips a sword into a scabbard at his side, then, with his hands wide open, secures a cap upon his head. Softly, with his wrist, he strokes the visor, then pulls it down over his eyes.

Gradually, as he clothes himself in his character's apparel, his features grow hard, as do his lips. They tighten. He throws his head back, as though his eyes were hampered by a visor, throws out his chest, places his left hand behind his back, palm up, with the right he adjusts an imaginary monocle and casts a look about him.

But now he looks worried. He realizes he has forgotten something. He steps out of his role for a moment to fetch a switch. It is a real switch, there in the grass—a flexible twig he uses for this purpose—then, assuming his pose again, he lightly taps the boots with his switch. He is quite ready now. He turns around.

Instantly, the little one assumes his role. He is less meticulous about it. He stands at attention only after his brother's first glance, then takes a step forward, freezes, clicks his heels—the clicking is soundless since he is barefoot—raises his right arm, looks straight at him, his face expressionless. The other responds with a brief salute, barely completed, supercilious. The little one brings his arm down, clicks his heels once more, and the older brother leads the march. Erect, chin out and pouting proudly, fingering his switch between his index finger and his thumb to tap it against his bare calves. The small boy follows him at a respectful distance. He does not move in the same stiff fashion. He is nothing but a simple soldier.

They cross the garden. It has square lawns, bordered by a line of flowers. They cross the garden. The commanding officer looks about as though inspecting it, from on high. The orderly follows looking at nothing. A dolt, a soldier.

They halt at one end, near a hedge of long-stemmed roses. The commandant first, then the orderly two paces back. The commanding officer strikes a pose, the right leg forward, bent slightly at the knee, one hand on the small of his back, the other, the one holding his switch, on his hip. He lords over the rosebushes. He has a nasty expression on his face, and he shouts out orders: "Schnell! Rechts! Links!" His chest swells. "Rechts! Links!"—Then he reverses them: "Links! Rechts!"—faster and faster, louder and louder. "Links! Rechts! Links! Rechts! Links!"—faster, always faster.

Soon the prisoners to whom he shouts his orders can no longer follow. They stumble, miss a beat. The commandant is pale with rage. With his switch he hits, hits and keeps on hitting. Not budging an inch, his shoulders still squared, his eyebrows arched, he shouts furiously, "Schnell! Schneller! Aber los!" using his whip with every order.

Suddenly, at the end of the column something seems to have gone wrong. He leaps menacingly, reaching his brother just in time. Now, the little one has stepped out of his role as orderly. He has become the guilty prisoner, back bent, legs unable to bear the weight of his body, face distraught, mouth twisted with pain, the mouth of one at the end of his rope. The commandant switches his whip to the other hand, closes his right fist tight, strikes him full in the chest—the ghost of a punch, they are playing. The little one reels, whirls, falls on the lawn. The commandant stares down at the prisoner he cast scornfully on the ground; he is foaming at the mouth. His fury is spent. He feels only disgust. He boots him—a fake kick since he is barefoot; they are only playing. But the little one knows the rules of the game by heart. The kick turns him over like a limp bundle. He lies there, mouth open, eyes glazed.

Then the big boy, pointing his switch at the invisible prisoners around him, orders, "Zum Krematorium," and walks off, stiff, satisfied and repelled.

The camp commandant lives close by, just outside the barbed-wire enclosure. A brick house, with a garden graced by a lawn, rosebushes, and window boxes painted blue, full of multicolored begonias. Between the hedge of rosebushes and the barbed wire lies the path leading to the crematorium. It is the path taken by stretchers transporting the dead. They go on all day, the whole day. The smokestack spouts its fumes the whole day long. The passing hours shift the smokestack's shadow upon the sandy garden walks and the bright green lawn.

The commandant's sons play in the garden. They play horses, ball, or else they play commandant and prisoner.

Roll Call

It is endless this morning.

The blockhovas are bustling about, counting and recounting. The female SS in their capes go from one group to the next, step into the office, exit from there with papers they are checking. They are checking this human accounting. Roll call will continue until the numbers come out right.

Taube arrives. He will head the search. He leaves with his dog to go through the blocks. The blockhovas are on edge, they lunge out with their fists and lashes right and left, indiscriminately. Each hopes the missing person is not in her block.

We wait.

The SS women, cloaked in their capes, examine the numbers, going over the human additions again.

We wait.

Taube returns. He has the answer. He whistles softly to call the dog that follows him. The dog is dragging a woman by the nape of her neck.

Taube leads his dog to the group from the woman's block. The count comes out right.

Taube blows his whistle. Roll call is over.

Someone says, "Let's hope she was dead."

Lulu

We were deep down in that ditch since early morning. The three of us. The rest of the detail was working farther on. From time to time the kapos prodded us, just to see how far we had gotten digging that same ditch again. We had a chance to talk. We were talking since early morning.

To talk meant that we could make plans about going home, because to trust we would return was a way of forcing luck's hand. The women who had stopped believing they would return were as good as dead. One had to believe, against all odds, incredible as it might seem. One had to lend to this possible return home certainty, reality and color by preparing for it, conjuring up each and every detail.

Occasionally, one of the women, voicing a thought we all had, interjected, "How do you envision getting out?" Then, realizing our situation, we let the question sink in silence.

To shake off that silence and the anguish it covered, another might venture, "Perhaps one day we'll no longer wake up to roll call. We'll sleep a long time. When we'll awake it'll be broad daylight, and the camp will be strangely still. Those of us who will step out first from the barracks will realize that the guard post is empty. All the SS will have fled. A couple of hours later, the Russian reconnaissance units will have arrived."

A new silence answered this anticipation.

She would add, "First, we will have heard the cannons' report. Far off at first, then drawing closer. The battle of Cracow. Once Cracow is seized, it will be the end. You'll see, the SS will take to their heels."

The more detailed her description, the less we were able to believe it. By tacit agreement, we'd drop the subject and pick up again our impossible plans characterized by the particular logic of mad schemes.

We were talking since early morning, happy to be a distance away from the detail, away from the kapos' shouting. Nor did we have to bear the truncheon's blows with which they punctuated their shouts. The ditch was getting deeper with every passing hour. Our heads no longer protruded over the top. Once we hit the marl, we stood with our feet in water. The mud we were slinging over our heads was white. It was not cold—one of the first mild days. The sun warmed our shoulders. We felt at peace.

A kapo came along, shouting. She signaled to my companions to get out, and marched them off. The ditch was deep enough now; there was not enough work for three. They leave waving a regretful farewell. They know the dread that fills us all when we find ourselves separated from the others, when we are left all alone. To hearten me, they say: "Come on, hurry up. You'll join us."

Left alone at the bottom of the ditch, I am filled with despair. The others' presence, the things they said, made it possible to believe we might return. Now that they have left I am desperate. I cannot believe I will ever return when I am alone. With them near me, since they seem so certain of it, I believe it could happen. No sooner do they leave me than I am frightened. No one believes she will return when she is alone.

Here I am, at the bottom of the ditch, alone, and so discouraged that I wonder whether I will ever reach the end of the day. How many hours are left before the blow of the whistle which marks the end of work, the moment to line up to go back to camp, in ranks of five, arm in arm, talking, talking to distraction.

Here I am, all alone. I cannot think of anything any longer because all my thoughts collide with the anguish that dwells within each and every one of us: How will we get out of here? When are we going to get out? I would like to think of nothing. But if this lasts much longer not one of us will get out alive. Those who are still alive say to themselves each day that they miraculously held out for eight whole weeks. No one can see further than a week ahead.

I am alone and frightened. I try to continue digging. The work is not moving. I attack a last bump at the bottom, even it out. Perhaps the kapo will decide it is enough. I feel my bruised back, its curve paralyzed, my shoulders wrenched by the shovel, my arms unable to cast spadefuls of muddy marl over the top. I am here all alone. I feel like lying down in the mud to wait. To wait for the kapo to find me dead. It is not so easy to die. It takes a long time, hitting someone with a shovel, or a bludgeon, before he dies.

I continue digging a while longer, scooping two of three spadefuls of soil. It is too hard. As soon as you find yourself alone you think: What good does it do? What's it all for? Why not give up . . . Better die now, on the spot. Only surrounded by the others is one able to hold out.

I am all alone, alone with my haste to join my companions, and alone also with my temptation to give up. Why? Why do I have to keep on digging this ditch?

"Enough! That's it for now!" A voice shouts these words from above. "Komm schnell!" I pull myself up, out of the ditch, by leaning on my shovel. How weary my arms are, how achy the back of my neck. The kapo is running. I must keep up with her. She runs across the road by the side of the marsh. There's the fill. Women like ants. Some carry sand to others who pound it flat, leveling the terrain. A huge, flat space, stretching under the sun. Hundreds of women are standing, like a frieze of shadows profiled against the light.

I follow the kapo who deals me a pounder and a blow, directing me toward a team of workers. I seek out my comrades. Lulu calls out to me, "Come here, next to me, there's a spot," and she makes room for me next to her, in the line of women who are pounding the ground. They hold the pounders with both hands as they raise them and let them fall. "Come here, to pestle the rice!" Where does Viva find the strength to joke like this? I cannot move my lips, even to venture a smile. Lulu is worried. "What's the matter with you? Are you ill?"

"No, I'm not ill, but I can't take it anymore. I'm all in today."

"That's nothing. You'll get over it."

"No, Lulu, I won't. I'm telling you I can't take it any more."

There is nothing she can say. It is the first time she hears me speak like this. A practical woman, she lifts up my tool. "Your pounder is real heavy. Take mine. It's lighter and you're more tired than I am on account of the ditch."

We exchange tools. I start pounding the sand, like the others. I look at all these women going on, making the same gesture with their arms getting weaker and weaker as they raise the heavy mass. Armed with their bludgeons, the kapos move from one to the other. I am overwhelmed with despair. "How will we ever get out of here?"

Lulu looks at me, smiling. Her hand grazes mine, to comfort me. And I repeat, letting her know it is useless, "I'm telling you I can't take it any longer. This time it's true."

Lulu has a good look around us, and seeing there is no kapo in the vicinity, she takes hold of my wrist, and says, "Get behind me, so they can't see you. You'll be able to have a good cry." She speaks in a timid whisper. Probably this is just what I needed since I obey her gentle shove. Dropping my tool upon the ground, but still leaning on its long handle, I cry my eyes out. I did not wish to cry, but the tears well up and stream down my cheeks. I let them flow, and when one of them touches my lips, I taste the salt and continue weeping.

Lulu goes on working and stays on the lookout at the same time. Occasionally she turns around and with her sleeve, softly, wipes my face. I keep on crying. I'm not thinking of anything. I just cry.

Now I no longer know why I am crying, but Lulu suddenly tugs at me: "That's enough now! Back to work. Here she comes." She says it with such kindness that I am not ashamed of having cried. It is as though I had wept against my mother's breast.

The Orchestra

It stood on an earth platform near the gate.

The woman conductor had been a celebrity in Vienna. All the women players were fine musicians. They had passed an examination to be chosen from among a great number. They owed this stay of execution to music.

With the onset of the warm season an orchestra was needed. Perhaps it had been the idea of the new commandant. He loved music. When he ordered a special concert for his own pleasure, he had an extra half-ration of bread distributed to the players. And when the new arrivals stepped out of the boxcars to proceed, in rank formation, to the gas chamber, he loved it to be to the rhythm of a merry march.

They played in the morning when the columns were leaving for work. When we passed by, we had to keep in step to the music. Later, they played waltzes. Waltzes we had heard elsewhere, back in an abolished past. To hear them here was intolerable.

Seated on stools, they keep on playing. Do not look at the fingers of the cello player, nor at her eyes when she performs, you could not stand it.

Do not observe the movements of the conductor. She parodies the professional she used to be when she led an all-women's orchestra in a famous Vienna café; clearly she recalls now who she once was.

All of them wear a pleated navy blue skirt, a light blouse, a lavender scarf on their heads. They are dressed up to set the pace for those who are on their way to the marshes, wearing the dresses in which they sleep, for otherwise their clothes would never dry.

The columns have left. The orchestra lingers a while longer.

Do not look, do not listen, especially if it plays "The Merry Widow" while, behind the second row of barbed wire, the men exit one by one from a barracks, stark naked, with the kapos hitting them hard, one by one, with their leather belts.

Do not look at the orchestra playing "The Merry Widow."

Do not listen. You would only hear the blows on the men's backs, and the metallic ring of the buckles when the belts fly.

Do not look at the women musicians who play while naked men reduced to skeletons exit driven by blows that make them reel. They are going to delousing because there are decidedly too many lice in the barracks.

Do not look at the violinist. She plays on an instrument that could be Yehudi's if Yehudi were not miles away, on the other side of the ocean. Which Yehudi did this violin belong to?

Do not look, do not listen.

Do not think of all the Yehudis who had packed their violins when being deported.

So This Is What You Believed

So you believed that only solemn words rise to the lips of the dying
    because solemn rhetoric flourishes naturally on deathbeds
    a bed is always dressed for funeral rites
    with the family assembled around it
    sincere pain and the appropriate demeanor.

    Naked on the charnel house's pallets, almost all our comrades said,
"I'm going to kick the bucket."
    They were naked on a naked board.
    They were dirty and the boards were soiled with pus and diarrhea.
    They did not realize that they were making the task of the survivors more difficult when they would have to report their last words to their relatives. Relatives expect something solemn. It is impossible to disappoint them. Trivial remarks are unworthy of inclusion in the florilegium of ultimate pronouncements.
    But it was even more unworthy to exhibit one's weakness.
    So they said, "I'm going to kick the bucket," in order not to rob the others of their courage and since they didn't expect that even one would survive they never left any kind of message.

Springtime

This flesh which had faded, displayed in the dry mud and dust, losing its glow and life, was withering and wasting away in the strong sunlight—brownish, purple, gray—blending in with the dusty ground so that it was hard to identify these creatures as women, to recognize empty breasts in these wrinkled paps.

Oh you who take your leave of them at dawn, on the threshold of a jail or of your death, drained of strength by long wakes, be glad you cannot see what was done to your wives, to their breasts which you dared touch for the last time, moved by their tender softness, you poised on the threshold of death in a tumult of emotion, leaving to die—what was done to your women.

It required an effort to make out faces when features were no longer illumined by shining eyes, faces the color of ashes and earth, carved out of rotting roots or detached from an ancient bas-relief, unaffected by the passage of time when it came to protruding cheekbones—a jumble of heads—incredibly small hairless heads—owl's heads with disproportionately salient superciliary arches—oh these sightless faces—heads and faces, bodies pressed against bodies stretched out in the dust of mud gone dry.

Amid the rags—compared to them, what you call rags would be draperies—amid the dirt-stained tatters, hands appeared—recognizable because they moved, the fingers bending and contracting as they foraged through the rags, searched the armpits for lice which they squashed between the nails of their two thumbs. Blood made a brownish stain upon the nails that squeezed the lice.

What was left of life in the eyes and the hands existed still in this gesture—but the legs in the dust—bare legs covered by running sores, ravaged by open wounds—the legs in the dust lay inert, wooden, heavy.

heads bent forward were attached to necks like wooden heads—heavy and the women who took off their rags at the first sign of warmth and sun, in order to delouse them, bared their necks which were nothing but knots and ropes, their shoulders reduced to collarbones, their chests where you could see the ribs through what used to be breasts—hoops

all these women leaning against one another motionless in the mud dried to dust, were rehearsing without knowing it

—they knew, you know—it is more terrible than that

were rehearsing the scene of their death on the next day—or close to it

for they were to die the next day or close to it

since each one of these women dies a thousand deaths.

The next day or close to it, they would become corpses in the dust which followed the snow and the mud of winter. They had lived through the winter—in the marshes, the mud, the snow. They could not last beyond the first rays of sunshine.

The first warm sunshine on the bare earth.

For the first time the earth was not a hostile element, threatening at every step—if you fall, or let yourself fall down, you will never rise again—

For the first time it is possible to sit on the ground.

The earth, bare for the first time, dry for the first time, stopped exercising its vertiginous pull to let yourself slip to the ground—let yourself slip into death as into snow—into forgetfulness—to let yourself go—stop ordering your arms, your legs, and so many minor muscles not to give up, in order to remain standing—stay alive—slip—let yourself slip in the snow—let yourself slip into death with its soft, snowy embrace.

The sticky mud and dirty snow were dust for the first time.

Dry dust, warm in the sun

it is harder to die in the dust

harder to die on a sunny day.

The sun was shining, the pale sun of the east. The sky was blue. Somewhere spring was singing.

Spring sang in the memory, in my memory.

This song surprised me so much that I was not certain of hearing it. I thought I heard it in a dream. I tried to deny it, not to hear it any longer, and my eyes sought desperately my companions all around me. They were glued to one another there, in the sun, in the space between the barracks and the barbed wire. The barbed wire so white in the sunlight.

That Sunday.

An extraordinary Sunday because it was a Sunday of rest and we were allowed to sit on the ground.

All the women were seated in the dust of the dried mud, a miserable swarm that made one think of flies on a dung heap. Probably because of the smell. The odor was so dense and fetid that we did not think we were breathing in air, but a thick, viscous fluid which enveloped and isolated this corner of the earth as though it had its own atmosphere in which only specially adapted creatures could move. Us.

The stink of diarrhea and corpses. Above this stink a blue sky. And in my memory spring was singing.

Why among all these beings have I alone kept this memory? In my memory spring was singing. Why this difference?

The new growth of pussy willows shines silvery in the sun—a poplar bends in the wind—the grass is so green that the spring flowers shine with amazing colors. Spring bathes everything with its light, light, inebriating air. Spring makes you dizzy. Spring is a symphony that bursts all over, bursts, bursts.

It bursts.—Bursts in my bursting head.

Why did I keep my memory? Why this injustice?

But also my memory gives rise to such miserable images that tears of despair fill my eyes.

In the spring, we walk along the Seine's embankment, looking at the Louvre's plane trees so finely etched next to the Tuileries' chestnut trees all in leaf.

In the spring, we walk across the Luxembourg gardens before

going to the office. Children run along the walks, their satchels under their arms. Children. How can one think of children in this place?

In the spring, the blackbird in the acacia tree beneath my window wakes before dawn. It is learning to whistle even before daybreak. It is not doing a good job of whistling yet. April has just begun.

Why am I the only one left with the ability to remember? And my memory finds only clichés. *Mon beau navire, ô ma mémoire* . . . Where are you, my real memory? Where are you, my earthly memory?

The sky was very blue, a blue so blue above the white cement pylons and the white barbed wire, a blue so blue that the web of electric wiring seemed whiter, more implacable

here nothing is green

there is no vegetation

here nothing is alive.

Far beyond the barbed wire, spring is flitting, spring is rustling, spring is singing. Within my memory. Why did I keep my memory?

Why keep the remembrance of streets with echoing cobblestones, of the fifes of spring played on the benches of the fruit and vegetable market, of the shafts of sunlight on the light parquet floor seen on awakening, the recollection of laughter, spring hats, bells ringing in the evening air, of the first light blouses and anemones?

Here the sun is not the spring sun. It is the sun of eternity, a sun of the world before creation. And I have kept the memory of a sun shining on the earth of the living, a sun warming wheatfields.

Under the sun of eternity, flesh ceases to pulsate, eyelids turn bluish, hands wither, tongues swell turning black, mouths rot.

Here, outside of time, under a sun before creation, eyes dim. Lips lose their blush. Lips die.

Words have all faded since time immemorial.

Words lost their color long ago.

Grasses—umbels—brook—a cluster of lilacs—spring showers— all vivid images have grown livid long ago.

Why did I keep my memory? I can no longer taste saliva in my mouth in the spring—the taste of a blade of grass you suck on. I cannot recapture the smell of his hair stirred by the wind, his reassuring hand and tenderness.

My memory is more bloodless than an autumn leaf.

My memory has forgotten the dew.

My memory is drained of its sap. My memory has bled to death.

This is when the heart ought to stop beating—stop beating—come to a stop.

This is why I cannot draw close to the one who calls me. My neighbor. Is she calling? Why does she call? All of a sudden the mask of death covered her face, violet around the nostrils, death deep in her eyes, death in her fingers that twist and knot like twigs devoured by the flames, and she speaks in a foreign tongue words I do not understand.

The barbed wire is so white under the blue sky.

Did she call out to me? She lies motionless now, her head fallen in the dirty dust.

Far beyond the barbed-wire enclosure, spring is singing.

Her eyes grew empty

And we lost our memory.

None of us will return.

None of us was meant to return.

2

Useless Knowledge

We came from too far to merit belief.—Paul Claudel

The Men

We felt deep tenderness for the men. We watched them circling the courtyard during recess. We threw notes at them over the wire fence, foiling surveillance in order to exchange a couple of words with them. We loved them. Our eyes told them so, never our lips. They would have thought it peculiar. It would have been like telling them that we knew how frail their existence was. We were hiding our apprehension. We said nothing that might have betrayed it, but we remained on the lookout, in a corridor or at a window, for each of their appearances, to communicate to them our ever-present thoughts and solicitude.

Some of us, who had a husband among them, saw only him, met instantly his glance among the crisscrossed looks in search of us. Those who had no husband loved all the men without knowing them.

Not one of them was my brother or lover. I did not love the men. I never looked at them. I avoided their faces. Those who encountered me a second time—furtively, when they got soup in the kitchen— were surprised that I failed to recognize their voice or figure. Face to face with them I felt immense pity and terror. Pity and terror in which I did not actually participate. Deep within me was a terrible indifference, the kind of indifference that comes from a heart reduced to ashes. I tried not to feel resentment. I resented all the living. I had not yet found inside of me a prayer of forgiveness for the living.

The men loved us also, but wretchedly. They experienced the sting of the decline of strength and manly duty since they could do nothing for the women. If we suffered seeing them unhappy, hungry, deprived, they did even more so, realizing their inability to protect and defend us, to assume their destiny on their own. And yet, from the start, the women had released them from all responsibility, unbur- dened them all at once from their manly care for women. They wished to convince them that they, the women, were not at risk.

Their femininity safeguarded them, as was still believed. And if they, the men, had everything to fear, the women found reassurance in being women. All they needed was patience and courage, two virtues they were certain to possess since these were part of everyday life. So they comforted the men by not allowing exhaustion, distress, and above all anxiety to surface. They would be worthy of them, who knew the threat weighing on their lives. On the other hand, the men tried to seem casual, as though life still followed a normal course. They attempted to be helpful, wondering what they might do. Alas! The wretchedness of the men's situation precluded any expectations on the women's part. Although their distress was just as great, the women still had some resources, those always possessed by women. They could do the wash, mend the only shirt, now in tatters, the men wore the day of their arrest, cut up blankets to make booties. They deprived themselves of a portion of bread to give it to the men. A man must eat more. Every Sunday, they staged an entertainment in the prison yard, which the men could watch standing behind the barbed-wire fence erected between the two quarters. All week the women were hard at work sewing and rehearsing for the coming Sunday. When the entertainment's preparation was threatened by the sinking of the spirit, or a bad mood, a woman was always there to say: "We've got to do it, for the men." For the men, they sang and danced, putting on a merry, carefree air. It was a heartrending show. Yet the liveliness it awakened would occasionally seem real, even for those who knew just how preposterous it was.

This particular Sunday was sadder than any other. The fort's commanding officer had forbidden the entertainment. The men were consigned to their rooms, the women to theirs. And this was not the sole reason why we felt absent, all of a sudden, at loose ends. Each one of us had a vague foreboding she did not acknowledge on account of the others, trying to dispel it by scrutinizing her companions' attitudes. However, since all of us played our roles to the hilt, no one could be duped.

We felt uneasy. Those who listened to sounds on the other side of the partition—the side of the men—attentive, their ears glued to the wall as in auscultation, would answer questions with "No, nothing to be heard." Not a sound, and our unease kept growing throughout the afternoon.

It was a Sunday in September, as sunny as a summer Sunday yet tinged with autumn melancholy; since early morning, everything about the air, the leaves of the trees we saw from our window, the wind's breath stirring the grass of the glacis, the color of the sky above the fort and the eyes' color as well, everything since morning had the dullness of those days referred to later as unusual days.

"And you, Yvette, do you see anything through the window?" "No, not a thing." Suddenly, we heard steps in our corridor, and the sound of the key turning in the lock. The head of the camp came in, accompanied by a sentinel. She was one of the prisoners, never walked alone. "Josée, what's going on?" "Nothing, nothing. What's the matter with you? Look at you, with your agitated faces? Nothing's going on. I've come for the men's underwear, that's all. Ready or not, you'll have to hand it in at once."

"Hand it back? Immediately? Why?"

Everyone got busy, making up bundles with shirts and socks, reopening the packet because they'd left out a handkerchief, happy to emerge from their passive waiting which crushed them since morning, as if able at last to do something, something useful.

"Are the men leaving?"

"I don't know. I know nothing." Josée did not want to say anything. Someone asked, "What time is it?" And all of us were to remember that at that moment it was four o'clock.

Josée left with the linens. With the door locked again, each went back to bed. The dormitory was stifling again, with its silence and waiting.

Every attempt at diversion or distraction collided with inertia, unexpressed anguish. What about reading something? No one answered.

"I hear some noise. They're walking down the stairs."

"What's going on?"

From the back of the dormitory heads are raised, questions converge upon the one with her ear to the partition.

"They're taking them down."

"All."

"No, not all. It has stopped."

A few months spent in a cell had added a supplementary sense to all of them, allowing them to interpret sounds and crumplings, breathing and steps.

Silence again. Waiting again.

Some tried to believe there was nothing to wait for. Why were we waiting? What did we await and why wait? But they could not give up the feeling of waiting and anguish. Silence, for another long moment.

Then steps are heard in the corridor, our corridor, the sound of boots, this time, and all the women stand up between the bunks, ready, when the N.C.O. comes in. He pulls out a piece of paper from his pocket and calls out names. At the sound of her name, each one lines up at the door, her countenance reflecting resolve and the bracing of oneself rather than the previous anxiety. The German calls seventeen names, folds the list, exits followed by seventeen women, and locks the door. To those who remained at their place the dormitory appears empty and resonant, with the particular resonance that fills a place where something is about to happen.

I had no husband on the other side. I had been summoned at the Santé four months ago. It was morning.

We were waiting, awaiting the return of our companions to give our anguish a name.

We hear them returning. The N.C.O. shepherds them in, and, when he has relocked the door, stiffening and resolve fade from their faces. Their features appear stripped of all expression, all conventional emotion, in the nakedness conferred by the sudden turning on of the light, or an atrocious truth.

We were awaiting them. A kind of slackening of our nervous

system takes place, something within us gives way when we see they're all here. We expected a story. No, they return to their bunks. Each goes to her place without a word, her eyes a void. And the others, who wanted to know, draw near, each to the one among the seventeen with whom she was particularly close, in order to question her. I remained where I was. I didn't go toward Régina, whom I liked, nor Margot. And not one of those whose names were called with mine on that morning at the Santé made a move. We knew.

Now the whole dormitory is awhisper. We learn details: "My husband handed me his wedding ring.—The commanding officer told them they'd be leaving tomorrow morning.—They're putting them into casemates for the night.—They pooled their cigarettes.—Jean was so pale, his eyes so hollow that he frightened me."

And I hear one, in a group close to my bunk, who whispers, "René told Betty that they were to be shot but that all had decided not to say anything to the women, letting them think they were being deported. Naturally, he could say it to Betty. Only we shouldn't repeat it."

Then, one of us stepped to the center of the dormitory and said in a loud voice, addressing all of us, "Friends, we still have some time before lights out. We should read some poems."

The younger ones set up benches. Everyone takes as seat. It's like the first meal after the funeral, when someone tries to find familiar words again, and is able to speak to the others of eating and drinking. And the narrator says: "Nothing elevates the spirit as having loved a dead man or a dead woman—one is fortified for life—and you no longer need anyone." At the sound of these words, each one realizes that despite the lie of the men, and the hypocrisy of the commanding officer, with this business of turning in the linens they had felt at once the nearness of death, its certainty. They were tender and brave, the men we loved.

And I was ashamed of having held this short respite against them. I was ashamed of having refused to love them. I had not wanted to look at them, see their faces, eyes, hear their voices, and now I could no longer distinguish one from the other. I wept with regret. And when today they speak of Pierre, who shot three Germans, or Raymond, the little guy crippled by a bullet in Spain, the whole group of the men we loved, indistinct and fraternal, rises in my memory.

I used to call him my young tree
He was as handsome as a pine
The first time I saw him
His skin was so soft
the first time I held him
and all the other times
so soft
that thinking of it today
is like not feeling one's own mouth
I used to call him my young tree
smooth and straight
when I held him against me
I thought of the wind
of a birch or an ash
When he held me in his arms
I no longer thought of anything.

How naked is
the one who's leaving
naked eyes
naked flesh
of one going to war
How naked is
the one who's leaving
naked heart
naked body
of one leaving to die.

On the jail's threshold
the morning of separation
March twenty-first

The weather is of parting
of loosened arms
and lips gone dry

The weather is
of clean-washed skies
and blooming daffodils.

I used to call him
month of May lover
of childhood days
happy because
I let him
when no one watched
be
my month of May lover
even in December
childlike and tender
as we walked clasped
in each other's arms
through the forest
always that of our childhood
we had no separate memories
he kissed my fingers
they felt cold
he spoke the words
words uttered by month of May lovers.
I alone heard them

One does not heed these words
Why
One listens to the throbbing heart
Believing these tender words
will sound a lifetime
So many months of May
throughout the lifetime
of two who love.

One month of May
they shot him.

I envy those
who gave their own
consenting to the sacrifice
As for me
I rebelled
hardly able
to keep from howling in his presence
He needed all his courage
too much
for a young man
leaving his wife
to go on living after him.

I did not give him up
death tore him from my arms
and also this cause
stronger than my love.

For this cause
he had to die
for my love
he should have lived.
You think it's easy
to be a woman and not jealous
of another.
You can kill her
but an idea
can kill you.
Unable to die with him
I did not die of it.

To mourn a hero
rather than love a coward
You must be right
you who have words for every occasion
Yet
there were some
neither strong nor weak
who never had to sacrifice themselves
nor betray
The thought crossed my mind
he might have been among them
and I felt shame
Would that I were certain
of being ashamed.
You've got to be
got to be
right.

I wondered
for whom
for whom did he die
for which one of his friends
Was there a living man
deserving of his life
he
most dearly loved.
Gently he returned
from whence he disappeared
returned to tell me
he died for the past
and all the future times
I felt my throat burst
my lips wanted to smile
since I was seeing him once more.

You cannot understand
you who never listened
to the heartbeat
of one about to die.

I also wept
because both of us had believed
love was a talisman
It was far worse than losing faith
it was as if I blamed myself
for having failed to love him with greater love.

I loved him
because he was good looking
a trifling reason

I loved him
because he loved me
a selfish reason

Yet
it's for your sake
I look for reasons
for me I had none
I loved him as a woman loves a man
without words to say so.

He died
since to be beautiful
a love story requires
a tragic ending.
Ours was magnificent
Why must your clichés
always triumph
in the end.

★

My heart dried up
From love and pain
From pain and love

day in day out
it withered
slain.

The Marseillaise Beheaded

The days were endless. Empty days. Coffee handed out in the morning, soup at eleven, bread at five. We spent our time watching the shadow of our window's seven bars upon the wall, slowly shifting from one wall to the next. When only three or four bars were left upon the peeling roughcast of the cell's left angle, the day was over, night was falling. It was the moment when the sentry walking round the courtyard left, the moment when the jail came alive. From one window to another, one side to the other, conversations began, quickly, before the arrival of the night watch. Each one addressed a familiar voice, over the crisscrossing of other voices.

Our window was so high—level with the ceiling—that in order to look out we had to climb up on the bed's iron headboard, stand on our toes, and hold on with all our might to the iron bars. It hurt our hands, the hollow of our palms bearing red marks left by the bars. One by one we made the climb to speak to the common prisoners of the next wing, administered by the French penal system. The greater part of the Santé, peopled by political detainees, not yet called resisters, was in the hands of the Germans. The common criminals labored in various workshops, returning to their cells in the evening. They too were on the lookout for the sentry's departure to speak to us. They received letters, read newspapers, and gave us news. When they found out something of importance, they whistled to call us and shouted: "Hey, girls, that's it. The English have retaken Tobruk. Mad dash!" The import of this victory escaped us. The Lybian campaign had begun after our arrest. We inquired: "And in Russia?" "They're still pushing ahead." "They, who?" "The Krauts."

That evening, Lucien and René were late. Their window was empty. All day we counted the hours which rang, at one-second intervals, from the neighborhood clocks. We pricked up our ears, trying to locate all these clocks. How numerous they were! I had lived in this neighborhood, but had never heard them before. You don't count the hours when you're free. We, on the other hand, spent the whole day keeping time, till evening. The day was but the expectation of the evening news: "What can they be doing today? What the devil can they be doing?"

"Perhaps they're in solitary."

"They'd let us know through their neighbors."

"Their neighbors are too far. We can't hear them."

"They'd sign through their window."

"You still don't see them?"

"No, nothing," answered the one who was gripping the iron bars while her cell mate, posted at the door, stayed on the lookout for an unexpected inspection by the female warder.

"Still nothing?"

We were desperate, the kind of silly despair which makes children weep when they're not given something promised.

"There, there! They got there at last!" The face of a breathless Lucien appears between the bars of his cell, on the other side of the courtyard.

All at once we feel comforted. The one clinging to the bars of our window shouts: "Why did you come back so late? We're almost out of time."

"We were on K.P. They had us install the big bathtub."

"The big bathtub? What's that?"

"The bran basket. For the head. At the guillotine. Tomorrow there'll be four. So, it's the great leap. You know, the four of the rue Buci."

We had no idea.

"That's right, you don't know. You were in here already. Four guys spoke up right in the Buci market, one morning, on market day, when all the women stand in line for shopping. Supposedly, one of the four jumped up on a stand, inciting everyone to put up a fight against the Krauts. Then he tried to run off with the three pals who were shielding him. But the cops caught up with them. They were brought up before a special court. All four condemned to death. It's for tomorrow morning. Right here, in the French part of the jail."

Sound of boots, clinking of arms. The night sentry must have entered the courtyard. Lucien's head dips down like Guignol at the marionettes. All of a sudden, everything stops. We hear the sentry's steps.

The four of rue Buci. Four of ours. If we could only find out their names . . . Perhaps we know them.

That night none of us slept. We heard every hour ring, saw the ceiling grow light, the day rise, the shadow of the first bars appear, blurred, hardly imprinted, on the wall.

"Four o'clock. Must be the time," says Henriette, at the sound of the fourth stroke.

Distant at first, because it comes from a wing behind ours, then increasingly clear, "La Marseillaise" bursts forth, stronger and stronger as the men move to the center of the courtyard which must be at the prison's core. Louder and louder, and now we can make out voices, four ill-tuned voices, but all four raised to the highest possible pitch. After the first verse—they must be waiting, standing at the foot of the guillotine—the voices die down—then they catch their breath to pick up the refrain, their voices raised high again, full and even. But after the first two words of the refrain, there are only three voices, still as even, articulating clearly all the words, then two, then one lone voice which swells and rises to the highest pitch, in order to be heard alone by all the prisoners, one lone voice in turn cut short. The head fell in the middle of a word. A word left hanging, severed, intolerably silenced. For one moment only, for the anthem rises again, carried now by the voices of the political prisoners singing from the depths of their cells.

It happened during the summer of 1942.

"Last week, an incoherent action, followed by several others, was decided upon by the new government: the execution in the courtyard of the sinister fortress of Montluc, in Lyons, of the Algerian patriot

Abderahmane Laklifi. He was beheaded Saturday, at dawn, accompanied to the gallows by the singing of all his comrades, behind the bars of their cells" (*L'Express,* August 4, 1960).

Morning of Arrival

Hell had vomited all its damned
who were greeting us now
Right away
we realized
why they failed to welcome us warmly
They missed the torments of hell
and saw us arriving
we who came from the world
as people who know
and can tell the difference
and right away
we would also know
and wish to forget life.

In hell
you do not see your comrades dying
in hell
death is no threat
you no longer feel hunger or thirst in hell
you no longer await anything
in hell
there is no more hope
and hope is anguish
in the heart empty of blood.
Why then do you say that it is hell,
here.

To Yvonne Blech

We were inebriated on Apollinaire
and Claudel
do you recall?

That's the beginning of a poem
I wanted to remember
for you, recite to you.

Words faded from my memory
which lost its way in the decay
of days gone by
it went away
together with our former loves
Apollinaire, Claudel,
perishing here
together with us.

Thank You to the Others

A ghostly rope dancer
practiced nights
on telegraph wires
Unaware of my seeing him
he kept on dancing
dressed as a phantom
and yet
no one else saw him.

I couldn't have made it
if no one had seen me
if you hadn't been there.

Actually
there's nothing to dying
decently
but
in diarrhea
mud
blood
a slow
drawn-out
dying

A silly sentimental ballad
on a summer evening
Life
the past you rue
No
Here we've forgotten how
to rue.

I saw men beaten
finally I could think
of him
dead

handsome still
straight as an arrow
dead of a death he chose.

When I saw what I saw
suffering
dying
as I saw
suffering and dying
I realized that nothing
nothing was too much
in this struggle.

This dot on the map
This black spot at the core of Europe
this red spot
this spot of fire this spot of soot
this spot of blood this spot of ashes
for millions
a nameless place.
From all the countries of Europe
from all the points on the horizon
trains converged
toward the nameless place
loaded with millions of humans
poured out there unknowing of where
poured out with their lives
memories
small aches

huge astonishment
eyes questioning
bamboozled
under fire
burned
without knowing
where they were.
Today people know
have known for several years
that this dot on the map
is Auschwitz
This much they know
as for the rest
they think they know.

Esther

I was in bed when a neighbor called me: "There's someone asking for you outside."

"Who?"

"A girl. At the door."

I step outside. A young girl is there, waiting. She does not seem to know me. I don't know her. I cast a look around me. The street of dirty snow which separates the block houses is empty. The girl is alone. I scrutinize her. A Jewess. She's wearing civilian clothing. She looks at me, walks toward me, and says in German:

"You're C.?"

"That's right."

"I'm Esther. I know you're a comrade."

I'm on my guard. "How do you know this?"

"I'll tell you later. Listen. We don't have much time. It's almost curfew." (After curfew the guards in the miradors shoot at any moving target.) "I'm Jewish, from Byelorussia."

I examine her. She is small, round, apple-cheeked. Twenty, perhaps less. Her hair is freshly shorn under her scarf. Jewish women are shorn every month; the others only on arrival, save for an error. She is clean, well-dressed. She understands my look, explains, "I'm working in Effekts."

It's the commando which sorts, puts away, inventories the contents of the luggage of the Jews, left on the platform at arrival. The Effekts commando is made up of Jewish women selected from those who enter the camp. The youngest and strongest from each incoming convoy are selected for work. They enter the camp. The others are sent to the gas chamber. The Effekts girls are well dressed because they pick clothes from those they handle. (Those Jewish men and women do not wear the striped uniform. They wear civilian clothes marked with a large, red lead cross in the back. The Effekts girls simply make the same mark on the clothes they take in exchange for their own.) They are not thin because they sell other female prisoners a pair of panties or an undershirt for a piece of bread or a portion of margarine, which constitute the evening meal. They are clean because they have a change of underwear, and are able to wash up with running water, right where they work. And the SS insist on their keeping clean since the things they handle will be distributed in the coming winter to German civilian war casualties. As to us, we never get to wash. Except for the Effekts privileged few, some ten or twenty girls, and the camp aristocracy—block leaders and their assistants, policewomen and sentenced German felons—no one ever washed.

I look at Esther, at the white scarf on her head. I stare at her teeth, gleaming in her face, and say: "You've got lovely teeth."

"That's why I'm here, to help you. What do you need?"

What do I need? Where do I start?

"Yes, you're in need of everything, isn't that so? I'll come back tomorrow. So long!"

The following day, she's back at the same time. She draws from her bosom a tube of toothpaste, a new toothbrush still wrapped in transparent paper.

"You'll wash your teeth in a bit of your morning tea."

A pink jersey.

"When it gets dirty you throw it away; I'll bring you another. That's all I was able to take today. Tomorrow, I'll bring you something else. A night gown so you won't have to sleep with your clothes on."

I look at the objects she's put in my hand. The toothbrush has some foreign markings. The inscription on the tube of toothpaste is in a foreign alphabet. The last convoys came from Greece.

I'm at a loss. Where shall I put all this? I have no pockets. If I leave these things under my blanket, I won't find them in the evening when I return from work. I look at the toothbrush, the new tube of paste, the clean jersey. They're much-needed objects yet they belong to a way of life that has been abolished, life when you brushed your teeth. And how does one share this? We share everything. But Esther is reading my face for signs of pleasure.

"Thank you, Esther. You're sweet."

"If you come back a bit earlier one evening, and you're not too tired, we'll be able to talk a bit."

She shakes my hand and turns around as she leaves, smiling broadly with her clean teeth, happy at the thought of having given me a bit of pleasure.

Who was this Esther? I never saw her again. The Effekts commando is often searched, and those unable to hide their pilfered goods are sent to the disciplinary column or the gas chamber. It depends on the whim of the SS. I found out she was from Grodno.

Thirst

After roll call, the ranks became columns setting out to work. Lined up five abreast, all we had to do was an about-face on the spot to be in perfect marching order, facing the gate, ready for takeoff. It didn't go that fast. We had to wait longer, marking time. The kapos busied themselves, forming their commandos. They counted us, five by five, and at one hundred cut the column. Each kapo sliced its portion of labor force. This morning, the cut had been made within our group, so that some of us were sent to work on a demolition detail, while the others were directed elsewhere. In the evening, when we were reunited at roll call, Carmen said to me, "Tomorrow, we'll go back there. I had a good look at the kapo, and I'll recognize her. Stay close to us. Watch out so they won't cut you off. There's water."

I'd been thirsty for days and days, thirsty to the point of losing my mind, to the point of being unable to eat since there was no saliva in my mouth, so thirsty I couldn't speak, because you're unable to speak when there's no saliva in your mouth. My parched lips were splitting, my gums swollen, my tongue a piece of wood. My swollen gums and tongue kept me from closing my mouth, which stayed open like that of a madwoman with dilated pupils in her haggard eyes. At least, this is what the others told me, later. They thought I'd lost my mind. I couldn't hear anything, see anything. They even thought I had gone blind. It took me a long time later on to explain that, without being blind, I saw nothing. All my senses had been abolished by thirst.

In the hope of seeing a glimmer of awareness in my eyes, Carmen had to repeat a number of times, "There's water there. Tomorrow you'll be able to drink."

The night seemed interminable. My thirst at night was atrocious, and I still wonder how I lasted till the end of it.

In the morning, clutching my companions, still mute, haggard, lost, I let myself be led—or rather they watched over me, since I was deprived of all reflex action, and without their help would have walked into an SS as easily as into a pile of bricks, or failed to keep my place in the ranks. I would have been shot. Only the thought of water kept me alert. I was looking for it everywhere. The sight of a puddle, of a slightly liquid mud flow, made me lose my self-control, and my friends held me back since I wanted to throw myself, face down, upon this puddle or this mud. I would have done so right under the dogs' fierce jaws.

It was a long way away. It seemed to me we'd never get there. I didn't ask any questions since I couldn't talk. A long time ago I had stopped trying to form words with my lips. Of course my eyes must have been full of anxious questioning. My friends kept on reassuring me, "Have no fear. It's the right commando. There's water there. We're telling you."

We got there at last. It was a tree nursery. "We plant trees. Little ones. Once a tree is planted we water it. We give it a full watering can," explained those who had been there yesterday. Indeed, there was a row of sprinkling cans near a well. I wanted to run to it at once, break ranks. Viva held me strongly by the arm. "Wait till the kapo has stopped counting us." The count made, the kapo assigned the teams. I wasn't assigned to the watering cans any more than any of my friends. We were supposed to carry the shrubs to the men who planted them. I was desperate. While each of my companions tried to comfort me, Carmen took things in hand. "Listen. Stay quietly with Lulu. Be good, very quiet." She spoke to me gently, as one does to the ailing. "Work. Here, take this." She put in my hand a frail shoot. "There's a Pole who draws water from the well. I recognized him, he was here yesterday. He fills the watering cans. We brought a whole portion of bread for him. See? In exchange for the bread, I'll ask him to put water there, behind the tree pile. Don't move. As soon as it's ready I'll let you know. No, don't make a move. I'll come back, right away." Fortunately, we weren't in a flat, exposed place. There were bends in the path and hidden corners, here a tool shed, there a lean-to for wood, so that we weren't constantly under the gaze of the kapos or the SS. Held up by Viva, and hidden by the others, I pretended I was working. Coming and going with them, carrying the same shrub, I did not have the strength to put it down in the furrow where a Pole would pick it up for planting. I could hardly stand, and did not know what I was doing. I believe I did not even have the sensation of thirst. Unconscious, dazed, I no longer felt or perceived anything.

Carmen came back. She and Viva, having made sure the way was clear, grabbed me under each arm, taking me into a recess between a piece of wall and the pile of shrubs we were supposed to carry. "Here!" Carmen said, showing me a pail of water. It was made of zinc, like those used in the country to get water from a well. A large pail. Full. I tore myself from Carmen and Viva, threw myself on the pail of water. Actually fell upon it. I knelt near the pail and drank like a horse, dipping my nose in the water, plunging my whole face. I can't remember whether the water was cold—it must have been, early in March, and having just been drawn from the well—but I felt neither the cold nor the wetness upon my face. I drank and drank breathlessly, and from time to time I had to lift my nostrils out of the water to take a breath of air. I did so without interrupting my drinking. I drank with no thought of any kind, without stopping to consider I might have to stop if a kapo happened by. I kept on drinking. Carmen, who was on the lookout, said, "That's enough." I'd drunk half the pail. I took time out without letting go of the pail which I was clasping tight in my arms. "Come," said Carmen, "that's enough." Without answering—I might have made a gesture, a movement—without stirring, I plunged my head into the pail once more. I drank and drank some more. Like a horse, no, like a dog. A dog laps water with its agile tongue. It hollows out its tongue in the shape of a spoon to hold the liquid. A horse merely drinks. The level of water was going down. I tilted the bucket to drink to the very bottom. Almost stretched out upon the ground, I aspirated the last drop, without spilling any of the precious liquid. I would have liked to lick the side of the pail, but my tongue was too hard, too hard even to lick my lips. I wiped my face with my hand, and my hand with my lips. "This time, you've got to go," Carmen insisted, "the Pole is asking for his pail." She was making signs to someone behind her. I didn't want to let go of my bucket. My belly was so heavy I couldn't stir. It was like an independent object, a weight or a package, hooked onto my skeleton. I was very thin. For days and days I hadn't eaten my portion of bread, since I couldn't swallow anything without saliva in my mouth, days and days I'd been unable to eat my soup, even when it was sufficiently liquid, because soup is salty, and it burned the bleeding ulcers in my mouth. I had drunk. I was no longer thirsty, yet still uncertain of not being so. I had drunk all the contents of the pail. Yes, just like a horse.

Carmen called Viva. They helped me up. My belly was enormous. Suddenly, I felt life pouring back into me. It was as if I were regaining consciousness, feeling my blood circulating through my body, my lungs breathing, my heart beating. I was alive. Saliva was returning to my mouth. The burning feeling round my eyelids was fading. Your eyes burn when the lacrymal glands dry up. My ears could hear again. I was living.

Viva took me back to the others while Carmen was returning the bucket. As my mouth regained its moisture, I recovered my sight. My head grew light. I was able to hold it up. I saw Lulu, who was looking at me with concern, staring at my enormous belly, and heard her tell Viva, "You shouldn't have let her drink so much." I could feel saliva forming itself in my mouth. Speech was returning as well. It was still hard to move my lips. At last I was able to utter, in a strange voice, on account of the stiffness of my tongue: "I'm no longer thirsty." "Did the water at least taste good?" someone inquired. I didn't answer. I hadn't felt the water's taste. I drank, that's all.

"We'll try to come back tomorrow," said Lulu. "We'll have to hoard some bread this evening," added Cecile.

The following day, disoriented by the jostling following roll call, we did not succeed in slipping into the tree nursery commando. It didn't matter any more. I was cured.

There are people who say, "I'm thirsty." They step into a café and order a beer.

Yvonne Picard
who had such lovely breasts
died.
Yvonne Blech
who had almond-shaped eyes
and eloquent hands
died.
Mounette died
who had such a lovely complexion
a full mouth
a silvery laugh.
Aurore
who had mauve,
mallow-colored eyes
died.

So much beauty and youth
ardor and promise . . .
All as brave as heroes of ancient Rome.

And Yvette also died
who was neither pretty nor anything special
yet braver than anyone.

And you Viva
and I Charlotte
who have nothing lovely left
shall soon be dead.

The Stream

Strange, but I don't recall anything about that day. Nothing but the stream. Since all the days were the same, a monotony interrupted only by heavy penalties and roll calls, since the days were the same, we certainly had roll call, and, following roll call, work columns were formed, I must have been careful to stay in the same column as my group, and later, after a long wait, the column must have marched through the gate where the SS in the sentry box counted the ranks passing through. And after? Did the column go right or left? Right to the marshes, or left toward the demolition work, or the silos? How long did we walk? I have no idea. What work did we do? Neither do I recall that. I remember the leader of the column because this memory is intimately connected with the stream. She was a German political prisoner who kept on shouting without ever catching her breath. This woman could really shout . . . She did so without any visible reason for it, shouting while stamping her feet, shaking her head, her stick, and hitting blindly, then suddenly freezing where she stood. She kept on shouting incomprehensible orders we were unable to carry out, then commanded us to sing while marching. Supposedly she was a former Socialist who had arrived at Birkenau after having gone through all the camps and all the prisons since Hilter's coming to power. She had been imprisoned for seven or eight years, long enough to go mad. Perhaps she had gotten used to shouting so as to pull the wool over their eyes and be promoted to kapo. When she waved her stick, hitting haphazardly, it would come down next to her target; at any rate, she let us dodge the blow. I can no longer recall what work we did that day. I remember only the stream. The memory of it obliterated all the other impressions of the day. To reconstruct it, I'd have to focus on summoning every detail. Since it was the beginning of April—a fact I know by performing a simple calculation: it was sixty-seven days after our arrival on January 27—seventy members of our group were still alive. I kept these figures in mind so I could be sure of them. But there weren't seventy of us at the stream, because among the survivors many were confined to the revier with typhus. Yvonne Picard had died already, Yvonne Blech also, Viva not yet; she died only in July. I was therefore with my small group: Viva, Carmen, Lulu, Mado. They entered the revir later, after coming down with typhus. In April, the five of us were in the camp, going to work together, together at roll call, walking together all five of us, arm in arm. So, it is quite certain that on that day I must have been with them. Yet, though I see them clearly in all the places where we worked together, I find it impossible to envision them near me on the day of the stream. I see their gestures when we were digging in the marshes, or scooping out a ditch, when we transported clods of frozen or muddy earth on hods called *tragues,* carried bricks, or pushed small tipcarts full of sand, when we cleared demolished houses, yet I cannot envision them on that day. In my memory—try as I do with all my might—there is only the stream and me. This is wrong, absolutely wrong. No one was there alone, except in solitary, and I knew no one who was imprisoned in this way. No one from our group, I mean.

It couldn't have been any other way. The column led by the half-crazed German kapo reached our place of work. The kapo made a count of the column—must have done so since it was routine—and we picked up our tools. But which ones and to do what? We started on our labor. With spades? With shovels, or our bare hands for the rails and the bricks? I can only recall the light on that day, because the memory of the light is associated with the stream. There was—it was always like that—the blow of a whistle for the noon recess, forming the ranks and lining up in front of the soup jerry cans. Did we eat our soup standing or sitting? I don't know. Perhaps we sat down, because the weather was fine. But sitting on what? If we had been sent to a demolition site we'd have found old doors, or boards to sit on. The weather was fine, but not good enough to sit on the grass. In fact, was there any grass? Probably, since it was near the stream. It must have been a field. After the soup—if my memory is true—the kapo shouted, "Now, if you wish, you may wash yourselves in the stream." Of this I'm certain. And yet I do not see the woman with whom I walked in the direction of the stream. And I couldn't have gone there on my own. Who was I with? I really don't know. We were always two by two, a pair that never parted. We must have gone there, all five of us, talking. We always talked. I don't see the others, not even Viva, who always helped me walk. I recall going down to the stream alone. It was in the month of April. I could tell the exact date since it was the seventy-seventh day after our arrival. We had taken the trouble to count the days from our arrival on Wednesday the twenty-seventh of January, in order to keep track of the dates. What dates? What did it matter whether it was Friday or Saturday, this or that anniversary? The dates we had to remember were those of Yvonne's or Suzanne's death, the death of Rosette or Marcelle. We wanted to be able to say, "So and so died on . . ." when they'd ask us after we returned. That's why we kept a scrupulous count. There were long discussions between us when we did not agree on the count. But it seems to me that we kept accurate records. We'd keep on checking all the time: "No, the dogs, that was two days ago, not yesterday." On Sunday, the columns did not leave the camp. That provided a point of reference and allowed us to reestablish a correct count when we lost track of the days.

I reached the stream's bank. It was only recently that its water had started to flow again. I even think that it was the first time that we saw the water of the stream. It must have been frozen so we had not paid attention. Otherwise, during all those weeks when I was so thirsty, I would have noticed it. It ran over pebbles, between two grass-covered banks. Yes, now I recall the grass. Ugly grass, and here and there a shrub with opened buds.

What amazes me, now that I think of it, is that the air was light, clear, but that one didn't smell anything. It must have been quite far from the crematoria. Or perhaps the wind was blowing in the opposite direction on that day. At any rate, we no longer smelled the odor of the crematoria. Yes, and what also amazes me is that there wasn't the slightest smell of spring in the air. Yet there were buds, grass, water, and all this must have had a smell. No, no memory of any odor. It's true that I can't recall my own smell when I lifted my dress. Which proves that our nostrils were besmirched with our own stink and could no longer smell anything.

I went down cautiously to the edge of the bank, thinking of how I'd adjust and coordinate my gestures so as not to waste precious seconds. The pause was a short one and we had to get the most out of it. The bank was not slippery, but I didn't wish to risk getting my shoes wet; they had finally become dry for the first time only a short while ago. Which means that this stream did not run through the marsh, for in April, as the ice melts, the marsh is nothing but a field of mud. Moreover, I now remember clearly the grass, and in the marsh there wasn't a blade of grass.

I figured out I could wash my face while standing barefoot in the water, a process which would hasten the subsequent washing of my feet. I sat down on the grassy slope, took off my shoes, which I carefully placed under my jacket. This means that neither Viva nor anyone from my group was close to me, for we'd have placed our shoes together. I had removed my jacket and my scarf—to wash my face and ears—but you couldn't consider taking off your dress to wash your neck and arms. The sky was clear, there was even some sunshine, but it wasn't warm. After piling up my shoes, jacket and scarf, I took off my stockings. I hadn't removed them since our arrival, sixty-seven days ago. I took them off and turned them inside out. At the toe end I felt some peculiar resistance. The stockings were glued. I pulled a bit too much, and on the other side a strange design appeared. I looked at this truly curious pattern. I looked at my feet. They were black with dirt, and at the tip strangely black, or rather violet, with dry thickening at the peculiarly costumed toes; except for the two big toes, all the others had lost their nails, which, detached from the skin, and glued to the stockings, formed this curious design. Naturally, there was no time to consider this detail. There wasn't a minute to waste if one wished to wash. Later, I understood that my toes must have been frozen. Or perhaps the others explained it to me when I told them of my amazement. To see one's toe nails encrusted in one's stockings is, I promise you, an astonishing sight.

Let's see, face, feet, legs. I should also wash my behind. I took off my panties and placed them on the pile formed by my jacket, scarf and shoes. My panties must have stunk. It was also the first time in sixty-seven days I had peeled them off. But no, actually I couldn't smell anything. There is something mysterious about the sense of smell. For example, I'd been back for a long time, and I bathed at that time twice a day—a real mania—scrubbing my body with a fine soap, I'd been back for weeks, yet I could still smell on me the odor of the camp, an odor of raw sewage and carrion. Yet, on that day, I removed my panties, stiff with dry diarrhea—if you think there was toilet paper, or anything like that, before the appearance of new-grown grass—yet the smell didn't nauseate me.

I went down into the running water, so cold it took my breath away. It hardly covered my ankles, but its contact amazed me, the forgotten contact of water on one's skin.

Now, where do I start? The face or the behind? Quickly, picking up water in my cupped hands, and leaning forward so as not to wet my dress, with its unbuttoned collar, I ran it over my face. Gently at first, because this sensation of water on my face was so new, so wonderful, but almost at once I got a grip on myself. There wasn't a moment to lose, and I started to scrub myself vigorously, particularly behind the ears. Why do mothers always insist on the ears? It's no dirtier than anything else.

What could I have been thinking as I tried to cleanse my skin a section at a time? Probably of the last shower I'd taken on the day of arrival? After shaving our heads, they sent us to the showers. I still had my piece of soap and bath towel. For the rest, we had to leave our things in our valises, keeping nothing. I had emptied a small vial of perfume on my throat, the gift of a friend who slipped it into one of the last parcels I received before departure. Up to that point I'd saved this perfume, satisfied with uncorking it and breathing in its aroma in the evening, before falling asleep. Naked amid my companions, I stared tenderly at the vial—Orgueil by Lelong; what a fine name for that day—and I poured it out slowly, between my breasts. Then, under the shower, I took care not to soap down the spot where the perfume had run in order to preserve its trace. I don't believe that sweet-smelling trace lingered for any amount of time. It is true, however, as I just said, that our sense of smell was quickly obliterated. I had started to wash myself thoroughly when a kapo shouted for us to hurry, and the water stopped running. I had entered the drying room where Viva, Yvonne and the others, half-rinsed, were sitting. It made them laugh. It was the last bit of laughter ringing out among us. "How good you smell!" said one of them. "Let me sit down next to you for a moment. We won't inhale delicate smells again." She must have been from the Tours region, so elegantly did she express herself. "Inhale," the word stuck in my memory together with the voice of the one who had spoken it, but I no longer know who she was, nor am I able to recapture her face.

So, on that day, at the stream, I must have thought of the last shower, and also of the pleasure of immersing one's body in gentle, warm water. Or perhaps I thought of all the ones who had died since our arrival without having been able to splash some water on their faces. All of this is but reported remembrances. Actually, I thought of nothing except the stream, and all my thoughts were focused on what I had to do to wash myself, to remove the dirt as fast and thoroughly as possible. I was rubbing myself quickly and strongly, fortunately unable to check on the results. It would have discouraged me. Enough with the face, time is running out. It was the first time, over there, that I would have liked to stretch time a bit. So, I had to consider that, as far as the face went, it was enough. Next I rolled up my dress, wrapping it round my waist, and keeping it in place with my elbows, so as to squat above the running water. My feet were beginning to be cold, and I was trying to rub them on the riverbed's pebbles. With my dress raised, my fingertips hardly felt how the hipbones of my emaciated body protruded. I was in too great a hurry to stop at these details. Scooping up more water in my cupped hands, I started to rub. My pubic hair, shaved on arrival, had grown back. It was matted by diarrhea, and I had a hard time disentangling it. If I could have restored it to its original length and curl I would have felt really clean, but I'd have to soak for hours. I rubbed, rubbed to the point of scratching myself, without achieving what I sought. It was discouraging. And the water was cold! It froze my belly. It was time to attack another spot. Anyway, I wasn't able to see what I was rubbing, whereas I saw my thighs, legs, feet, black with dirt. Seen in the transparency of the water, where they'd been bathing for quite a while, they hadn't altered in color.

As for the face, the behind, I'd thought it all out, but been unable to bring myself to use a handful of sand in lieu of soap. The skin of the thighs and legs is harder. My hand full of wet earth, I started to rub the right thigh, directly above the knee. My skin was getting lighter, redder. Yes, it really looked lighter. I rubbed with all my might, particularly the knee. I had to go on rubbing elsewhere when I noticed some drops of blood. I was rubbing too hard, and the sand was too rough. I was about to turn my attention to the other knee, when the kapo blew her whistle. Fall in! The pause was over. Quickly I pulled my panties back on, dried my feet on the grass, pulled up my stockings with its nails, got into my shoes. I grabbed my jacket and scarf to get into ranks. It must have happened like this, but I have no memory of it. I only recall the stream.

This shall be the last time I'll see Viva. I have such an exact knowledge of death that I could tell the hour of Viva's. Before tomorrow morning.

This shall be my last visit to the Birkenau revir to see Viva. Only for Viva would I find the courage to go there.

This shall be the last time I'll see Viva.

Without her curls I wouldn't have recognized her. How her hair has grown! Such a long agony, Viva.

She's there, already lifeless, stretched out on bare planks. The stinking boards have stripped her skin, revealing the bone at her shoulder tip. She used to have beautiful shoulders, Viva.

Without her hair I wouldn't have known her. Skin tightly glued to her jawbones, glued to her eye sockets, to her cheekbones. Death is imprinted on Viva's face. Death makes skin look delicate. Delicate and tightly stretched, strangely transparent.

I say softly, "Viva." Viva no longer hears me, no longer sees me. I take her hand in mine without eliciting any response, not even a tiny shudder. Her hand is cold. Death has already taken hold of her hand. Her pulse is far, far away. Death will rise from her hand to her eyes. Sometime between now and tomorrow morning.

Tomorrow morning, in front of us lined up at attention for roll call, Viva will pass before us on the small stretcher, with her feet sticking out and her hand hanging between the stretcher's arms. And perhaps one of those standing in the ranks for roll call, and knowing that her turn is coming to be carried on the small stretcher, perhaps one of them will say, looking at Viva's beautiful black curls, "She lasted a long time, that one." A whole winter, a whole spring.

Yes, she will have struggled a long time, Viva. She will have helped me a long time.

This shall be the last time I'll see Viva.

Not a tear came to my eyes. I've had no tears for a long, long time.

Lily

"Lily isn't here? Where's Lily?" asked those who had spent the morning working in the fields.

The others asked them to lower their voices, pointing to Eva.

"They came to the lab for her."

"There were two of them."

"Do we pick up her soup?"

"Her cousin took care of that."

Eva was seated, eating. She looked at nothing. And we did not look at her. Next to her, Lily's place was empty. The stool, the bare wood of the table, the bowl full of soup getting cold. Lily had been served. No one looked at the soup thickening in the bowl. No one looked at Eva, who was quietly, sedately eating, looking calmer than usual perhaps.

Everyone had finished eating. They were clearing the table. At Lily and Eva's table the one who was picking up the bowls had skipped Lily's place, letting the soup grow cold, as though she didn't see it.

At the sound of the whistle we left the refectory and fell in outside to march back to work. No one approached Eva, no one spoke to her. To speak to her would have meant giving her marks of sympathy reserved for those who have suffered a misfortune.

Two SS had come for Lily in the morning. She was standing in front of a scale, weighing earth in small containers and entering the weight on a chart. The SS had called her name in a loud voice, standing at the entrance. She had stopped weighing but had still written down a number, and then asked "Me?" in German. Lily spoke very good German.

"Komme!" said one of the SS.

"Now?"

"Ja, Schnell!"

Yes, you, quickly. Lily had taken off her gown. A comrade had helped her. It was a lab coat, buttoning in the back. In the morning we helped one another button up all the way down the back, and in the evening we did the same to undress. Lily took off her lab coat. Underneath she had on a striped, clean dress, tight-fitting, even a little short. Lily was twenty years old. Her stylishness triumphed over captivity. She had refashioned the striped dress.

The SS were in a hurry, but there was nothing brutal about them. Finding themselves in a laboratory where everything appeared to them to be scientific and complicated, seeing chemists dressed in white lab coats, working in silence with precise gestures, surrounded by a serious atmosphere, impressed them. Lily did not hurry. Since she spoke German, she was asking the SS where and why they were taking her. One of them took out a folded sheet of paper from the outside pocket of his tunic, looked at the other one, seeking his approbation ("Do we tell her?") and answered, 'Politische Abteilung" (political department, the police or Gestapo). Alleging a toilet call, Lily warned her cousin, who was drawing in the next room. Eva had already been warned. One of the chemists, walking and moving in elaborate fashion, had brought a test tube to Eva's office. Thus Eva knew yet kept on wondering. Why was Lily summoned by the police? We all wondered.

Lily left after a brief farewell. We saw her through the windows walking proudly between the two SS. She was wearing a dress. It was summer. In the summer we didn't wear jackets. The road was sun-kissed. Our eyes followed her as long as we could see her, walking between the two SS with her back very straight, knowing perhaps why she had been summoned. As for us, we didn't know, and were wondering. They didn't summon you to the police headquarters for nothing. In fact, we had no idea why someone should be summoned by the police. Lily was the first.

We saw her walking between the two SS. Saw her shiny black hair, shorn recently (Lily was Jewish: the heads of Jewish women were shaved frequently), hair that was growing back shiny-black, like the shiny coat of a dog. Her hair grew low over the nape of her neck, and was as long there as on top of her head. Lily left it alone, didn't even it out. When your hair has been shorn many times, you don't ever want to cut it, even to clear your neck.

Lily walked between the two SS. Perhaps she knew. The two SS didn't know.

Now each one of us in turn would go up to Eva's drafting table, cupel or test tube in hand. Eva made lovely drawings: watercolors of various leaves and flowers, various types of roots, their characteristics marked by small arrows directing the viewer to an India ink explanation, written in fine hand on the plate's edge. When Herr Doktor, the SS laboratory head, was not there, Eva drew flowers, foliage, birds and houses. She also made portraits. Later, each one of us recalled that on that day we thought: fortunately Eva made a portrait of Lily. But on that day we did not know.

At noon, Lily had not returned. Nor by evening. Between ourselves we said, "They're questioning her." Interrogations lasted a long time. No one voiced what she thought deep inside herself, things she didn't dare express, and reproached herself for thinking. We talked a good deal in order not to think, communicated our suppositions. As soon as Eva appeared we'd stop. Eva was now more alone than ever, and not only because she no longer had Lily. How could we speak to Eva? To avoid saying Lily's name was not natural, to utter it was to show apprehension, and perhaps, after all, Eva was as calm as she appeared, then why give her cause to worry? We also knew it was cowardly to reason in this manner. Eva could not be calm. Later she told us she had not slept the first night. In the dormitory, her cot and Lily's were next to one another. Keeping watch, she had waited, hoping to recognize among other night noises the steps of the SS bringing Lily back from interrogation. Nor did she sleep the second night, when she no longer hoped to hear Lily returning.

The following day, we still avoided Eva. At noon, Lily's place was still empty, but her bowl had not been filled. It was better to keep the soup warm . . . From my table I could see Lily's back, the nape of her neck with its stiff hair, black and shiny like that of a dog, over the collar of her dress. Even when she was not there, when her stool was empty, it seemed to me that she sat in her seat, with her studious back, the neck of a boy whose parents don't give him the few pennies needed to go to the barber, hair growing back, hanging shiny and stiff as that of country lads.

Only on the third day did we find out. We all went over to Eva. We kissed her. We weren't able to say anything. Eva wasn't crying. Her face was drawn, the look in her eyes even more haunted than before. Lily was her only remaining relative. Her whole family had been gassed. The entire small Slovakian town she came from had been gassed. Then, the others at the table spread out. The stool had been removed, and you could no longer see that Lily was missing.

We knew now. How did we find out? Almost impossible to say. Doubtless through the men. Not through Eva, in any case. She never said anything to anybody. She never mentioned Lily to anyone. Everyone knew without anything having been said.

We worked in a laboratory a few kilometers from the big camp. One day, German scientists had decided to study the koksaghyz, a plant they had seen in the Ukraine and which they decided to introduce into Poland. A central Asian dandelion, its root yields a latex from which the Russians, who grew it for industrial usage, derived a rubber comparable to Para rubber. This interested the Germans. They wanted to try growing it in the conquered territories, and they had brought back sacks of seeds from Russia. This project required chemists, biologists, botanists, agronomists, translators, draftsmen, laboratory assistants, all assembled at Auschwitz's research center. Thus, they had taken from Birkenau, a death camp, the women who belonged to these professions. For these women—less than one hundred—it meant salvation.

We were glad to be there because it meant we could wash, have clean clothes, work in a sheltered situation. The cultivation of koksaghyz would yield no result before 1948. We were at some remove from the camp, and did not smell the odor of the crematoria. We did see smoke rising from the smokestacks. So strong was the fire at times that immensely high flames issued from those stacks, reaching toward the sky. In the evening, they cast on the horizon the red glow of blast furnaces. We were well aware that these were not blast furnaces, but crematoria ovens; they were burning people. It was hard to be comfortable and not to think day and night of all the people being burned day and night—thousands of them.

Surrounding the laboratory, there was a garden where prisoners—from the men's commando—cultivated flowers and vegetables for the SS. The gardeners made funeral or nuptial wreaths. This is how we knew that an SS was getting married or had died. Some SS died of typhus.

The gardeners came from the men's camp each morning to work in the garden. It was strictly forbidden to speak to them. Naturally, we did anyway. Behind a greenhouse, moving some potted plants or watering our seeds (the cultivation of the koksaghyz was the responsibility of the laboratory, or our commando), we were able to speak to the men. They brought us news. Men were better organized than we were in the matter of news. Some of us had a friend among them, even a fiancé. This was Lily's case. Her fiancé was Polish. They became engaged by exchanging a few words without looking at one another, without seeming to talk, since an SS could appear at any moment and catch them breaking the law. It was for him, for her fiancé, that Lily took care of her appearance. When she came out of the lab, a basketful of roots on her arm which she pretended to be taking somewhere, when she stepped out, having caught a glimpse of her fiancé through the window and having seen him kneeling near a forcing frame, precisely on the side of the path she would be taking, Lily put a white collar on her dress, a collar she was hiding between her breasts. Wearing a white collar on a striped dress was strictly forbidden. Moreover, to find a piece of cloth for a collar, thread and a needle, was a difficult, complex task. However, there was a human chain between the men's camp sewing workroom—where female prisoners worked for the SS—and the lab with which the garden commando had established a liaison operation.

When her fiancé brought Lily something—cigarettes from his ration, or a stolen cucumber—he hid it under the pumpkin leaves, near the well. He would also add a short note. Lily picked up what her fiancé had left, slipping it into her basket, together with the kok-saghyz roots, and also placed a note, which her fiancé would retrieve later on, from under the pumpkin leaves. It was strictly forbidden to write to the men, forbidden to write in general. But how could one speak, how else might we speak to one another, except by passing several times with a basketful of roots on our arm—the same basket, full of the same roots which each one of us in turn carried out to speak to the men, putting it back in its place behind the laboratory door when she returned so that another might pick it up to do the same. This is how Lily began to write. She spent evenings writing, and each evening she wrote she was happy.

On that day, Lily's fiancé hadn't come. He'd been assigned to another commando. He explained to a comrade where he would find Lily's letter. Walking through the entrance gate to the camp—the gate with a motto inscribed above it, "Work Makes You Free"—after coming back from work in the evening, the comrade had lost the note, folded many times to be very small. It had slipped from under his trousers—not from his pocket, nothing was ever carried in the pockets. Pockets were searched first, obviously. An SS picked up the note, and having summoned the comrade, had taken him to the Politische where he was interrogated. He said it was his note. Good. And who was the one who signed it "Lily"? He didn't want to say. They had beaten him and beaten him. It was easy for the police to locate a Lily in the lab. Still, they had beaten him. Then all the men were called to the camp's central square, in front of the kitchens. The commanding officer announced that the man who had received a letter from some "Lily" would be shot. This letter was obviously a coded message to communicate political information—because for the

Gestapo everything was coded, and love letters must convey political instructions. So Lily's fiancé stepped out of the ranks to stop his friend from being shot in his stead. Both men were jailed. The following day, two SS came for Lily. She had left between the SS, walking on the sun-drenched road, knowing perhaps, or perhaps quite unaware. All three were shot.

In Lily's letter to her fiancé, there was this sentence. "We are here like plants full of life and sap, like plants wanting to grow and live, and I cannot help thinking that these plants are not meant to live."

A man who worked at the Politische told us this.

The Teddy Bear

The Polish girls decided we had to have beans. A cup per person. The Russian girls were working on bagging the crops. It was easy to buy something from them. When they returned in the evening, they emptied their shoes of the split peas they had hidden in them—shoes were oversized there. One could exchange a cupful for a piece of bread.

Of course what they wanted to make was beans and cabbage. The Frenchwomen were skeptical . . . The gardener, a Polish fellow, would provide the cabbage. Then there'd be potatoes in sauce. The potatoes would be filched from the kitchen. If we could find beets, we'd start with borscht. And they described the recipe for borscht, how succulent it was, particularly with cream. But much as we planned and imagined all kinds of tricks, we couldn't get cream.

Each one's contribution had been set at two onions—to be purchased from the Russian girls (another ration of bread we'd have to relinquish)—a piece of margarine, a package of noodles and two lumps of sugar. The Polish girls would throw in the poppy seeds they received in their parcels, which arrived more regularly than ours. A Christmas meal couldn't possibly be imagined without noodles and poppy seeds.

Hanka collected everything. It was risky business. A search, by uncovering our operation, would have meant the confiscation of our provisions, on top of a punishment inflicted on the whole commando. But Hanka had four years of camp experience. She was canny.

We meant to celebrate a traditional Christmas. A Polish Christmas, since there was a larger contingent of Polish women. The Russians, also numerous, were not invited.

November had been misty. The sun's orb plunged lower each day, orange in the grayness of the plain as it touched the ill-defined line of its setting. In December, the camp was covered with a crust of ice which shone in the moonlight at night. When we stepped out to the latrines, we heard the sentinel stamping on the icy ground as he paced behind the silvery, frost-encrusted barbed wire. Occasionally it was an SS, humming opera arias to himself. Or breaking into lusty singing, as though he were frightened. The effect in the blue immobility of the night was fantasmagoric. Then snow fell. We had to have snow for Christmas.

At the end of the day, each one of us, perched on her cot, busied herself with presents, sewing, drawing, embroidering, knitting. The tiniest tatter, or bit of wool, was obtained by infinitely complex maneuvers. During that time, throughout the final evenings, the cooks, who had much planning to do, set up their pots on the laboratory stove, so as merely to warm the courses on the great day just before the meal. It was so cold that conservation was assured. Wanda was taking care of the tree. She also promised a surprise.

Finally, Christmas Eve came.

We were through working at four. Christmas Eve would begin with the first star, according to Polish tradition. We had little time for primping or ironing a dress when our turn came. Since there was only one iron, we had to wait while it was warmed on the stove (where could that iron have come from?), meanwhile combing our hair. A few experts devoted their efforts to setting hair. "Cécile, it's my turn, after Gilberte.—No, mine!" We enjoyed the new growth of our hair which, however, did not enable the volunteer hairdressers to set large curls. Some of us slipped on silk stockings of mysterious provenance. How extraordinarily slender and shiny legs could be! The others looked on with envy. We put on white collars cut out of shirt bottoms to wear on our striped dresses. Dark-haired girls crinkled paper, making flowers to affix to their hair. We got vaseline from the infirmary to smear on our eyelids. In the dormitory everyone was getting edgy, as if waiting for a ball to begin: "Are you through with the needle?—Who can lend me a hair brush?—Did anyone see my belt?—Hurry up and pass the iron here, we haven't had it yet."

Someone came to say everything was ready, and we'd better hurry. The first star . . . In a moment's time, the room was full.

We could hardly recognize one another, hair coiffed, faces made up. The lab chemists had made cheek and lip rouge, as well as powder, but they produced a single shade, so that, seeing all these faces painted the same color, the same way, was strangely disturbing. The sameness of our striped dresses became even more apparent. Suddenly we were filled with the feeling that all our efforts had been made in vain, that our preparations, excitement, and expectation of a real Christmas Eve feast had been to no avail. We had dressed up with great care, as though to welcome guests, guests who were not forthcoming. We were still among ourselves, with faces that were not ours. A moment of sadness broken by somewhat strained bursts of laughter.

The refectory tables, pulled together end to end, formed a large horseshoe. The bedsheets, washed specially for the occasion, served as tablecloths, and under the cloths they placed a thin layer of straw—another ritual. Paper garlands hung from the ceiling. At the center of the room a tree was gleaming, covered with cotton-wool balls for snow, decorated with ornaments made of chocolate wrapping, festooned with streamers and glowing with candles. The laboratory store room had been ransacked. Prettily wrapped parcels rested at the foot of the tree: gifts.

The stools were lined up all along the tables, but we wouldn't sit before sharing the host: wafers of dough with blue, pink, mauve, white, pale-green seals which the Polish women mutually presented to one another. Each broke off a piece, ate it, and then both kissed one another, exchanging wishes that drew tears from them. All we could hear was: "Do domou"—"back home"—words returning again and again. Next Christmas back home. At home . . .

The Frenchwomen didn't have hosts. They graciously accepted the ones proffered, and tried to repeat the magic words: "Do domou, do domou"—at home. The Polish women explained: "We share the host as a symbol. It means that we also share the bread." The Frenchwomen welcomed this explanation with forbearance. It was hardly the time to remind one's companions of any resentment one might harbor due to the selfishness of this one or that.

The cooks made their way between the groups, filling the plates
—lab glassware. It would have been unseemly to serve a Christmas
meal in our tin cups. They had had to give up on the borscht and
were deeply disappointed.

The women kissed one another. They never stopped kissing and
exchanging hosts and good wishes. Each had ninety-four accolades to
give and to receive. As to us—the Frenchwomen—we were a bit ill at
ease, because Polish women kissed each other on the mouth, as Slavs do.

At last we sat down. The beans and cabbage were cold, but there
was lots of it. We were served potatoes with onion sauce, noodles
which, in Poland, are spiced with nuts and honey, my neighbor
explained. The essential ingredient was poppy seeds. Thank God,
there was no lack of that. The noodles were firm. Few among us
could finish that dish. And we had lost the habit of eating our fill.

Wanda's surprise came with the dessert. It was beer, a whole barrel
she had "organized" (stolen) from the SS kitchen. No one could match
Wanda when it came to "organizing" things. It was dark, sweet beer.

My neighbor offered me a cigarette from her cigarette case. She
had a cigarette case . . . It opened by a click of the nail, a gesture that
I suddenly remembered but here seemed the height of refinement.
The cigarettes had been sent by the male prisoners, who received a
regular smoking ration.

The meal was drawing to a close. Someone switched off the
lights. All we could see in the dark was the glow of cigarette tips. One
by one, the candles were lit. The fir tree emerged from the shadows
surrounded by a ghostly halo. And the chorus of Polish women raised
their voices in song.

It was a nostalgic, polyphonic hymn, whose words escaped us.
In the darkness enlivened by twinkling candles, the melody seemed
strange and haunting. They kept on singing, and we slipped into a
dream state. We were dreaming of a faraway Christmas Eve, over
there, back home. In our dream, our memories and hopes seemed
remote and frail. And what about our comrades who weren't lucky
enough to belong to this privileged commando? How did one spend

Christmas Eve in a death camp? There was in the death camp, since mid-December, planted at the center of the square, a tall fir tree covered with real snow. At the top of the tree, one could see a red star lit by an electric bulb. The fir tree stood next to the gallows.

The chorus grew silent. Lights were switched back on. Each one was joining in the merriment dictated by the feast day. The chorus was congratulated. Indeed, they had performed beautifully. Then, a lot of paper was ripped to uncover a cake of soap, a rag doll, a handmade lace bow, a woven rope belt, a colorfully bound memorandum book.

At the end of a table, a young girl petted a small teddy bear she had been given. A pink teddy bear with a ribbon round its neck.

"Look," Madeleine said to me, "look! It's a teddy bear! A small child's teddy." And her voice broke.

I stared at the teddy bear. It was a terrifying sight.

One morning, as we passed near the railway station on our way to the fields, our column was stopped by the arrival of a Jewish convoy. People were stepping down from the cattle cars, lining up on the platform in response to the shouted orders of the SS. Women and children first. In the front row, a little girl held her mother by the hand. She had kept her doll tightly squeezed against her body.

This is how a doll, a teddy bear, arrives in Auschwitz. In the arms of a little girl who will leave her toy with her clothing, carefully folded, at the entrance to "the showers." A prisoner from the "heaven commando," as they called those who worked in the crematoria, had found it among the objects piled up in the showers' antechamber and exchanged it for a couple of onions.

At First, We Wanted to Sing

We arrived on a morning in January 1943.

The doors of the cattle cars were pushed open, revealing the edge of an icy plain. It was a place from before geography. Where were we? We were to find out—later, at least two months hence; we, that is those of us who were still alive two months later—that this place was called Auschwitz. We couldn't have given it a name.

At first, we wanted to sing. You cannot imagine these heartrending voices, veiled by the mist-enshrouded marshes and their own weakness, repeating words which no longer summoned any images. The dead do not sing.

. . . But no sooner are they resurrected, they do theater.

This is what happened to a small group which had survived six months of the death camp and had been dispatched some distance from there, as a privileged commando. There were straw mattresses to sleep on, water to wash up with. The work was not as hard, sometimes in a shelter, sometimes sitting down. We who could hardly stand on our legs as we issued from death—to cross a small meadow, carrying an empty basket, required an extraordinary exertion, the exercise of willpower—began to regain human appearance. After a while, we started to think of theater. One of us recounted plays to the others, who managed to work close to her, digging with their spades or hoeing. They'd ask: "What are we going to see today?" Each telling was repeated several times. Each one wanted to hear it in turn, and the audience could never exceed five or six. However, the repertory was beginning to be used up. Soon we started considering "putting on a play." Nothing less than that. Without texts, without the means to get some, with nothing. And above all, with so little free time.

When I returned home, I met men who'd been prisoners of war. Listening to their stories, I took the measure of the incommunicable. These men have things to tell. We'd also have much to recount, yet we can't speak of the nature of our anguish. For those who were in Auschwitz, waiting meant racing ahead of death. We weren't waiting. We were clinging to a hope made up of so many fragile pieces that not one of them could have resisted close scrutiny had we kept a modicum of common sense. To have lost that common sense, and persisted in the madness of hope, saved some of us. Their number is so small it proves nothing.

When I listen to the stories of prisoners of war, I pity them for having been victims of events beyond their control, yet I know that for my part I chose the situation that turned me into a victim. When they tell of the ways in which they filled the void of many years, I cannot help but be filled with envy. They received books, acted in plays, put on shows. They had nails and glue. They were able to live in the world of the imagination, once in a while, for only a couple of hours, but these were hours that mattered.

You may say that one can take away everything from a human being except the faculty of thinking and imagining. You have no idea. One can turn a human being into a skeleton gurgling with diarrhea, without time or energy to think. Imagination is the first luxury of a body receiving sufficient nourishment, enjoying a margin of free time, possessing the rudiments from which dreams are fashioned. People did not dream in Auschwitz, they were in a state of delirium.

And yet, you might counter, each had a stock of memories? No, one couldn't be sustained by one's past, draw on its resources. It had become unreal, unbelievable. Everything that had been our previous existence had unraveled. To speak was our only escape, our mad raving. What did we speak of? Material, usable things. We had to omit anything that might awaken pain or regret. We never spoke of love.

And suddenly, in the small camp, we were coming back to life, and everything was coming back to us. We wished we could read, listen to music, go to the theater. We were going to put on a play. After all, we had Sundays off and an hour in the evening.

Claudette, who worked in the laboratory where she had a table, pencil and paper, undertook to reconstruct from memory *Le Malade*

Imaginaire. No sooner was the first act completed than rehearsals began.

I write this as though it were simple. You may think you've got a play down pat, that you see and hear all the characters, but it's no easy task for someone who's just recovered from typhus and is constantly hungry. Those who were able to do so helped out. Recapturing a line was often the victory of an entire day's quest. And the rehearsals . . . They took place after work, after supper—supper was two hundred grams of dry bread and seven grams of margarine—at the time when, in a dark, freezing hut, you experience more keenly than ever a profound weariness. Persuading and bullying, calling on the spirit of camaraderie, managing flattery and insults, such were the means resorted to on a daily basis by our camp volunteer theater director. Personal pride and the spirit of rivalry also played their part. We wanted to show our Polish companions, who sang so well, what we were capable of.

Every evening, stamping our feet and waving our arms—it was in December—we went on rehearsing. In the dark, the right kind of intonation assumed a strange resonance.

The day set for the show—the Sunday after Christmas—was drawing near. However, it was impossible to set things up ahead of time because of the supervisor, an SS female officer, whose only virtue was that, utterly absorbed by her love affairs, she gave us some breathing space. Eva, the draftswoman, was making a poster to be placed on the hut's inner door on Saturday, after the last round of the SS. Why a poster when everyone was informed of our plans? Because we were at last living our illusion. A colored poster, on which one could read: *"Le Malade Imaginaire,* after Molière, by Claudette. Costumes by Cecile. Directed by Charlotte. Set and props by Carmen." Then the list of characters and players. Lulu in the role of Argan. Our play, however, was only in four acts. We had not succeeded in re-creating Molière's structure, scene by scene. Yet, as I recall, nothing had been left out.

Having forgotten for the first time all our concerns about our daily soup, bread rations and various chores, we busied ourselves from early morning with our exciting preparations. Cecile achieved miracles of ingenuity with sweaters transformed into doublets and casaques, nightgowns and pajamas turned into breeches for male roles (the only details of dress which were not made from uniforms—how we were able to obtain the latter is too long a story). The striped dresses had proved beyond metamorphosis. Fortunately, we had at our disposal something like cages made from tulle netting. These were used in the selection of seeds from our plants. (As I explained earlier, we were assigned to an agricultural experimental station in which a latex-giving dandelion, the koksaghyz, discovered by the Germans in the Ukraine, was being acclimated to Polish soil.) The tulle was cut into ruffles, lacy cuffs and cannions, bows and stoles. A sky-blue matelassé robe—a priceless item of our wardrobe collection—became Bélise's sumptuous bustled gown. A yellow-green powder whose composition I didn't know (it must have been an insecticide) was used to good effect for the doctor's wonderfully bilious makeup. A shout rang through the dormitory: "Anyone who owns a clean black apron (the black apron was part of our uniform) please let us have it at once! The wardrobe mistress is waiting!" With the help of six aprons Cecile was able to drape a doctor, setting upon his head a tall, cone-shaped cardboard hat, blackened with ink and surrounded by wood shavings forming the stiff curls of a wig. Claudette, the author of the adaptation from Molière's play, was pleased with the result, but found it hard to be reconciled to the fact that the male characters had neither wigs nor hats, and Belise no fan. "At the time of Louis XIV, how can that be!" Alas, our hair, shorn at arrival, was but a few centimeters long. However, we had walking sticks beribboned with tulle.

The refectory tables, stripped of their legs (otherwise the stage would have been too high in the low-ceilinged hut), placed one against the other, formed a platform. Blankets, skillfully hung together by Carmen, who had a hammer, nails and a bit of string, which she had been pining for before she was able to filch them from the SS gardener, made a perfect stage curtain, not the least of our achievements. Other blankets, nailed to the window, darkened the room. The only light we had was directed onto the stage, where Carmen, our electrician as well as stagehand, had installed a trouble lamp and a projector. "Where did she steal all this stuff?—I'll tell you later . . ." For the moment, she was busy driving in nails and tying things up. Our theater even had the traditional wings: blankets and string. And a prompter, holding the text, if you please.

The traditional three knocks were heard. The curtain went up (no, opened). The Polish women were the audience. Most of them understood French.

The curtain opens. We see Argan, seated on boxes hidden by blankets, himself swathed in blankets, shaking his bell made from an empty food can in which a piece of glass has been inserted. When someone first suggested that a pebble should be used, Carmen protested: "No, I don't want a pebble. A pebble doesn't sound right."

The curtain rises. It's magnificent. It's magnificent because Lulu is a born actress. It's not only that her accent from Marseilles reminds us of Raimu, but her face's true naïveté is deeply moving. She's the incarnation of human generosity.

It's magnificent because some of Molière's lines, having surfaced intact in our memory, come to life again, unchanged, full of their inexplicable, magical power.

It's magnificent because each one of us plays her role with humility, without trying to push herself to the foreground. Perennial miracle of modest interpreters. The miracle of an audience having suddenly recaptured childhood's purity and resurrected the imaginative faculty.

It was magnificent because, for the space of two hours, while the smokestacks never stopped belching their smoke of human flesh, for two whole hours we believed in what we were doing.

This belief was stronger than the only one we lived by then, that of freedom, which we would struggle to attain five hundred days later.

The Trip

We were in a train. A real train. With seats, windowpanes that go up and down as you wish, a knob you can turn right or left—useless since the train is not heated—and scenery stretching out on each side. There were eight of us.

For the first time in years we felt we were going on a trip. Taking a trip. Such an unsettling impression that we forgot we were traveling without tickets, that no steward would enter our compartment, isolated at the very end of the coach.

Still, it was a real trip. So real that we also forgot the SS who accompanied us, and who were dozing on the other side of a semi-partition. A real trip. Didn't we have luggage in the racks above our heads, valises we could reach for, open up to look for and find familiar objects, such as a comb or an old lipstick which once belonged to us and was ours again, as though it had never left us? Seated on our wooden benches, we felt good. Really and truly a beautiful trip.

And the feeling of freedom, however erroneous, freedom restored, abolished all that had been forfeiture of our civil rights. We were rediscovering the gestures of free people, those gestures that are the very essence of freedom. To look at our faces in a pocket mirror, to go to the WC and turn the lock that would bring out the word "Occupied." The astonishing thing is that it did not seem astonishing to us. Everything was normal. We were finding ourselves again, as though, having come upon some item of our clothing hanging on a hook by the front door and putting it on again, we had recovered our previous personality, the being we were before. All the more astonishing since we had not put on other clothing. We still had on the striped dress and striped jacket, the scarf tied under our chins, the loose galoshes, many sizes too large, laced with string. Incredible, these galoshes they gave us on departure. So large that it was obviously on purpose. They prevented us from walking or running off as surely as a ball and chain. Our uniform was another shackle.

We were in this train which kept on going, would go on going till the following day. We thought this trip was marvelous and wished for one thing only, that it might go on for a long time, for an eternity of time. We longed for an endless voyage. At the end of this one—and what kind of end would it be? we had no idea—we didn't expect anything good. But we were content at that moment and took comfort in this contentment without thinking of what would come next. At times we were surprised by not feeling greater amazement. We did not question what was happening because we had lost the habit of questioning and took all that came about without bothering to inquire. Still, this trip was astonishing.

It started early one morning, just before daylight, in the laboratory where the day's work had begun a while back. An SS came in, and a rumor spread through the work teams: they've come for the French girls. Our first reaction was one of disquiet. Flora, our SS, was to accompany us to Birkenau. Just the name Birkenau filled us with trepidation. What reassured us was the sight of a cart waiting for us. We would never have climbed into a truck, choosing instant death over such a thing. Trucks took people straight to the gas chambers. The SS—it was the ugly mug, the one who filled us with boundless terror when we were in Birkenau a few months ago—had pulled a list of names from his pocket and called out ten names. Ten of us stepped out and lined up. He then gave us time to pack our things, but Wanda said, "Don't bother taking anything with you. Give it all to the comrades here, because over there they'll take it all away." So we left the nightgown obtained by means of elaborate planning and infinite stratagems, the spare pair of panties and extra pair of stockings, the rubber bands to hold them up. We kept a small cloth bag which held our toothbrush, piece of soap and knife. The Polish women, far more experienced than we were in the matter of transfers, assured us that they would not confiscate food, and so the commando had left work at once and met in the refectory where all of us searched through bins, and our own storage boxes, to take out bread—above all bread, which, as every experienced prisoner knows, is essential—sugar, onions, and also cigarettes. Cigarettes were entrusted to us since we had become adept at smuggling them through any kind of search.

Each one of us would have to carry a few loaves of bread of one kilo each. We had never been so rich.

We got busy tying all this up when Flora appeared at the refectory door. "Schnell." Then all of us, standing at attention, sang *La Marseillaise*. As if there were nothing else to sing. The Polish women knew it in French, and even better than we did, without skipping a line. Then *Ce n'est qu'un au revoir* which was more than painful, unbearable, because it was what we sang to the men, in jail, when they were taken away in the morning. We were also sad to leave our comrades, on a day when the snow was supernaturally dazzling. "Ready? Let's go!" shouted Flora. We picked up our bundles and stepped out.

The Birkenau SS called out our ten names once more, counting the ten women, and we climbed into the cart. The others, following us to the very edge of the camp, waved their hands and scarves. The cart started out on the narrow earthen path between the fields of turnips, and we, looking backward, waved our farewells to the comrades watching our departure. They followed us with their eyes so long as they could still see us.

When they vanished behind a fold in the terrain we turned back to the front and started singing again. Not because we felt merry, but there are times when there's nothing left to do but sing. Carmen, who knew more songs than any of us, would keep on leading us in one song after the other. We sang at the top of our voices, straining our throats to the breaking point, as we held on to the rails of the cart which was crossing snow-covered fields. Flora sat in a cocoon of blankets, while the ugly mug drove the team of horses.

We had to make a stop at the grade crossing. Carmen sang out, "Always a crossing—a grade crossing—blocking your way—away, away." We sang along with her, pretending to be merry. But no sooner had the electrified barbed-wire enclosures appeared, the roofs of the block houses buried under the snow, than we could not continue. The cart and horses, weighed down by our silence, stopped in front of the quarantine hut.

We had climbed down while Flora and the SS had their orders checked at the sentry box. It smelled of wood. We could hear French voices coming from the next room. The survivors of our convoy were quarantined in this hut. And soon, under the pretext of having to use the toilet, some of them slipped out to join us, asking, "Where are you being sent to? Why did they call you?" We didn't know. We knew nothing. Then one of them, who had just overheard something the SS had said, came running. "You're being sent to Ravensbrück. They're going to make you strip in order to search you, and then you'll dress again. If you have things, pass them to us. We'll give them back to you after the search is over. We'll slip them under the door." We entrusted our cigarettes, knives and letters from home to them.

An SS returns with the woman in charge of the block, a hysterical German woman who will not stop shouting, and a kapo, her arms full of striped dresses. We undress. We're naked. The SS doctor comes in with Taube, a sinister SS we know, and with a Jewish female doctor, a prisoner, who brings in the thermometers. She distributes them to us, and we stay there, naked under the eyes of the SS who inspect us. The SS doctor makes us pull out our tongues. Taube, who is not a physician, examines us also, makes us turn round and round—can you imagine us, naked, with thermometers up our asses, whirling like tops—and feels us. The woman doctor asks us to hand over the thermometers and writes down our temperatures. Lucie and Geneviève have a little over 38. They will not be leaving, and cry bitterly. We try to reach an accommodation with the doctor, have her correct the figures on her sheet. She shouts and shouts, and we beg her not to attract the attention of the SS, whereupon she shouts louder than ever.

Our comrades observe this scene through the holes they made in the wood of the partition by prying out the knots.

Papers are brought in that we must sign, stating we have not been mistreated, nor have suffered any illnesses (such as exanthematic typhus), and that our personal belongings and jewelry have been returned to us. A signature! Under these conditions! . . . Nevertheless we sign these papers and are ushered into a dormitory to get dressed again.

The dresses are so filthy, soiled with blood, diarrhea, pus, that we experience the very same nausea we had upon arrival, last year, when we were handed repulsive, louse-filled uniforms we kept until our appointment to the laboratory commando six months later. We raise our voices in protest. The hysterical German woman breaks into sharp shrieks. When the SS returns, we call the dirty togs to her attention. She, in turn, calls Taube, who shouts some orders at the kapo, sending her out to fetch other dresses. All that time we're there, naked . . . The other dresses are hardly less filthy. That's that.

The SS decides we are inadequately clad; she gives an order for unearmarked striped jackets to be brought. All this in minus-twenty-degree weather. We're ready at last, having pulled on seven-league galoshes.

We are led to a hut across the way—as we file past our comrades, they hand us back our cigarettes, knives, letters, which we smuggle up our sleeves—and as soon as we reach the door we are seized with a biting cold. The woolens we secured against all odds, exchanged for some onions stolen from the vegetable patch, or our rations, have now been taken away from us.

The hut across the way is where they store the clothing of newly arrived prisoners. Amazed, we find in this heap—we have reached seventy-five thousand today, in Birkenau—items that look like ours. Some things are missing of course, but we proceed from surprise to surprise. One of us gets back her wedding ring, another her watch. One, whose shoes they cannot locate, will be asked her size and issued a brand-new pair she won't be allowed to wear since they don't conform to our uniforms.

As we see our valises and recall the day of arrival, we enter a peculiar state of being in which everything seems both natural and transfigured. Last year, when we were brought here—the month was

also January, and the camp was also buried under snow—there were two
hundred thirty of us. Fifty remain, and eight, who are leaving the camp,
are being handed back their clothing and made to sign release papers.

Outside, Taube is getting restless. He is talking to another SS and
we believe he's saying we might miss the train since we've got to
hurry. Here's the commanding officer in his small verdigris car. He's
restless too. Squatting on the steps, Carmen—it's so cold we can't
hold our valises in hands gone numb—Carmen struggles with
shoelaces she can't thread, and her shoes are so loose that, were she
unable to lace them up with a bit of rope, she couldn't take a step.

And this is when we witnessed the most extraordinary scene.
Taube—the Taube we've seen send thousands of women to the gas
chamber, set his dog on many of us, whom the beast devoured, take
out his revolver and shoot the Jewish women of block 15 because they
were not entering it fast enough (as if a thousand women could step
in fast through a single door) one morning, just like this one—Taube,
whose high silhouette filled us with fear, Taube, the most cruel of the
SS—kneeled before Carmen and, with his pen knife, sharpened the
end of the laces so they'd slip through the eyelet holes. Having carried
out this operation, he got up and said softly, "Gut." We'd have been less
surprised had he led us to block 25, the antechamber to the crematorium.

The commanding officer is getting increasingly restless. Four SS,
whose arrival we hadn't noticed, are waiting to one side. Taube picks
up our valises, hands them to the officer, who piles them up at the
back of the car. He grabs all he can hold; the rest still feels heavy; the
two men get into the car, shouting an order in the direction of the SS
as the car takes off. The SS have us file in ranks of two, then march
behind us. We set off in the direction of the railroad station.

From the windows of the quarantine block, our comrades wave us
farewell.

We had a hard time walking in these galoshes, bearing bundles.
We followed the very same road we had taken for the first time a year
ago. It had not lost its aspect of a road devoid of hope, and we were

filled with strange emotions. So, we were leaving Auschwitz. Leaving
it dressed as prisoners, something we had never considered before.
Everything was a long shot, incredible, incredibly strange. It was as
though this were a dream, yet there was also the certainty it was real,
while the feeling of dreaming persisted.

We took a shortcut over the freight trains' tracks, walking between
parked cars so as to reach a shed where we might take shelter. We felt
increasingly cold. Crammed with loaves of bread, our bags were
breaking our wrists.

The verdigris car is here. The commanding officer and Taube are
taking their bearings. They call our SS, whom we follow looking
ridiculous while mimicking their gait in our galoshes, and loaded
down with bundles. Men in striped uniforms are waiting also, looking
miserable as men always do here. "How do they manage to stand on
their feet?" one wonders looking at them.

Emerging on the curving tracks, a train appears, slows down,
stops along the platform, its cars shaking to a stop. We're trying to
guess what kind of car will stop before us—this is a mixed train, travelers and merchandise—and we fear, without hoping for something
better, that we'll travel in a cattle train, as we did last year coming
here. How bitterly cold we felt then!

But the miracle continues. The commanding officer walks toward
a third-class car, tells us to get in, passing our valises and bundles to
our SS. Once the bags are in, he climbs in himself, places our luggage
in the overhead racks, and assigns us politely to our seats, reminding
the SS, however, that they are to keep us from leaving the train at the
station stops. He jumps down and slams the door shut, and had he
wished us a good trip we wouldn't have been any more taken aback
than we were.

We were in a train traveling through Silesia. We were glad it was
daylight, happy to see something of Katowice, a town built of dirty
bricks and lined with sad-looking avenues. A woman wheeling a
baby carriage stared at the train. No cars in the streets. Snow lying
on windowsills.

Traveling along the tracks next to ours, a convoy of tanks and cannons passed us, eastward-bound. Our SS rise and explain, "Panzer divisions. On their way to Russia."

I was dying to approach them, start a conversation, find out, as little as it was bound to be, what's an SS. Why and how does one become an SS? The others go along with that. I go. They turn out to be Slovenes, forcibly enrolled in the SS. They say they know nothing about Auschwitz—all those smokestacks . . . Otherwise . . . They offer us cigarettes, light them for us. When we stop they go to the railway canteen, return with ersatz coffee distributed by Red Cross nurses to the soldiers. We had never seen a look of pity or a human expression in the eyes of an SS. Do they strip off the assassin on departing from Auschwitz?

Night falls. Behind the windowpanes the landscape grows dim. A landscape of factories, blast furnaces (or could they be crematoria?), soot-encrusted buildings, soot-covered countryside dotted with enclosures fenced off by barbed wire. Either all of Germany is covered by camps, or all the camps run along this railway line. A desolate landscape.

We're cozy in our compartment. We've pulled out sweaters, socks, handkerchiefs from our valises. Simone is looking at a book that belonged to her sister. She doesn't dare open it. Still, she's glad this book remains, a reminder of her sister, who died in camp last summer. Gilberte doesn't say anything, looks at nothing. She won't find anything of her sister's. Lulu holds on to Carmen's hand, deeply moved by their good fortune. They're the only remaining sisters.

Night has fallen. The train is not lighted. In the darkness we look for our knives, cutting up bread for margarine sandwiches. After our meal we light up cigarettes, one to a person. We feel good. It's nighttime. Leaning against one another we fall asleep, lulled by the creaking of the train.

In the morning, Berlin's suburbs.

"Lieutenant William L. Calley, who killed one hundred nine Vietnamese and is to be tried, had taken in and sheltered a Vietnamese girl, lost, starving, wearing tattered rags. To see naked, starving children roaming the streets was a heart-rending sight for Lieutenant William L. Calley. He had adopted this little girl, fed and clothed her, taken care of her. One day, returning from action, he did not find her there. She had escaped. Lieutenant William L. Calley was deeply distressed." (This was the statement made by the lieutenant's sister to the *New York Post,* November 28, 1969.)

Berlin

Now the train stopped at all the stations. Despite the cold, at every stop it made we rolled down the windows to see—the panes were covered with frost—and hear. The platforms were teeming with workmen going to their jobs. Scarves wound round their necks, haversacks on their shoulders, they were hurrying to their occupation, not minding anything else. Their breaths added to the fog tiny clouds of white mist flitting above them. Their shadows slid against each other, silently fused. It wasn't quite daybreak. Suddenly we heard someone shouting in French, "This way, pal!" We called out at once, "Hey, hey, over there! Hey, Frenchmen! You're French? We're French-women!" A man turns around, gives us an unpleasant look, muttering, "Merde!" then takes off at a run to jump into a train across from our track.

"For the first Frenchman we see . . . what a greeting!" says Lulu.

We were deeply disappointed. How is it possible? Women wearing striped uniforms call out, and this free man does not even ask who they are, where they're coming from. We came from Auschwitz. Everyone should have realized it. We discovered an abyss between the world and us, and it made us very sad.

At the next station stop it was almost daylight. We could have a better look at the travelers on the platform. Their general appearance, clothing, berets told us they were our fellow countrymen. This time, however, we were careful not to call out to them.

"Germany must be full of French 'volunteer' labor," declared one of us.

Our train was coming into Berlin. Along the tracks, buildings destroyed by bombing raids were still lived in. Here and there one could see a stovepipe sticking out through the transom of a cellar, or rising from a shelter built onto a wall that remained standing. The city deployed its frightful appearance.

"It looks completely destroyed . . ."

"They're getting their just deserts."

We felt the very same satisfaction we experienced in Auschwitz when we used to watch interminably long ambulance trains, their white roofs painted with a large red cross, returning from the east with their load of wounded soldiers. Nurses walked through the corridors of those slow-moving trains which at times came to a stop, staying in place for a long time. We could see the wounded stretched out upon their berths. "Serves them right." Some of them, standing up, their heads bandaged, looked out. What did they say seeing us?

Our train was stopping under the glass roof of the station's hall. Our SS readjusted their holsters, started picking up their things, hanging their rifles on their shoulders and ordering us to be ready to alight. From the end cars, men in striped uniforms were coming down, probably the same ones we saw at the Auschwitz platform. There were quite a few of them, some sixty or so. They were also being transferred to another camp. They were terribly thin in the particular way we knew, one we could never get inured to, and they lined up in ranks like automatons. Next to them we felt strong and alert. We were looking them over. Among them there might be an acquaintance, who knows? But they all looked the same on account of their hollow, feverish eyes, their swollen lips. All of them were unrecognizable.

Our SS did not know their colleagues in charge of escorting the men. They had nothing to do but be in charge of the eight of us. Without counting us, or having us line up two by two, they led us toward an underground passage. They must have been peasants who had never seen a subway before. After attempting to consult a subway map, comparing the itinerary to something scribbled on one of their pieces of paper, they decided to dispatch one of them in search of the right information. Grouped next to the map, we examined eagerly our surroundings, those civilians going about their ordinary life, taking the subway. A sign underlined by an arrow pointed to the toilets. We asked our SS whether we could use the facilities. They acquiesced. Waiting for us at the top of the stairs, they lit up a cigarette. The huge wooden soles of our clogs which forced us to step sideways on steps more narrow than our clumsy shoes, and our cumbersome bags, made the trip down perilous. We made the downward climb with the deliberate slowness of invalids.

The toilets seemed very comfortable to us: rows of washstands, doors carefully aligned. The attendant in charge, an old woman, saw us enter her mosaic-decorated palace, which smelled of disinfectant, without registering any surprise. Obviously, one saw all kinds of things in Berlin at that time, and the old woman's worn face no longer reflected any amazement. "Poor kids!" she said, however, in a voice as worn as her features, and she unlocked for us the coin-operated cabins.

We opened our valises to find something to wash up with. We had no towels, no gloves, no brushes, nothing useful for the occasion. Everything had been stolen. One of us said, looking through her belongings: "We could change our clothes and escape."

"And where would we go? We don't know anyone in Berlin and we can hardly talk broken German."

"Berlin must be full of French people."

"You saw them a while back. You don't imagine they'd help us . . ."

The opportunity was too unexpected for us to plan taking advantage of it. We were used to planning, calculating all our moves for so long we couldn't imagine setting off on a risky adventure without any preparation.

Having washed up, run a comb through our hair, we closed our bags and made our way up toward our SS, who were peacefully smoking. "Had they given us the opportunity to escape?" "They're much too stupid for that," declared Carmen.

With our valises at our feet, we waited for our subway train. People were flocking to the crowded platform, but they stepped away from us, fearing no doubt to catch lice. They avoided looking in our direction. We whispered for all those who were passing by, "We're French political prisoners; we're not criminals," in clearly phrased

German, a sentence we had worked on for the occasion. A little girl,
who was holding her mother's hand, a woman our age, tried to wrest
herself free to run away. She was afraid of us. Her mother held on to
her gently, saying, "These are unfortunate women. Give them a
smile," and she herself smiled kindly. The little girl turned in our
direction and tried to smile. We could have kissed the mother. Mother
and child walked away.

The subway arrived. Our SS and the other SS, who were conveying the column of male prisoners, cleared a path through the throng
of commuters, then took up their positions at the doors of the car
they reserved for the prisoners. People drew back submissively. Our
SS saved the back of the car for us while the men remained standing
in the middle. By the light of day—it was an elevated subway line—
the faces of the men seemed even more pitiful. "We should give them
some bread," said Lulu. They accepted the bread with indifference.
Not one look, not a movement of their lips, no sign in response to
our gesture. They appeared even more miserable.

At each stop, the SS guarded the doors of our car to keep travelers
from getting in. The trip was a long one. We wished it might be longer,
very long. We were under the impression that we were crossing the
entire city. Ruins, ruins everywhere. This distressing sight filled us
with hope. "Victory can't be far off now. They can't hold out any
longer." It would have been too much to expect us to feel pity for the
children who must have been buried under the rubble. We felt pity
only for the Auschwitz children, who had hardened our hearts against
the others.

We stepped out of the subway when we reached another railway
station. Prisoners of war, watched by two German soldiers—older
men—were clearing the rubble. Their complexion was as green as
their tattered uniforms. We hailed them. They turned out to be Ital-
ians, skinny, so skinny! Not as thin, however, as deportees. We wanted
to speak to them—between prisoners you always find a way of com-
municating, this at least is what we learned in Auschwitz—but the

soldiers who kept watch over them began to shout. Our own SS said nothing.

The platform was crowded. Our SS elbowed their way and ours to an empty compartment, remaining standing in the corridor. They wouldn't let any of the regular travelers get in, despite the latter's grumbling. Two German female soldiers, in gray uniforms, succeeded in convincing our SS of their right to sit down. They pushed us to make room. "Aren't you afraid to catch our lice?" I asked them when, despite our inertia, they slipped into seats next to ours.

"Ah! Frenchwomen! I know France. I was in Amiens. The French are dirty," and she drew away as far as possible so as not to come in contact with us.

"We never had lice in France, but in Auschwitz we were covered with them. The Auschwitz lice carry typhus." They exchanged looks with each other and left the compartment, hurling some kind of invective at our SS.

A quite different landscape was spreading before us, sandy soil sparsely covered with clumps of pine trees. Not far from Berlin miradors appeared, dotting a vast space fenced off by barbed wire. We looked carefully for the name of the next station: Oranienburg. The word meant nothing at the time. Only later, when we recalled that the German pacifist leader Carl von Ossietsky had been there when he received the Nobel Peace Prize, did it acquire meaning. "It's darned close to Berlin. They've got some nerve." Other barbed-wire enclosures followed, and we were wondering whether it was still the same camp. Men in striped uniforms could be seen working all over.

After a little over an hour of travel we reached our destination. It was a short halt, marked by a small building next to the grade crossing: Ravensbrück. We had to wait till our train left to walk across the rails. Our SS had us line up two by two and assume a regulation demeanor. No longer could they carry our luggage. "It's stupid to lug these heavy bags just to store them in the Ravensbrück checkroom. We should have left them in the Berlin lavatories." Pretty little cottages, spread through the pine trees, gave the place a resort look. They were the villas of the camp's SS officers. They had been built, stone by stone, by the labor of the first female prisoners. This is what we were told later by the camp's other prisoners.

"You'd think you were in Fontainebleau," said Cécile.

"Oh, Fontainebleau! We used to go camping there every Saturday with our group."

"If I ever come back, I'm through with camping . . ."

The distance between the stop and the camp enclosure seemed very long: a high wall painted green.

"It's less terrifying than electrified barbed wire," said Poupette.

The Misanthrope

The gypsies were really amazing. They walked through the camp, in the evening, after roll call—in the summer, because in winter no one lingered outside after roll call—and sold all kinds of things they had filched here and there, from the checkroom, the kitchens, including cigarettes pinched from the pockets of the SS. A slightly gaping pocket and the trick was done. They approached us and, with a quick gesture, half-opened their dresses to show us what they had to offer.

It was all one price: a ration of bread. A ration of bread for one cigarette, a ration of bread for an onion. A ration of bread for a pair of panties or a shirt. We even ran into some who were offering a piece of broiled meat. Appetizing, golden brown. However much they'd swear on their mother's head it was stolen from the SS kitchen, we never purchased it. We feared this roast originated in the crematorium.

That evening, the little gypsy girl who had approached me drew from her sleeve, then quickly put back there, out of sight, a very small book.

"A ration of bread," she said, in French.

"You speak good French. Where do you come from?"

"I'm French, from Lille."

"And what's this book? Show it to me at least."

She drew out the small book, letting me look but not hold it. It was Molière's *Misanthrope* in the petits classiques Larousse collection. I couldn't believe my eyes. *Le Misanthrope*. Someone had actually taken a copy of *Le Misanthrope* on a trip to Ravensbrück . . .

I gave up my bread ration. "You might consider lowering your price a little. It's not as easy to sell as a pair of panties." Nothing doing. She had seen the gleam in my eyes. Whoever paid so dear for a book?

Hugging my copy of *Le Misanthrope* to my bosom, I joined my comrades in our barrack. They were getting ready to have supper, that is, to eat their bread spread with margarine.

"You're not eating?"

"What did you do with your bread?"

"Bought a cigarette with it again!"

"I wouldn't have smoked it all by myself. No, I bought a book."

I took *Le Misanthrope* out from its hiding place in my bosom.

"Then you're going to read it to us?"

Each one of my companions cut a slice of bread from her ration.

How beautifully Alceste spoke. His language was precise and strong, and his whole air lavish.

"Her tongue is as sharp as yours, Cécile, that Célimène," said Poupette, who was meeting Célimène for the first time in her life.

Since Auschwitz, I always feared losing my memory. To lose one's memory is to lose oneself, to no longer be oneself. I had invented all kinds of exercises to put my memory to work: memorize all the telephone numbers I used to know, all the metro stations along one line, all the boutiques along the rue Caumartin between the Athénée theater and the Havre-Caumartin metro station. I had succeeded, at the price of infinite efforts, in recalling fifty-seven poems. I was so afraid they might escape my mind that I recited them to myself every day, all of them, one after the other, during roll call. It had been so difficult to reconstruct them! Sometimes it took days for a single line, a word, which simply would not come back. And now, all of a sudden, I had a whole book I could memorize, a whole text.

I learned *Le Misanthrope* by heart, a fragment each evening, which I'd repeat to myself at roll call the following day. Soon I knew the whole play, which lasted almost throughout roll call. And until departure, I kept the play within my throat.

The Heart Beats at Ravensbrück

The weather was beautiful on that autumn day. Beautiful for whom? In the shop the sewing machines were stitching jackets and more jackets, by the hundreds. Each at her place, each sitting at her machine, the seamstresses were leaning over their work. The pieces went from the one assembling them, to another who sewed in the sleeves, a third who attached the collar, a fourth who made the buttonholes, and the last who did the lining. A chain. As many chains as rows of sewing machines, between which walked a supervisor, an SS dressed in gray, who kept on shouting—needlessly, since the whirring of the machines covered her screams—and dealing out blows. Forbidden to look up, speak, stop working. The only way to slow down the chain was to break one's needle. In that case you could leave your stool, go up to the supervisor and ask for another needle, which she'd deal out together with a clout or a fisticuff. Each one of us would break her needle in turn. And yet, the uniforms kept piling up in spite of our slowdown, and all that was left to do was to sew the shield with the double S onto the lapels.

The machines kept on rumbling, rumbling in the heads of the prisoners, rumbling and running over their thoughts, their memories of a soft, russet day in autumn—before—rumbling and rotating their plans for a life of freedom, if they could ever recover it. The rumbling of the machines echoed throughout the workroom.

Suddenly an SS appears at the entrance, blows her whistle to cover the noise and make it stop, and shouts: "Halt! Alles raus!" Everybody out. The machines come to a halt, first those closer to the door, then the others, then the last. The women rise, fall into ranks. "Why are they taking us out? What do they want? Surely we'll be punished."

They step out into the courtyard, reform their ranks, wait. They are awaiting the women of the night shift, who were asleep in their barracks and arrive now crinkled from sleep, asking questions. No one can tell them what is happening, what will happen. The workroom staff is now complete, lined up in front of the barrack in the soft autumn light.

The women wonder what is expected of them. They are waiting. At last the head of the camp arrives, accompanied by an SS doctor. An order is issued: "Take off your shoes and stockings! Quickly!" The women step out of their shoes. "Lift your dresses!" The SS officer who heads the camp grabs a woman by the arm, lifts her dress up to her thighs to show the others what to do. Double quick!

Barefoot, holding their shoes in the left hand and the hem of their striped dresses in the right, the women file past the SS. "Schneller!" yells the head of the camp. He wants us to walk faster.

They have all understood. They brace themselves. Quickly the young ones make their way to the outside edge of the ranks, shielding the older women, who walk in the center. Those hardly able to set foot on the ground, too lame to walk and who, recommended by friends, got appointed to the uniform shop where one is able to work sitting down, those too weak for hard labor such as carrying sand or coal, all of them are made to march now.

The SS want us to walk faster, yet they also wish to have a good look at everyone. They order the women prisoners to file past them several times. A look at their legs can be decisive. They pull out of the ranks those with swollen legs, or feet deformed by edema. And the parade goes on, dresses held up, feet bare on the sharp slag. Schnell! Schneller! The women pass before the SS. Tense, their faces distorted as they attempt to walk normally, to move with ease, faces distorted as they try to hide their fear. Each time round, the ranks thin out. Those who have been pulled to one side will be going to the "fasting camp." It is a hut situated outside the main enclosure, where you are not given anything to drink or eat, where you are condemned to a slow death. Fear and tension grow in proportion to the swelling of the group set aside.

One woman is staring at her knee. If only looking could heal the stiffness of a knee unable to react to its owner's command . . .

The chin of another is shaking. She's clenching her teeth to stop the trembling, but the gritting of her teeth can't control her chin.

One woman is preceded by her head. She's fleeing. A flight forward. The impossible flight.

And all are walking like the damned upon the tympanums of cathedral portals.

The camp's commander-in-chief, his fists on his hips, is livening up. "Ha, ha! The heart is beating, what?" He's having a really good time.

Take Your Place, Get Set

This last summer, the streets of the camp were not safe. It was dangerous to be there between morning and evening roll call. At any time one could expect a raid.

The factories of the Third Reich were in dire need of manpower. The camps furnished them with what they required. It all happened very quickly. Upon an invisible signal, whistle blasts burst forth from every direction at once. The streets between the barracks were cordoned off by the "red bands" (the Polizei, prisoners who were in charge of maintaining order in the camp, and who stood out because they wore red armbands). All the female prisoners who were in the streets, or standing at the door of their barracks, were immediately pursued and hemmed in. With the Polizei in hot pursuit, they took flight in every direction. In their attempt to make an escape they collided against the road blocks, whereupon they were collared by sheer force, shoved, kicked, pummeled, bludgeoned, and forced into the column formed at the center of the camp. This was called "transportation departure."

Opinions varied in the matter of these transports. Some believed it was better to be anywhere other than Ravensbrück. They feared the end, predicting that, once defeated—and Germany's defeat was no longer in doubt in the summer of 1944, after the Allied landing—the enraged SS would give themselves up to unfettered cruelty. "You'll see, they won't let us go just like that. They'll blow up the camp, mine the sewers. They'll set off a conflagration of incendiary bombs. They'll poison the water before taking off and going into hiding. They must already have prepared some safe hiding places." Others refused to contribute in any way to the buildup of German industry, even though, on the eve of the war's end, their contribution was bound to be insignificant. These women reasoned in the following manner: "We are more secure right here. The Allies are bombing the factories. They'll never bomb Ravensbrück. We're under cover here. The SS will vanish before the arrival of the Allies because they are deathly afraid of being made prisoners. The other day, the small case of an Aufseherin sprang open: it was full of civilian clothes." However, both parties agreed on one point: it was important not to be separated from one's group. We had to leave together or remain together. Each one of us had experienced fully the fact that an isolated individual is defenseless, that you cannot survive without the others. By "the others" we meant those members of our group who hold you up, or carry you when you can no longer walk, those who help you hold fast when you're at the end of your rope.

My group had arrived at a decision: we should not leave.

To avoid the raids and the transports, it was best to be part of a column of work, one of these columns that take off after roll call, going outside to dump coal, carry sand or stones, cut down trees in the forest. Of course we did not really wish to work, to do any work. After three years in captivity, we had to conserve our strength if we wanted to reach the end, and the end seemed close at hand. Thus, every morning, when the columns assembled, we resorted to all manner of stratagems, constantly improvising new ones, to hide so as not to be taken off to work. Once the columns had left, we had to dig ourselves in till evening roll call. Up to that time we had succeeded in doing so.

Why did I find myself on that particular day all alone in one of the camp streets? We never made a move without being together, eye and ear on the lookout. Why then was I alone on that day, when the whistle blows burst from every side of the camp, and the Polizei cordoned off each street? Without even knowing how it happened, I found myself in a column formed by the SS kicking women into place, while the kapos, wielding truncheons, kept them in line. How did I get caught so stupidly? Fool that I am. Oh, how dumb, stupid!

There I was in the midst of unknown faces. Russian women, Polish women, no one I recalled ever seeing before, no one who spoke French. Gradually, by dint of shouting and cudgeling, the column was established. It will not unravel. Perhaps everyone has become resigned. My spite doubles, as does my anxiety. I will not see my comrades again. Where are we being taken? One never knows. To what kind of factory? One never knows. I'm on the outer edge of my row, giving a searching look, watching for a possible way out. The kapos are guarding the surroundings, nonchalantly now, drained from having had to race about, wielding their truncheons. Two SS women officers keep their eye on us, come and go from one end of the column to the other. We're waiting. We're waiting for Pflaum, says the "slave trader," so called because he is in charge of the transports, because he deals with the industrialists who require a labor force. Once he gets here the numbers will be written down and the convoy formed. We shall leave. I'll be gone and my comrades won't know where I am. We are waiting.

A third woman SS joins the first two, and all three stay there. I look, never taking my eyes off them. If only something could catch their interest, preferably at the other end of the column, so that . . . I observe closely the one with her back to me. In the way she stands firmly on her legs I have the definite impression that she has shifted her attention, and suddenly, in a flash, as happens in dreams, I hear Jouvet's voice in his conservatory class, Jouvet saying to a student who's stepping onto the platform to start a scene, "No, do it over again. You haven't really entered. Come in. Wait. Now. Take your place. Good. Don't make a move. Get set! You're in place now. Now, you may start speaking. And as for us, we know that you've got some-thing to say. Now we shall listen to you. Now we know you're about to speak." Take your place. Get set! The three SS were in their place. I could tell by their backs, their boots, their shoulders that they had started a conversation and would not budge. They were set. I took an instant flying leap out of the ranks, rushed down a street in front of me. My run seemed to summon a Polizei, whom I brushed aside, racing, running deep into the inner core of the camp, up to our bar-rack which I reached, breathless, exhausted from having raced, run so fast, been so frightened. I collapsed amid the group of my comrades opening their arms to embrace me. "Where did you go? You got caught, didn't you? When we heard the whistles blow and saw you weren't here, we were scared. Oh, how scared we were!" I had been terrified too. It took me a long time to catch my breath, hear my heartbeat slow down.

Departure

All of a sudden, the Sunday afternoon torpor was shaken by tremors whose epicenter remained invisible, tremors swelling, growing into a hubbub, a mad agitation, then a general commotion. Groups of prisoners were running in all directions, the red bands were racing through the camp streets, calling the heads of the various blocks, conveying an order, which was immediately transmitted to the barracks, looking for the lone prisoner or groups of friends who were walking about, chatting, and holding at arm's length the shirt they had just washed—waving it to dry is faster—or who, seated along the walls, under the barracks' windows, shook their hair to air it and take advantage of one of the first sunny days. All at once everything stirred, grew animated, tossed out questions. "You're French? Then quick, go to the Lagerplatz. All the Frenchwomen at the Lagerplatz! Fall in!" "Belgians! To the Lagerplatz! With all your belongings!" What did it mean, all your belongings? A tin cup, a spoon, a toothbrush, a bit of soap for those able to get some; perhaps some letters from home, dating back to May 1944; an object as precious as the sliver of a mirror or a knife, obtained through endless negotiations . . . Absurd treasures, each one representing extended longing and careful calculations; recipes collected on bits of paper gleaned through endless guile and incredible bargaining.

Women issued by the hundreds from the blockhouses and the hidden places where they sought shelter to spend as peaceful an afternoon as possible, a happy moment to be enjoyed for once, on a Sunday free of punishment, a day when the weather was good enough to wash one's hair and have the possibility of drying it in the sun.

Across the way from the kitchens women prisoners fell into square formation. This was accomplished as the din of wooden soles scraping against the tightly packed slag of the paths, the multilingual shouts uttered by the red bands and the kapos in directing the prisoners to where they expected them to fall in, the commands crisscrossing over their heads, rose to a climax. "What's going on?" They were all filled with a vague disquiet. "What are they up to?" The rows were formed in a state of confusion, and it took a long time for them to assume any kind of shape and keep it that way. SS officers arrived, counting the prisoners after the heads of the blockhouses had done so. They came and went. Questions and rumors circulated from one row to the next. "Why did they call only the women from France, Belgium and Luxembourg?—They're also calling Dutch women.—And Norwegian women.—Are there Norwegian women? Do you know any?—The camp is being evacuated.—Then why not everybody?—Why try to understand? You know very well that it is impossible to understand what they're up to."

During that time the rows were falling apart and the red bands were stepping in. But no one was paying any attention to their shouts.

We were waiting, and this became boring.

"Look! It seems something is moving at the end, over there."

"Yes, they're taking them to the showers."

"So, it's not evacuation after all. They wouldn't have us shower only to cast us out on the roads."

"As though this were the first time they have us doing something senseless."

"Still, they may be illogical, but . . ."

The ranks were falling apart gradually, row by row. Row by row the women entered the showers. Those who had come in first were already leaving, and the kapos lined them up through the main avenue. When we got there, there was no water left in the showers. They still had us strip. "Take off your dresses. Keep on your shoes. Return the tin cups." The SS doctor was there, surrounded by a few male and female SS, all examining us. We still failed to understand anything, nor why they were setting apart those women who had been shorn recently. Some, few in number, had been shorn recently on the pretense that they had lice. The SS shoved them into another line, and the unfortunate creatures, separated from their comrades, were in a state of despair. The others, all of them naked, their shoes in one hand, filed past the doctor, who palpated some of them, haphazardly, soon merely looking them over as they passed. At the end of the inspection a female prisoner, assigned to the showers, handed out to each woman a package containing striped clothing similar in every way to the one they had just shed, with one exception: it was unnumbered. We issued from the showers in groups of five, lengthening the line formed in the Lagerstrasse and filling it out as the squares in the Lagerplatz were being thinned.

We kept on waiting and wondering: "Can you make heads or tails of these shenanigans?" Suddenly a rumor runs throbbing through the ranks: "We are being liberated. The French women are to be set free." Weary smiles greet this news. "And why not, didn't they liberate a contingent of women last month, the ones who left with the Canadians?" "They may have left, but did you hear they ever arrived?"

"Free us to go where? They're liable to cast us out just like this . . . with the SS and the dogs."

Other rumors were more detailed: "There are trucks waiting at the camp entrance.—Yes, they got here last night.—Trucks? Did you see them?—No, but Martha said so. She saw them."

"I'll believe it only when I see them with my own eyes."

"And what then? . . . How do we know they're for us, these trucks?"

"At any rate, something's going on . . ."

"They might spirit us off to who knows where."

"You, my dear, could demoralize a whole regiment."

New groups issuing from the showers increased our column. "We didn't get new clothing. We never showered. They told us to tear the numbers off our uniforms and throw them into a basket. There's no more water, or dresses."

Daylight was fading. Someone said: "I think it's raining. I felt a drop." We stretched out our hands to check. It was a just a drizzle, nothing to reckon with. Our early excitement had waned. We were beginning to feel cold, tired. Time was slowing to a crawl, yet there was nothing to do but mark time. We had run out of conjectures.

All of a sudden, Pflaum materializes on his bicycle. He stops, hurls the bicycle to one side, saying to one of the SS women officers guarding the column, "They're not leaving this evening. To the Straff-block for the night!"

The news spread like wildfire. "We're being taken to the Straff-block." Our hearts were gripped with fear. The disciplinary block-house, at some distance behind the enclosure, filled all of us with terror. We had no idea what went on there, but we knew they were things to stand in dread of.

Slowly, wearily, the column walked toward the barrack, disappearing within. The place was empty. What had they done with the occupants, those punished for transgressing? The wooden floor had just been washed; it was still wet. We were greeted by the smell of humid wood. "To bed! Bedtime!" shouted the German woman in charge of the blockhouse.

"They're saving on the bread ration." The dinner bread had not been handed out. No one seemed much concerned. Exhausted by hours of waiting, all of us longed only to lie down. When Mado and I entered the barrack all the beds were taken. All that was left for us to do was to sit down on the wet floor of the refectory, at the back of which they had piled up the tables and stools. Forming small groups, newly arrived women sat on the floor, throwing out questions from one group to the other. "You really think so?"

"Oh, come on! It looks pretty certain at this point."

"To evacuate the camp, they wouldn't have taken off our numbers."

"Nor have us go through the showers."

"When we left Auschwitz, they gave us back our things."

"Last year they had more time. It looks as if they're short of time now."

"Yes, but where are they going to take us? We heard American troops are fifty kilometers away."

"That's just it. They'll deliver us to the next American action station."

"You're crazy. They're still fighting and you think they'll take us across the line of fire."

"There'll be a truce to let us through." Skeptical laughter greeted this statement. What an optimist, that one!

Some of us were stretched out, unable to speak, at the end of their rope with fatigue. Others, leaning against the wall, their hand raised to their heart as though to help it beat, counted each intake of breath, wondering whether they'd last till morning. Here and there talk went on, oscillating between somewhat strained hope and fear, all of it phrased in the interrogative mood.

"What's the first thing you'll ask when you're free?"

"To eat. A whole chicken all to myself. A roasted chicken, thoroughly cooked, with the meat falling off the bones."

"I'd prefer something crunchy."

"I'd stick a whole thigh in my mouth . . ."

"With the juice running down your lips . . . Oh, no. I'll be too happy to be able to use a knife and a fork, to cut my meat on a plate."

"I'd like a sweet, thick, hot chocolate, with bread and butter. As much butter as bread, holding the imprint of all my teeth."

"I think I'd start with a hot bath, perfumed with lavender salts."

"Just like a kept woman!"

"I couldn't. I'd get into bed first. I wouldn't have the strength to take a bath."

"There's nothing like a nice hot bath!"

"On the following day. First, I'd get into bed and have them bring me something to eat there."

"I believe that if I were to go to bed at once, I wouldn't wake up the following day. I'd sleep for days and days."

"What I would like is a cigarette. A real one. All to myself."

Occasionally, once in a long while, we'd been able to secure a cigarette. Gypsies, who stole them from the SS, sold them for a ration of bread. Each of us who contributed to the purchase was entitled to one puff. We had to bear our comrades' censure: "Aren't you crazy?

To exchange food for a cigarette when you don't have enough to keep from dying . . ."

"And you, what would you like?"

"Nothing."

"Nothing?"

"No, nothing. Just to believe it happened. To be certain of it. To get used to the idea."

"One must get used to it quite fast."

"Get used to getting up late, to coming and going as you please . . . No, that can't come back quickly."

"Let this be the least of our worries for the time being."

"You're right, we're not there yet."

Fatigue was overcoming the strongest among us. Voices were growing softer, low-pitched. Silences interrupted the murmurs, and in the intervals created by these silences one could hear the heavy breathing of the women leaning against the wall, mouths wide open, eyes staring into space. At every moment, a woman would step out of the dormitory, another rise from the corner she occupied. On their way to the toilets, they stepped over those seated on the floor. They inquired: "Does anyone have a tin mug? We need water for Margot who's going to faint?"

"Old woman Suzon won't make it. She's breathing hard. We're getting scared."

Cries, faint at first, rose over the murmurs.

"It's Jeannette. She's delirious, burning with fever."

"I wonder how she ever passed inspection. It's obvious she has typhus."

"Would you have liked them to keep her from leaving?"

Seated next to other typhus-infected women, all motionless, shaking with fever, their lips drained of color in their yellowish, almost brown faces, Jeannette was sagging.

The chattering started again: "I'll arrive without warning. Peek-a-boo! Here I am!"

"You won't be able to do otherwise. Do you imagine the telephone is working in France?"

"We won't arrive one by one. People will be waiting for us at the station."

"It'll be extraordinary to get there in time for the First of May."

"You want to march in the parade?"

"Of course. We've already missed the liberation."

"I'm not about to march in any parade. Thank you. I've had my fill of marching here."

"It won't be in ranks of five . . ."

"Five abreast or ten, I'm through with marching."

"It's as though you were saying that you'll never get up early again because you had to rise at four in the morning here."

"That's right. I've seen enough sunrises to last me a lifetime. If I see another, it'll be coming back from an onion soup at Les Halles. And even . . ."

"We're going to find things changed when we return."

"Oh, you know, much was changed already when we left last year."

"True enough. You haven't even been here a year."

"We were stupid enough to be picked up at Romainville with the Americans at the Porte d'Orléans."

"What's weird is that we left quite cheerful. We were sure we'd been given a round-trip pass just to see what it's like and bring you news of home."

"The winter's been endless. It seemed to take forever since the liberation of Paris. They fought till the bitter end."

"D'you imagine they'd have fought to the end to let us go free, just like that?"

"When I left the house my wash was on the stove."

"It's got to be cooked by now."

"No, the cop turned off the gas."

"A regular guardian angel."

"Someone would have come to your place and put things straight."

"No, no one knew where I lived."

"You could have sent a postcard."

"Idiot."

"Come to think of it, there's something I'd like to do. Go to the Ravensbrück canteen to purchase some postcards."

"Couldn't do it. You have no marks."

"I wouldn't waste one minute in these parts. When I'm free it won't be to visit the neighborhood."

"I can't wait to be out, but I'm in no hurry to get back. I know what to expect, and who does not expect me. If I get back, I'll be the sole survivor of my family."

"You'll come to stay with us. There are at least thirty of us."

"Where are you from?"

"From Poitou. When I get back home, I'll ask for a dish of mongettes."

"What's that?"

"Beans. White beans cooked with crackling. My mother prepares them so well . . . It's so smooth, melts in the mouth!"

"You always speaking of eating, never of drinking. I'd like something good to drink, really good."

"A good coffee."

"D'you think they'll give us some coffee before leaving? Am I ever thirsty . . ."

Suddenly everything grows quiet. Pflaum appears in the door, breathing hard like someone who had to run. The head of the block, who sleeps in a hovel near the door, goes toward him. "Send them back to their blockhouses. They're not leaving," he says in German, and goes back where he came from.

"What is it? What did he say?"

The slightly hesitant voice of a woman seated near the door chimes in. "He said, 'Send them back to their blockhouses. They're not leaving.'"

A moment of stupefaction. A cry. A death rattle. A longer cry. As though everything was collapsing.

The blockhova walks through the refectory and shouts, "Up! Roll call!" Roll call! Each one of us feels caught in a nightmare. The block-hova shouts again, "Fall in! March out! Go back to your barracks!"

Those who were asleep come out from the dormitory bewildered. "What's up? Are we leaving?"

It must have been four in the morning. Dark night. Heavily, stupidly, the ranks are being formed. It was cold, a penetrating dankness following a night warmed by the closeness of our bodies. The block-hova yells louder and louder: "Line up with your blockmates for roll call!"

The women were stepping outside, reeling, dazed. The sick, who might have made a final effort to walk to freedom but now could no longer stand on their feet, were being pulled by them. Some, almost unconscious, moved their lips asking for an explanation. No one could say anything, explain anything.

Step by step, helping one another, we join our former comrades lined up for roll call. They look at us in amazement, not asking questions. They've lost the habit of questioning long ago, the old prisoners, Czech and Polish women.

After roll call, the routine was reestablished, but weirdly. They no longer sent us out to work. The red bands no longer policed the streets. This simulacrum of departure had sapped the entire system. The soup was ready at odd times. Sometimes there wasn't any; sometimes there was too much.

We were at loose ends, bewildered. We went here and there, trying to decipher by the looks of the SS something of their own confusion, or their intent. One no longer saw many SS. We went looking for those who worked in offices, thinking they might know something. Every day we witnessed the death of this one or that, at the end of their tether, who might have lived had they been liberated on that day. They died as a result of the emotion, and the disappointment. Died of having allowed hope to beat in their hearts.

One never met a face that wasn't a question, a face burning with questions: "Do you think we're going to leave? What's your opinion?"

"Nothing. What can one think?"

"Listen. We've got to be liberated. I can't hold fast any longer. I'm at the end of my rope."

She was looking at me with supplicating eyes, her voice hardly perceptible, her lips retracted, her pupils enlarged: "I'm going to die," her eyes said. "I'm going to die if I don't leave this place at once."

"It won't be long now. Try hard."

"No, I can't any longer. I mean it. This time I can't."

It was true. Impossible to deny it. She was hanging on to me, like a wilted plant. And what about all the others? With their hollow eye sockets, their leaden-hued eyelids, where might they find the necessary strength to hold fast, even for a few days? Their begging look was the only living part of bodies already seized by death.

Finally, exasperated by these questions which I could not answer, I decided to say: "Yes, yes, we're going to leave. We'll leave on the 23rd."

"When is that, the 23rd?"

"Next Monday."

"Why the 23rd? You know it? How do you know that?"

"I know. Don't ask me how. We'll leave on the 23rd."

"I wonder if I'll be able to stick it out."

"Of course you will. Go lie down."

After having counted the days in her head, she inquired once more: "Why the 23rd?"

"Because everything that happens to me happens on the 23rd."

The young man who, for a number of days now, took a seat next to mine in class, had managed to be by my side when I was going out and to ask, without daring to look at me, "Which way are you going? May I accompany you?" He was walking next to me in silence. We were going down the Boulevard Saint-Michel. It was in the evening, after a rainfall. We walked in silence. He was trying to start a conversation. I could see, by looking at him surreptitiously, that he found it increasingly difficult to say anything. It amused me, and I did nothing to help him.

At the corner of the Boulevard Saint-Germain, along the Cluny iron fence, there was a florist's stand: a wicker basket, covered by a rug woven of green strands imitating grass, displayed tiered bouquets of violets; a piece of blackboard, stuck among the violets, proclaimed: Today April 23. Saint Georges's Day.

"It's my name day," said the young man at last.

"Your name is Georges?"

Grown bolder, he added, "I'm lucky to have met you on my name day."

"Saint Georges is a fine saint. He's magnificent in his black cuirass, riding a rearing horse, his gorgeous golden hair floating down to his shoulders as he plunges his lance deep into the dragon's throat."

"If only I could please you as much as he does," said the young man, mastering his timidity to the point of taking my arm. I thought he was very handsome. Later he told me he wanted to offer me a bouquet of violets but had stopped himself for fear I'd laugh at him.

It was also on a 23rd, May 23rd, that I was called to his cell at the prison of the Santé, where I was also incarcerated. They were taking me to him for a last farewell. My handsome Saint Georges, dying while fighting the dragon, my magnificent Saint Georges, shy and courageous.

But at that moment, in Ravensbrück, when I was extending the hope of a departure on the 23rd to those who craved some reassurance, I did not indulge in remembrances. The time had not come to let oneself go.

Why did I say we'd be leaving on the 23rd? I'm not superstitious. Was it impatience? Charity? Was it because I could no longer bear those eyes begging for a ray of hope, a crumb of conviction? And since I was stating with the firm self-confidence of an accomplished actress, "We're leaving on the 23rd," they went off comforted.

We left on the 23rd, the 23rd of April. If Mado weren't alive to attest to this fact, I wouldn't dare recall my prophecy.

The Farewell

We woke up hearing the key turn in the lock. It was the moment before dawn. A dim light seeped into our cell. Standing framed in the doorway, a soldier called my name, ordering me to get dressed in a voice whose intonation transformed the words he spoke, casting a mortal meaning on each syllable. "Get dressed, if you wish to see your husband one more time." He stopped before stressing "one more time." A mortal meaning. He stepped out into the corridor, leaving the cell door half-open while I was getting dressed. My cellmates had gotten up too. They handed me my clothes, helped me with gestures full of sweetness and pity, their only way of expressing their care and compassion. Framed by two soldiers on each side, I walked through long, dark corridors, full of turns and intersections, following a labyrinthine itinerary. The soldiers' boots resonated on the floor tiles. We walked fast. I would have liked to walk even faster. They led me to a cell with the door open. Leaning against the wall, Georges was expecting me. I'll never forget his smile.

We hardly had enough time to tell one another everything we wanted to say. A soldier called out, "Madame!" in that same tone which cast a mortal meaning on each word. I gestured: Wait. One more minute. Let us have another minute, another second. He called me again, but I would not let go of Georges's hand. The third time he called, I had to go, just like Giraudoux's Ondine whom the King of the Sylphs had to call thrice while she was bidding farewell to the Chevalier who was about to die. After the third call, Ondine would forget her mortal existence and return to the underwater realm. I knew that, like Ondine, I would also forget, since to go on breathing is to forget, and to continue remembering is also to forget. The distance between life and death is far greater than the one between earth and the waters to which Ondine had to return in order to forget.

The soldiers took me back to my cell. They wanted to push me in because I remained motionless on the threshold, keeping them from closing the door. I went into the cell. My companions came toward me. I was reeling—just a little, as when one loses one's balance—and they laid me down on my cot. They asked no questions. And I told them nothing, nothing of what I said to him who was going to die.

I said to him
how handsome you are.
It was the beauty of his forthcoming death
growing more visible with every passing moment.
It's true
that dying brings out people's
beauty.
Haven't you noticed
how they look
the dead, these days
how young and strong they are
this year's corpses.
Death is growing younger
every day
this year
Yesterday it was a fellow
barely nineteen.
I know there's nothing like death
to make the living handsome
give them back their childhood faces.
He was handsome
with the beauty of death
growing more handsome with every passing moment
death which would alight upon him
rest on his smile
his eyes
his heart
a beating
living heart.

All the more dreadful
because of his greater beauty
all the more dreadful because
all
are young and handsome
lying side by side
beautiful for eternity
fraternal
aligned
as when men are reaped
like ripe wheat in its season
of ripeness
man's season
in the summer of rebellion
when men are beaten down
like sheaths of wheat
facing bravely the blade of steel
chests exposed
punctured pierced
hearts rent
yet this is the choice they made.

That's what made him so beautiful
to have chosen
chosen his life, chosen his death
staring both in the face.

The Final Night

Except for some minor details, everything was supposed to happen in the same say as on the previous Sunday. Hubbub, shouts, falling in line opposite the kitchens in the early part of the afternoon. It was also a Sunday.

We form serried ranks. They are being counted. Crisscrossing of orders, carried out at a more languid pace than on the previous Sunday, with much less shouting. However, just as on the previous Sunday, nothing had transpired, nothing let us foresee that the departure scene was to be staged all over again. All at once, the French-women, the women from Belgium and Luxembourg were to report to the Lagerplatz. The ranks are counted again. The heads of the various blockhouses hold their registers up to their chests, checking numbers provided by real women against figures entered in their ledgers. All this accounting takes forever, all these verifications.

"So, are we going back to the showers? I hope there'll be water this time."

There were neither showers nor sorting. Only one more formality. Since, following last Sunday's orders, we no longer had numbers on our dresses or jackets—at least I suppose this was the reason—they decided to take down our identity. Tables made from boards set down upon trestles had been erected in a sidestreet. Two prisoners from the Politische were seated, notebooks open before them. We waited lined up in ranks. Those at the end were questioning those at the head of the line. "What are we to do? What are they writing down? What are they asking?"

Those at the head of the line told the others, and this information passed row to row: "They ask for name, date of birth, father's name and surname, date of birth."

"Whose date of birth?"

"Your father's."

Better be prepared, and answer without hesitating. Some of us needed a bit of time to gather our wits. For those hiding under an assumed name it was not easy to invent a father, with a first name and his date of birth. Those who had already answered these questions on arrival had to remember what they had said, or written down on the registration form. "I can't recall for the life of me the first name I invented for my father.—You're not registered under your real name?—They never found out my real name, not even the French police.—That won't make matters easy for tracing your family in the future.—And if you had died?—I'd be dead without being dead. That's what immortality is all about.—Do you believe any of this matters? Looks like a hell of a mess."

"This time we're leaving. No doubt about it."

"You sound as though you didn't know them. In the fortress where we were, they went to get a prisoner one morning. They went through all the monkeyshine of a regular discharge. They gave her back her handbag and her papers, even went so far as to wish her a good trip. Next she found herself on death row. I wonder what happened to her. She hasn't been transferred here with us."

"You've nothing jollier to offer?"

"Find my father's first name and the date of his birth."

"Just say anything that comes to mind. I can assure you their circus doesn't matter one bit any longer. They don't even remember what they did with their papers."

"They must have burned them all so the Allied forces won't find them."

"If that's so, why do they need more papers? Couldn't they free us without our identity? We'll be traveling without passports anyway."

"It's not the first time you see them putting together perfectly useless files."

"They're putting on a good face before taking to their heels. Once we've left, they'll vanish. They don't want to be made prisoners."

"They'll fly off, pftt! Just like that! You think it's some kind of movie."

"The other day, an SS—did you notice that for some time now they're never without a small case?—let her case fall. It opened, scattering her belongings on the ground. It was all civilian dress; a skirt and blouse, a jacket, shoes. A complete change of clothes. Jeanne saw it. Clearly, this is a well-planned disappearing act."

We were moving slowly. The identity statement took time since the registrars were Czech or Polish women. They didn't understand what we were saying and had no idea of how to spell the names. Don't let them count on us to help them. Although we have nothing against them. If the identity papers turn out messy we'd only be glad.

The ranks were unraveling. SS women officers were there to keep an eye on things but they looked bored and no longer interfered to keep order or a strict lineup.

"It really looks like the end."

Certainly the discipline had become loose. Those who were really weary sat on the ground; others moved from group to group to chat. Suddenly, without knowing where it came from, a handcart pulled by two of the Red Bands appeared at the end of the drive. The SS women called out to us, and the ranks waiting to file past the tables moved in the direction of the cart with its pile of cardboard boxes. The Red Bands and the SS proceeded to distribute the boxes. One each. They turned out to be Canadian Red Cross parcels. Each one of us started to open her package, quite unconcerned about proceeding to the identity tables. Finally, however, what had to be done was completed in a state of utter confusion. Later we formed columns once more, standing five abreast along the Lagerstrasse.

It was the end of the day. As on the preceding Sunday it was raining, a fine drizzle that made the entries in ink run all over the identity ledgers. We were waiting while eating the contents of our parcels: biscuits, slices of dry bread, a can of corned beef, and many other things all squeezed together in the box. We were waiting, still waiting. Something we would have to do until the end . . . We all looked though our boxes announcing what we found there. They were all exactly the same. There was even a pack of American cigarettes in each one. That's what I opened first. I extracted a cigarette, held it somewhat awkwardly between my fingers, thinking they should have provided matches. Obviously, no one had thought of it. These parcels were meant for soldiers, and soldiers can always light up. I craved lighting my cigarette. Moving deliberately slowly, I approached an SS, asked her for a light. Without a moment's hesitation or surprise, as naturally as in civilian life, she drew a lighter from her pocket, stretched her arm out in my direction. I took the lighter from her, lit my cigarette, inhaling the smoke under her very nose. I returned her lighter, which she took saying "Danke." The end indeed.

The cigarette was not as pleasant as I'd anticipated. It was my first, and I should have expected it. I smoked it to the end, however, pushing myself a bit. I was getting dizzy.

Everything was beautifully packaged in this parcel. There were numerous covers of an unfamiliar make, covers to unscrew or to force up with a small metal tongue. Having partaken of everything that seemed available in its simplest form—biscuits, chocolate, sugar—some of us went after the butter, sticking two fingers in and placing a bit of butter on our tongue to suck like a piece of candy. "It's salt butter.—I'm eating something, I don't know what it is, but it's good.—Show me! Ah, the blue box. It's peanut butter. It'll give you strength."

We were waiting. The waiting seemed endless. The rain had stopped, clouds blown away. Night had fallen. The projectors were turned on. As on the preceding Sunday, we saw Pflaum arrive on his bicycle, let go of the handlebars, and toss the following words at a woman SS: "They're not leaving tonight," pointing to the blockhouses where we would spend the night. And as on the preceding Sunday, anxious questions burst out from all sides:

"What did he say? Did you understand? You who know German, did you hear?"

"He said we're not leaving tonight."

"They're up to the same tricks as last Sunday."

"You see, we're not leaving," said a very young girl to me, her face distorted by disappointment.

And I, unmoved: "I told you we'll leave on the 23rd. The 23rd is tomorrow."

"You think we'll leave?"

"Tomorrow. I'm sure."

The grateful look in her eyes testified to her desire to believe me, yet it was also fading with sorrow.

"Be brave, go on! It's our last night here."

The column set off, crossing the whole camp to a remote section where they put us up in some empty huts. Immediately, all the women grabbed a cot. This time they had enough for all of us. We were at the end of our rope, and sufficiently aware of what a night of sleep meant not to stretch out at once. Their precious parcels in their arms, all the women went to bed. All except me.

The parcel contained a box of instant coffee. The directions said you could use cold water. A cup of coffee, a cigarette! Everything I wanted most. I still had a brown-red enamel mug, with a handle much like that of a beer stein. I kept it handy. I poured into the cup a double portion of the coffee powder, measured with the help of a small cardboard spoon enclosed in the box. It was described as the correct amount for the size of my cup. But it seemed such a small quantity. I added some. I let the faucet run drop by drop, carefully, so as not to spoil the powder and get really strong coffee. The sugar took a long time to melt in cold water. I was waiting patiently. One can always wait for a real pleasure. Unfortunately I could no longer light the cigarette I wanted to smoke while drinking my coffee. Too bad. It would have to wait till tomorrow. I drank small mouthfuls of coffee, but failed to experience the anticipated pleasure. It tasted bitter. The first cup of coffee . . . I would have to get used to pleasures all over again, tastes, the taste of coffee, of tobacco. Perhaps it was also a matter of the concoction; instant coffee was unlike real coffee. As with the cigarette. I forced myself to finish what I had in my mug, which I rinsed under the faucet before reaching the cot my friends had kept for me. No sooner was I lying down that I experienced a strange sensation. I wondered what was going on inside of me. My

throat tightened with anxiety. My heartbeat was so strong it filled
my ears. They hummed to the point of aching, and my aching heart
jumped in my chest. I was suffocating, although I kept my nostrils and
mouth wide open in order to draw breath.

"Where are you going?" asked Mado, hearing me clamber down.

I pointed to the lavatories. Mado must have failed to see my gesture in the dark. She fell asleep again at once. I was suffocating. I
needed air. I succeeded in making my way to the hut's entrance, and
opened the door. I was panting, fainting. Standing against the door
frame, with my face turned to the night outside, I held on to my
heart with both hands to keep it from tearing. My dress constricted
me. I unfastened the buttons. My copy of Molière's *Misanthrope*, that
hard, small thickness I'd gotten used to carrying aginst my chest, and
which had even kept me warm last winter, was now a burden to me. I
threw it down at my feet. I was trying to draw air into my lungs, yet
with each inhalation I thought I was about to die. The last night in
Ravensbrück. My last night. I was going to die just as I'd finally
leaarned the whole text of *Le Misanthrope* by heart, and no longer
needed it. I felt I was losing my mind. I was about to die as stupidly as
those who make dumb bets. My heart was jumping in my throat,
tight to the point of strangulation. I imagined that every breath I was
taking would be the last one. I hurt, hurt, hurt. Standing in the door
frame, my face frozen by the night air, blood hammering in my temples—oh, how my temples ached—my forehead covered with sweat,
the ice-cold sweat of anguish, unable to keep my mouth from twisting,
my heart from its wild knocking, I kept on thinking this was really
too stupid. It was dumb to die here, on the threshold of this hut, the
threshold of liberation. Now I knew it would happen, too many signs
pointed to its coming.

The night was clear and cold. The moon had risen above the barracks, very large, very close. Its light turned the roofs blue, made
them shine. As I was gasping, I looked at the night, summoning all
my willpower to help me hold on to my heart till morning. Hold fast,

hold fast, you fool. It wasn't the first time I issued orders to my heart. Up to now, however, it had been to urge it to continue beating.

Gradually, the heartbeats became less frequent, and my breathing regained its normal rhythm. The night was over. Although I had remained on my feet throughout, I was immensely happy to have held fast till the end of night, so happy that I felt no fatigue. So far as sleeping went the night was over, but it wasn't morning yet. The stars shone cold in the night sky, where the moon had scaled the heavens. Two kapos arrived, blowing their whistles, and in the blink of an eye everyone was up. My comrades were looking for me: "Where were you? Were you sick?" They brought me the parcel I had left on the bed. "Nothing, it was nothing. It's over."

I didn't tell them at once why I'd been sick last night. I was much too ashamed, ashamed of having been afraid of dying. An old deportee like me . . . Twenty-seven months of camp spent saving my energy, controlling my heartbeat, gauging the least gesture, regulating each step, so as to hold on to life one more hour, one more day. And then, to behave like a novice, a fool.

Two SS women arrived following the kapos, ordering us to form ranks in front of the barracks. They were shouting without obtaining any results. The prisoners stepped out, lined up, and, all of a sudden, withouth knowing why, everything kept on unraveling, everyone was stepping back. SS and kapos went on shouting at the top of their lungs, grabbing women here and there in order to enforce rank formation, but to no avail. The women refused to follow orders as though an invisible force were pulling them back.

My group never hastened to come out. We were never the first nor the last to do so. We learned from experience that bludgeon blows fall on the first and the last. In the middle, there is usually a lull before the bludgeons, drained of strength by the first wave of blows, resumed their ardor.

When we stepped outside, we didn't understand why the ranks unraveled as fast as they were being formed, why they reformed farther on, under the kapos' grip, only to draw back in utter disarray. We stepped into the column, as close as possible to the gate. We didn't move and couldn't understand why those ahead of us panicked. No one wished to be in the first row, so that, withough having moved, we found ourselves among the first. It was then that the reason for the rout became obvious.

Just in front of us, four helmeted SS men were positioned, one knee on the ground, behind machine guns pointed at the path for an enfilade. Pale flashes of moonlight burst from the guns' barrels. Our minds were made up without discussing the matter. "If they're going to shoot . . . A minute earlier or a minute later will make no difference. Better be shot at once." I, who had feared death during the night, was not at all frightened now. All five of us were very calm. After so many years, nothing could shake our self-control. We held on to one another, arm in arm, five abreast, firmly staying in the front row, and shouting to those behind us: "Take your places. They're leaving."

The column was formed. SS and kapos stopped shouting. There was a moment of silence following a lengthy marking of time, then the kapos shouted "Los!" ("March!"), and the column marched unflinchingly, straight toward the machine guns that did not fire a shot.

This must have been the commanding officer's final joke.

It was only when I undressed that evening in Denmark that I realized I'd forgotten my copy of *Le Misanthrope*.

The Morning of Our Freedom

The man who appeared before our eyes was the most handsome man we'd ever seen in our lives.

He was looking at us. He was looking at these women who looked at him, without knowing that, as far as they were concerned, he was so perfectly handsome, handsome by having human handsomeness.

Standing there, on the stoop, at the entrance—the amazing thing which we had not yet fully realized was that an entrance might also be an exit—he must have been expecting our arrival. He was alone, next to a group of men wearing trenchcoats and fedoras.

The door was flung wide open. The reflecting mirror above the entrance cast its light into the darkness. The man looked searchingly as far as the light would let him. There a first row of heads looms up, stepping forward into the light, followed by row upon row of other heads. The man looks at nothing but those heads, growing larger under his scrutiny, and he begins to doubt that these heads and eyes are real, so fascinated is he by these heads made more livid by the light. He can't look away from them, forgetting the bodies, the feet. When he'll finally catch a glimpse of the bodies and feet, he'll experience even greater doubt.

He looks at this strip of pale spots formed by the heads against a dark background, this strip which unfurls slowly, moving forward silently. Now he can make out faces, and eyes fastened on him, but those eyes are so used to remaining expressionless, even facing the most incredible spectacles, that they fail to register what they feel at the sight of this man. Astonishment. Interrogation.

The column is moving forward. No emotion. Nothing. In general, the faces are deeply marked by protracted suffering, by ancient, drawn-out struggles. It is as though willpower and pain had imprinted themselves on those faces—perhaps as they entered this place, passing

by the threshold where the man is standing—and hardened there forever.

The column is moving forward. The door is open, the gate lowered. The column comes to a stop at the gate. The women look at the
man, wait, and the man is also waiting. He waits for the last rows to
come to a halt at the end of the path illuminated by the projector. The
entire column has stopped. All the women are able to see the man, yet
all look at him with unseeing eyes, eyes that must have stopped expressing
anything a long time ago, carefully remaining blank. And perhaps
there really was no emotion in any of these beings—for, by dint of
having had to brace themselves constantly, constantly exercise self-
control, they were no longer capable of feeling.

The man looks at the women. In his case, you sense he is trying
hard not to show feelings that overwhelm him.

The women look at the man and do not see him. That is to say
they do not perceive those features which make him a certain kind
of man. All they see is a man, an effigy of a humanity they forgot
existed. And this is far more amazing than this man's very presence.

The whole column has come to a halt. The stamping has stopped.
We're waiting.

He speaks. He, the man. The trenchcoats topped by soft fedoras
do not deign to turn in our direction, pretending to have nothing to
do with him or us. The man asks—a sentence spoken in textbook
French, each syllable carefully pronounced, as though set apart, colored by a foreign accent unfamiliar to our ears trained to recognize all
the accents of Central and Eastern Europe—he asks: "Vous êtes
françaises?" stressing the mute *e* in every word. Is he addressing us?
Could it be that someone should actually ask us anything at all? No
one answers.

At last, a voice rises from the front row: "Oui."

"Vous êtes toutes les Françaises?" He insists on "les."

The voice from the front row answers, speaking distinctly as one
does with foreigners:

"No, all the Frenchwomen aren't here. Those who are sick are in the infirmary."

The man says, "Yesterday, I picked up all the sick women from the infirmary. One hundred and ten sick women."

The voice from the front row anwers: "In that case, we're all here."

(But it was an error. The commanding officer of the camp had indeed handed over a hundred and ten sick women, no doubt about it—was there anyone among those standing in the column who was not sick?—but they were not the ones laid up in the infirmary. Those were not sufficiently presentable. They were left with the twelve thousand prisoners—Polish, Russian, Czech, Yougoslav women— found by the Russian troops a few days later.)

Only when he begins to speak do the women realize that the man is wearing khakis, a uniform with fawn-colored boots and gloves, a white armband with a red cross on one arm, and on the other a blue armband with a yellow cross—a different type of cross. He smokes holding his cigarette between straight, outstretched fingers, nothing military about it, just an ordinary man. One of the women from the first row will say later, when she tells the story: "You know that special smell of Virginia tobacco." We were familiar with the Red Cross armband. But what about the other one?

The man looks at us for a long time with eyes full of disbelief and says, still hammering out every syllable, "Now, we are going to Sweden."

We are going to Sweden, and no response comes from the long stripe of light spots dotted with pools of darkness, women's eyes. Not a shudder, not a sign of life.

Did these women expect to leave, to go to Sweden? No. Hardly an hour ago, when the SS chased them out of the huts where they spent the night, corraling them for departure, and they found themselves facing a large number of armed SS, with their short, gleaming bayonets affixed to the barrels of their guns, they were certain, as the ranks formed under the menacing presence of machine guns pointed in their direction, that this couldn't be the much-awaited departure, but rather the campsite evacuation—columns marching for days and days, with women falling on the road in utter exhaustion, and shot in the temple or the forehead by an SS. We had heard of the evacuation of Auschwitz, in January, under the snow falling and covering the corpses, many at each step along the roads of Silesia. We'd also seen men from a western camp. They had covered hundreds of kilometers on foot, and lost most of their companions on the way. Here, north of Berlin, we were in the Reich's last corridor between the Russian and the American lines moving closer together. Where could we be evacuated? It wouldn't matter to the SS. They had hurled thousands of prisoners on the roads, making them walk aimlessly. They know that people die walking.

We walked through the camp where people were still asleep. The moon shone icy on the roofs. A lamppost cast its light upon Pflaum, who was holding papers and calling names. Why? Was he calling those he wanted to leave separately? We didn't know what had been planned and were afraid because everything that was Pflaum was terrifying. Then the column moved toward the gate, and we saw the man.

We are going to Sweden . . . A yellow cross on a field of blue, on the man's sleeve, that's Sweden. The gate is lowered. We wait.

We are going to Sweden. Our eyes may not respond, but we are recovering our sense of sight. There are vans outside, in front of the gate. White vans painted with a red cross. Our mouths remain silent. Not a single "Ah!" not one exclamation of surprise. No joy. Motionless, we wait.

We are going to Sweden. The man said it only once, but this sentence echoes within us, like a subdued song composed of a couple of notes, always the same, dropping like pearls and starting over again.

We are going to Sweden. A motorcycle is parked in front of the gate. We hadn't heard it arrive. It is there, with its caparisoned driver—boots, helmet, leather gloves—a knight in armor with a red cross against a white background on his chest and back. A real knight, chasubled with crosses, looking as though he had emerged from the pages of a history book.

We are going to Sweden. We must believe it since the man says so, since the white trucks are standing at the gate, since the knight who has come to free the captives is leaning forward on his machine.

Silently we wait, so calm that we ourselves are surprised by it. We, who used to think that, were this day to come, we'd faint from joy.

The barrier is lifted like the arm of a grade crossing. Pflaum is busy with his papers. He steps into the office, comes out, speaks to the trenchcoats in green fedoras—the Gestapo. We wait. We are watching for a sign from the man's lips. We are going to Sweden.

The man keeps quiet. It is Pflaum who makes a gesture with his hand: Forward! The column sets off, walks through the gate.

Then, the voice of one of us rises. "Comrades! Think of those we are leaving here. Let's have a moment of silence for them." And this voice asking for silence breaks the silence.

Actually, the Swedes arrived here the day before, in order to be ready. As we exit, they hold some of us up under the arms, guide us by the elbow, help us into the cars. Lottas carrying satchels, first-aid kits, instrument cases, flasks, busy themselves taking care of the weakest among us. Captain M. discovers the women whose eyes and faces he had seen from a distance. Now he is able to see swollen legs covered with sores, miserable bodies, feet shod in unimaginable footwear.

After we settled ourselves, parcels and blankets in our laps, he walked through every car, asking, "Are you comfortable?—Yes." At last the women were able to speak. Standing in the frame of the car door, more handsome still, he added, "Finished, the Gestapo." He smiled and all of us smiled back.

I know now why Captain M. was so handsome on the morning of April 23, 1945, on the threshold of Ravensbrück. I know why the children we saw in the small Danish railway station were so beautiful. I know why the flowers, the sky, the sun were beautiful, and human voices deeply moving.

The earth was beautiful in having been found again.

Beautiful and uninhabited.

And so I came back
You did not know,
did you,
that one can come back from there

One comes back from there
and even from farther away

★

I've come back from another world
to this world
I had not left
and I know not
which one is real
tell me did I really come back
from the other world?
As far as I'm concerned
I'm still there
dying there
a little more each day
dying over again
the death of those who died
and I no longer know which is the real one
this world, right here
or the world over there
now
I no longer know
when I am dreaming
and when
I do not dream.

★

I used to dream
of despair
and drinking bouts
long ago
before
I surfaced
from the depths of despair
that particular despair
thinking I had dreamt
the dream of despair
Memory returned to me
and with it suffering
which made me wander back
to the homeland of the unknown

It was still an earthly homeland
and no part of me can flee
I know myself through and through
a knowledge
born from the depths of despair
You find out soon enough
you should not speak with death
for it is useless knowledge.
In a world
where those who believe they are alive
are not
all knowledge becomes useless
for the one possessed of that other knowledge
it is far better to know nothing
if you wish to go on living
know nothing of the price of life
a young man about to die
has to pay.

I've spoken with death
and so
I know
the futility of things we learn
a discovery I made at the cost
of a suffering
so intense
I keep on wondering
whether it was worth it.

★

You who love one another
men and women
the man of a woman
the woman of a man
you who love one another
can you how can you
proclaim your love in the press
in photographs
shout it in the street which sees you pass
display it in the window
as you walk by
close to one another, glued together
your eyes meeting in the mirror
your lips joined
how can you
exhibit your love to the waiter
the taxi driver
who finds you so likable
both of you

lovers
say it to each other wordlessly
with a gesture
Dearest, your coat, don't forget your gloves
stepping aside to let her pass
she smiling, eyelids lowered then raised
proclaim it to the onlookers
and those who do not look
with the self-confidence you have
when someone is waiting for you
at a café
a public garden
the self-confidence you have
when someone is waiting for you in this life
say it to the animals in the zoo
together
this one is so ugly that one is so beautiful
sincerely agreeing
or not
no matter
do you even think of it
how can you and why
tell me
I know
that all the men have the same gestures
in regard to women
your gloves, dearest, you're forgetting your flowers
dearest suited me well too
I know that all women
feel the same rapture
he used to take my hand
wrap a shielding arm round my shoulders
how dare you
with me

I no longer have to smile
thank you darling you are so nice
darling suited him fine too.

And this desert is peopled
by men and women who love one another
love and shout their love
from one end of the earth to the other.

I came back from the dead
and believed
this gave me the right
to speak to others
but when I found myself face to face with them
I had nothing to say
because
I learned
over there
that you cannot speak to others.

Prayer to the Living
To Forgive Them for Being Alive

You who are passing by
well dressed in all your muscles
clothing which suits you well
or badly
or just about
you who are passing by
full of tumultuous life within your arteries
glued to your skeleton
as you walk with a sprightly step athletic awkward
laughing sullenly, you are all so handsome
so commonplace
so commonplacely like everyone else
so handsome in your commonplaceness
diverse
with this excess of life which keeps you
from feeling your bust following your leg
your hand raised to your hat
your hand upon your heart
your kneecap rolling softly in your knee
how can we forgive you for being alive . . .
You who are passing by
well dressed in all your muscles
how can we forgive you
that all are dead
You are walking by and drinking in cafés
you are happy she loves you
or moody worried about money
how how
will you ever be forgiven

by those who died
so that you may walk by
dressed in all your muscles
so that you may drink in cafés
be younger every spring
I beg you
do something
learn a dance step
something to justify your existence
something that gives you the right
to be dressed in your skin in your body hair
learn to walk and to laugh
because it would be too senseless
after all
for so many to have died
while you live
doing nothing with your life.

I have returned
from a world beyond knowledge
and now must unlearn
for otherwise I clearly see
I can no longer live.

After all
better not to believe
these ghostly tales
for if you do
you'll never sleep again

if you believe
these ghostly phantoms
revenants returning
yet unable to tell
how.

3

The Measure of Our Days

I recall everyone
even those who left.
—Pierre Reverdy

The Return

During the return voyage, I was with my comrades, the survivors among my comrades. They were sitting next to me in the plane and, as time gathered speed, they became diaphanous, more and more translucent, losing their color and their form. All the links, the lianas tying us together were loosening. Only their voices remained, but even they began to fade as Paris was getting closer. I watched their transformation under my very eyes, saw them grow transparent, blurred, spectral. I could still hear them, but was no longer able to comprehend what they were saying. When we arrived, I could no longer recognize them. They were sliding, vanishing in the crowd of the people awaiting us, then for a moment only they regained their appearance but it was so impalpable, unreal, fleeting that it made me doubt my own existence. They played this will-o-the-wisp game during the whole time we were treading our path from one office to the other, getting lost, then found again, joining me, uttering words I could not grasp, vanishing once more into the crowd of people awaiting us, finally sinking out of sight within this crowd. They had lost their reality so completely during the voyage, when I witnessed their metamorphosis from one minute to the next, saw them fade away, imperceptibly, inexorably, become ghostly, that I failed to take note at once of their disappearance. Probably because I was as transparent, unreal, fluid as they were. I floated through this crowd which was slipping by me, all around me. And all at once I felt alone, alone in a void with no oxygen, a void where I tried to breathe, where I was suffocating. Where were they? I realized they were gone when it was too late to call them, too late to run in search of them—how could one run in this slippery crowd? Moreover, my voice failed me and my legs grew numb. Where were they? Where are you, Lulu, Cecile, Viva?

Viva, why call her now? Viva, where are you? No, you weren't in the plane with us. If I confuse the dead and the living, with whom do I belong? I had to acknowledge—and it was a drawn-out conclusion, which filled me with anguish as I was formulating it, leaving me wandering, sliding, floating—I had to acknowledge I had lost them and from this moment on would be alone. Where should I look for help? Nothing would come to my rescue. It was useless to shout, call for help. Everyone in the surrounding crowd was ready to rush to my assistance, were there in fact to help, but they were offering only what they could do, in the way they could do it, which, so far as I was concerned, was of no use at all. The only human beings who might have helped me were out of reach. No one could take their place. With the utmost difficulty, the ultimate effort of my memory—but why speak of memory since I had none left?—an effort I cannot name, I tried to recall the gestures you must make in order to assume once again the shape of a living being in this life. Walk, speak, answer questions, state where you want to go, go there. I had forgotten all this. Had I ever known it? I had no idea what to do and where to begin. The whole project was beyond me. Better to give it up. Give up or postpone. First, I had to think. I was floating in the crowd that bore me without even knowing what it was doing since I weighed nothing and my head was empty. To think? How can you think when you have no words at your disposal, when you've forgotten all the words? I was too absent to be desperate. I was there . . . How? I don't know. But was I really there? Was it me? Was I . . . I was there and it would be wrong to say I did not know what to do. I did not think, nor did I wonder whether there was anything to do. To know, wonder, think, these are words I use now.

How long did I remain seated on this bench where people might assume I was pondering or resting? How long did I spend in not pondering, in trying to recall what one is supposed to do to recall? To say I was shivering with cold as when racked with fever, that I was at the end of my tether, is easy to declare today in lieu of explanation. The truth of the matter is I felt nothing, did not feel myself existing, did not exist. How long did I remain thus, in a state of suspension? (As

you can see, I have found my words since that time.) A long, long
time. I kept a vague image of that time, one in which there isn't a
light speck allowing me to distinguish between wakefulness or sleep.
A very long time.

If I try very hard, I believe I recall lying down and people coming
to see me. They kissed me, spoke to me, told me things, questioned
me. As to questions, they stopped quickly because I never answered
any. I hear their voices coming from a great distance. When they
entered my room, my eyes clouded over. Their thickness intercepted
the light. Through this veil, I saw them give me an encouraging smile,
but I failed to understand their smile, their attitude, their kindness—
later I assumed it was kindness. It was almost impossible, later, to
explain with words what was happening in that period of time when
there were no words. Why are they coming to see me? Why are they
speaking? What do they want to know? Why do they want me to
know certain things they're ready to tell me, things they came to tell
me? Everything was incomprehensible. And it was a matter of complete indifference to me that everything should be incomprehensible.
I had no curiosity, no desire to know anything. They brought me
flowers and books. Did they fear I might get bored? To be bored . . .
All their ideas came from another universe. They're afraid I'll be bored
so they bring books . . . They set down books on my nighttable and
the books stayed there without my even thinking of picking them up.
The books stayed there a long time, within reach, out of my grasp. A
long time. Finally, I was told that my absence from the world had
lasted long enough. My body was weightless, as was my head. Days
and days without thinking, without existing, yet knowing—today I
can't remember how I knew—or rather feeling, in an indefinable
kind of way, that I did exist. I was unable to get reaccustomed to
myself. How could I reaccustom myself to a self which had become
so detached from me I was not sure I ever existed? My former life?
Had I had a former life? My life afterwards? Was I alive to have an
afterwards, to know what afterwards meant? I was floating in a present
devoid of reality.

Friends continued to visit me, bring me books that piled on top of the ones I already had. Occasionally, lifting myself upon my pillows, I looked at these books without making any connection between them and the act of reading. Useless objects. What does one do with them? And then I'd forget them and return to my absence.

Slowly, unbeknownst to me, reality assumed its shape around me. Unbeknownst to me, for I made no effort to return to the surface of reality. I did not have the strength to make the tiniest effort. It was all by itself, by means of its weightiness, that reality resumed its contours, colors, significance, but ever so slowly . . . I would discover, following long lapses of time, a new feature, a new sense. Gradually, I recovered my senses of sight and hearing. Gradually, I began to recognize colors, sounds, smells. Tastes came later. One day I saw—yes, saw—the books on my nighttable, on the chair next to my bed. All of them were within reach, but my hand did not reach out for them. For a long while I looked at them without ever thinking of touching them, picking them up. When finally I ventured to pick one up, open it, look through it, it was so poor, so beside the point, that I put it back on the pile. Beside the point. Yes, everything was beside the point. What was this book about? I do not know. I only know it was beside the point. Beside things, life, essentials, truth.

What's not beside the point? I asked myself this question and was in despair at being unable to answer it. I say in despair for failing to find an adequate word for what I want to say. I was not in despair, I was absent.

I waited a long time before attempting another reconnaissance in a book. The second was as disconcerting as the first, and I became increasingly desperate, or rather increasingly driven into my absence.

What's not beside the point? Is there nothing left for me in books? Are all of them nothing but futile repetition, pretty, vivid descriptions, one word after another utterly devoid of import?

My discouragement in regard to books lasted a long time. Years. I could no longer read because I felt I knew already what was written in this book, and that I knew it in an altogether different way, a deeper, more trustworthy knowledge, manifest, irrefutable.

Just as I had to look down in order not to see people's faces, because they shed their trappings before my eyes, letting me see everything through the face the moment I set eyes on them, an experience so embarrassing that I was forced to lower my gaze, I also distanced myself from books because I could see through words. I saw the banality, conventionality, emptiness. Yes, I saw the skillfulness. But what does this one know that he's trying to impart? And why doesn't he say so?

Everything was false, faces and books, everything showed me its falseness and I was in despair at having lost the faculty of dreaming, of harboring illusions; I was no longer open to imagination, or explanation. This is the part of me that died in Auschwitz. This is what turned me into a ghost. What can still be of interest when falseness becomes apparent, when subtlety is gone, with no gradations of light and shade, nothing to guess at in people's eyes or in the pages of books? How can one continue living in a world stripped of mystery? How can one exist in a world where lies are brightly, blindingly colored, separating themselves from truth, as in decomposing amalgams where each ingredient finally assumes its own color and density?

I raised these questions over and over again without coming up with an answer. Why go on living if nothing is real? Why regret your inability to be comfortably fooled? I was struggling against an insoluble dilemma. Nothing was of any use to me. But what's the good of knowing when you no longer know how to live?

How did it happen? I don't know. One day, I picked up a book and read it. I wish I could say how it happened. I can't remember. I can't even remember the book's title. It would sound good were I to name a masterpiece. No. It was one of the many books, the one that gave me back all the others. I'll have to try to remember. It's so hard that I'll give up for the time being. Whoever thinks of marking the subterranean course where he gets lost for many years before reaching a spot of light? He knows he will never return to this subterranean passage, so why look for it?

I fought against injustice
it gripped me
handed me over to death
I fought against death
fiercely
so that it could not whisk me away from life
but death
seeking vengeance
robbed me of the will to live
and handed me a certificate
signed with a cross
I have it here
to be used by me next time.

My heart lost its hurt
its reason for beating
life was returned to me
and I am here in front of life
as though facing a dress
I can no longer wear.

A child gave me a flower
one morning
a flower picked
for me
he kissed the flower

before giving it to me
and asked me for a kiss
this boy the color of licorice
who smiled at me
in Sicily.
There is no wound that will not heal
I told myself that day
and still repeat it from time to time
but not enough to believe it.

Gilberte

As for myself, I felt at a loss at once, as soon as I came back to Paris. On arrival, we went through some strange places, covered playgrounds transformed into offices, with makeshift tables and bustling personnel. Yes, I believe that first place was a school. Since I don't know Paris, I couldn't say where it was. We had to provide them with our identification, go here to list sicknesses we had had, there to pick up some papers. Then they took us over by bus, this time to the center of town. Another row of tables, more questions, more papers. It was in a hotel, as I realized later on. The one impression I kept is that of a crowd, a crowd in which I was lost. I remember vividly that at first you were either in front or in back of me, that I would turn around to see if you were still there, that those who were in front of me turned around to give me a smile. How did it happen that, once we had gone through the line at the tables with their bustling personnel, I found myself alone, all alone in a crowd, without a single familiar face to turn to? Later, I realized that you, the Parisians, had families waiting for you, and with the formal procedures completed you were in their hands. No one said, "What about Gilberte?" Or else, when you noticed I wasn't there, I had disappeared, engulfed by the crowd. You must have been as bewildered as I was. I was the only one from Bordeaux. I remained fastened to my spot, at the end of the row of tables, in a desert where no one paid the least attention to me. It was like standing in traffic at the crossroads. I just stood there, stupefied, lost. You were no longer next to me. All of a sudden I had lost a limb, an essential organ. I could not see or hear anything. It was like drowning. Everything had sunk. There wasn't the smallest bit of wreckage to hold on to. Someone among the women and men busying themselves behind the tables, filling out forms for those still in line, must have noticed me. I woke up in the soft darkness of a room. There was a large double bed in the center where I had lain

down fully dressed. I was weary, so weary. When I woke up, night had
fallen. My throat tightened as in fear. And yet, I wasn't afraid. I wondered what I was doing there, why I was in this place, how I got there.
A deep fatigue nailed me to the mattress. I didn't have the strength to
move. Very briefly—oh! for an instant—I considered finding out
where I was, a very distant desire, too remote to propel me to get up,
look for the electric switch. I fell back asleep. When I woke up again,
it was still night. I had to go out, but couldn't bring myself to do so.
After a long period of hesitation, feeling my way, I proceeded to
switch on the light. The room was a hotel room, furnished with
copies of period pieces, in grand-hotel style. It was a large room. I let
the flowered wallpaper and the chandelier—a bronze angel, no, a
Cupid, holding a beaker—benumb me. "I've got to get up, I've got
to get up," I kept on saying to myself without making a move. Finally,
I got up. A half-open door led to the bathroom. The toilet was there
also. I opened the faucets, watched the water run. I was thinking of
nothing, absent, lost. I experienced the same anxiety that had taken
hold of me once when I had almost been separated from you. I had
been pushed by a kapo, against my will, into a column of nothing but
Russian and Polish women. Not a single familiar face. I was desperate,
undone by the thought of being transferred to another camp without
you, leaving you, severed from my group, among strangers who
chatted without paying the slightest attention to my presence. I
couldn't understand a word they were saying. They appeared resigned
to leaving the camp. Of course they were together, and I was alone
among them . . . The thought of being separated from you chilled my
blood, paralyzed me, robbed me of incentive. I was in despair, as lost
as a child separated from its mother in a crowd. Thanks to a scramble I
was able to dart off—how did I do it? the boldness of despair—run
toward a barrack where I found you, where you were waiting for me,
devoured by anxiety. As soon as I found myself among you, I was
comforted, reassured, warmed. I remember it as one of the most
powerfully joyful moments of my life. And now, here I was, alone in
this room, overwhelmed by despair. I had dreamt of freedom

throughout deportation. Was this freedom, this intolerable solitude, this room, this fatigue? I went back to bed to seek some warmth from the pillow, a presence, and I fell asleep again. I don't remember how I woke up and had the courage to step out of the room. I'd left the light on, and the flowers of the wallpaper had acquired a reassuring aspect. I opened the door and ventured out. There were endless corridors. They took sharp turns, made detours ending nowhere. I didn't dare go too far for fear of getting lost. I went as far as a corner. Should I go farther? Frightened, I regained my room, which I recognized by its open door. I had gotten used to its decor, the colors of the bedspread. It had become my shelter. There was a dresser, a washstand, a bathtub, but I had nothing to wash with. There were no towels, no hot water. I sprinkled some water on my face and hands and sat down on the bed. I waited without awaiting anything. I was there, inert, not wondering whether there was anything I ought to do. I heard no noise, had no idea of what time it might be. I could have walked over to the window, opened the curtains, tried to get my bearings. I was drained, without initiative. I never thought of going down for information, to find out what I was to do. Was there something to do? What? I felt neither hunger nor thirst, only fatigue and bewilderment. The feeling of solitude was overwhelming. I couldn't remember the circumstances that brought me to this room. The only question that arose in my mind was: Where can Lulu, Cécile, Charlotte be? It was more of a monotonous repetition than a real question looking for an answer. It didn't try to remember a single address. I was lost, didn't know what to do, had no will to do anything. How long did I stay in the room? I don't know. Days, nights. A long time. The corridor had frightened me. I no longer had the courage to venture there. I remained a long time seated on the bed without a thought in my mind. I think I must have fallen asleep again.

When I woke up, I was hungry. I welcomed this feeling of hunger as a form of deliverance. I was hungry, therefore I was. My disorientation was so total I could not imagine a way of getting out of this situation. I was hungry, where could I find something to eat? What could

I do? Stay in the room and wait? Perhaps someone might come. In a
hotel, there are chambermaids. A strange hotel where no one comes
to see what's going on. I carefully inventoried the contents of the
room. To whom did the coat on the chair belong? It was the coat I
was given in Sweden. Like yours, I believe. Gray. I didn't recognize
this coat. Nothing gave me a clue, a key. I discovered a bell. It
couldn't have been connected. I rang three or four times without anything happening. The telephone on the nighttable was also disconnected. I was lost but no longer anxious. Lost, without energy. Having
completed my exploration, I went back to bed. There was nothing
else to do. I remained there a long time. How long? I couldn't say. I
had no notion of time passing, only that I'd been in the room a long,
long time. When I got up again—and why did I?—the feeling of
being hungry was sharper. At first I did not recognize it. When I realized that it was hunger gripping my belly, I was reassured. This feeling
of hunger was strong enough to make me get up, but not strong
enough to impel me to walk to the end of the corridor. It had to have
an exit . . . Finally, I made up my mind to go out. I opened the door
and stayed on the threshold, watching, waiting, wondering whether I
should go right or left, hesitating. I was holding on to the trim, not
daring to let go. I was there, undecisive, scared. I did not budge. I was
still hesitating between coming out and going back to bed when a
man passed by. He addressed me: "Where are you from?"
    "Auschwitz."
    "I've come back from Mauthausen, but that's not what I was
asking you. Where are you from? From what part of France?"
    "Bordeaux."
    "Do you have family?"
    "My father. I must still have my father."
    "Are you waiting for news?"
    "No. No one knows I'm here."
    "How did you get here? You're not alone . . ."
    "I was with my friends, Lulu, Cecile, Charlotte, Mado. We were

taken to Sweden by plane. I lost them at the tables, downstairs, on arrival."

"You've been here for a long time?"

"I don't know."

I was getting tired from all these questions. The sound of this man's voice seemed so strange . . . I did not have the strength to speak.

"You should send your father a telegram. You can send telegrams from the office downstairs."

The thought of sending my father a telegram made me feel even more lost. No, not that. What would I say to him? "Have returned. Gilberte." And my father would think: "And Andrée? What did you do with Andrée?"

"No, I can't send a telegram."

"You can't stay here forever. You'll have to go home."

"Yes, I must go home."

Why had I focused my whole purpose during the three years of captivity on going home? Did I really believe this was what I wanted? Undoubtedly, because of all of you. We had to go back. Go back . . . Seen from over there, going home seemed so improbable. One should not put one's trust in miracles . . . Yet, if I suceeded in holding out until now, it must have been because I had willed this return. It would have been so easy not to come back. We had to come back. All of you used to say, "We've got to make it back." And you were making plans. I did not make plans, but I was caught in the common decision: return. We had to return. Why? Alone in this room, abandoned, lost, I no longer knew why we had to return at all costs. "Obviously, I'll have to go back." I was terrified. Go back, and then? I did not envision the then. I could not see at all the reason for going back. To see my father again . . . Of course I wanted to see my father, but I was so full of apprehension at the thought of facing him I would have given anything to push this moment back to some inaccessible point in time. My father . . . How would I find him again? He had been interned in Merignac, a camp near Bordeaux. Even before my arrest, the Gestapo used to pull out hostages from that place every time the

Resistance staged a terrorist attack against the occupying forces.
Was he even alive? I was afraid of all the alternatives, of finding
him and not finding him. And I could not bear taking a step to find
out.

"Come. We'll have lunch and then you'll send your telegram,"
said the comrade from Mauthausen.

I followed him through the corridors. The elevator was not
working. We went down the grand staircase covered with a red carpet,
and he showed me the way to the dining hall.

Having seen to my being comfortably settled, the comrade from
Mathausen said, "Wait for me. I'll bring your tray." I must have been a
pitiful sight. I was sitting in the center of a dining hall full of people,
more lost than ever. I didn't dare raise my eyes to look at people at the
other tables. Many seemed to know one another; they chatted, called
out from one table to another, creating a hubbub in which I couldn't
make out a single word. I saw faces through a mist which made them
seem remote and indecipherable. The comrade from Mauthausen
came back carrying plates. He set one down before me. "Eat, you're
hungry." He poured me a glass of wine. "Drink, it'll pick you up."
The wine was bad, or at least seemed bad to me. The soup . . . I
believe it was soup, or perhaps noodles. I'm not sure. I ate without
paying attention. More than anything else, I wanted to cry, find
refuge in tears. I thought of crying, thought of it as something sweet.
If only I could cry . . . Since I left Dédée over there I'm no longer
able to cry. Do you cry? I could have shed endless tears after Dédée's
death. After the death of Viva, of Grandma Yvonne, of all our companions from Bordeaux, those who had been imprisoned with Dédée
and me since the beginning. And for Berthe, whose dead body you
carried, coming back from the marshes in the evening, Lulu,
Carmen, Viva and you. Tears are a boon denied the likes of us.

The comrade from Mauthausen kept on talking. He was interested in me, asking questions, wanting to help. "Eat some bread. It's
good to eat bread after what we've gone through." Was the bread
good? I no longer felt hungry. I wanted to cry, and felt my lips tighten

as when you break into tears. I tried hard to tighten them some more in the hope that tears might follow, but they did not flow.

There was jam for desert. "Take it if you want," I said to the comrade from Mauthausen, who was happy to hear me speak at last. Fortunately, he did not expect me to ask him questions. He was from the Basses-Pyrénées. "So you can imagine, when you said you were from Bordeaux! We're fellow countrymen. You see, if my telegram gets there in time . . .—I don't know if my brother is in Biarritz or Pau; he was supposed to move; people moved a lot during the occupation—I'm waiting for his telegram to know if I'm buying a ticket for Pau or for Biarritz . . .—if my telegram gets there in time, we could travel together . . ." All of a sudden I wanted to leave as soon as possible. He was nice, this comrade. His questions showed friendliness, not a trace of curiosity. I couldn't say whether he was young or old, tall or short, I never saw him. I only felt his presence, his desire to come to my assistance. His voice sounded very remote, as though filtered through fog. Everything was veiled in mist. I myself was in this fog wherein I'd lost all my landmarks.

"You're through eating? Come. You'll send your telegram."

He took me to a counter. There was a pile of forms to fill out. The comrade handed me one, together with a pencil he pulled out of his pocket. He was already well organized. Pencil in hand, I remained standing there, my empty head full of fog. I couldn't find a single word. "All right! Write the address. There . . ." The address. I no longer knew my father's name, nor mine. The comrade took the pencil from my hand as well as the form. "I'll write it for you. What's your father's name?" I was able to articulate the name, the address. "And the text?"

"The text . . . I don't know."

"You're sure he's in Bordeaux, your father?"

"If he's alive he's in Bordeaux."

"Do you prefer to inquire and wait for the answer?"

"No, I've got to leave."

"In that case take the four o'clock train. You can still catch it.

There's a train at four which gets to Bordeaux around midnight. I
know. Whether I go to Biarritz or Pau that's the train I'll be taking."

Four o'clock. Midnight. This evening. Already. I started shaking
with fear. He was resolute, this comrade. I no longer wished to leave,
and I did not know what reason to give him.

"It's not a good idea to leave at four and arrive in the middle of
the night if you're not sure there's someone home. What if you left
tomorrow morning and got there in the daytime? Is the station far
from your home?"

"Quite far."

"There can't be taxis in Bordeaux."

"The streetcars must be running. They did during the war." I'll
take the streetcar."

"Fine. Then I'll write, 'Arriving Bordeaux Saint-Jean tomorrow
Saturday . . .'"

He knew tomorrow would be Saturday . . . He was really organized, that fellow.

"'Arriving tomorrow Saturday four thirty. Kisses.' There you go.
How do you sign?"

"Gilberte."

"You want me to read it back to you?" Not necessary. He handed
the telegram to a woman behind the counter. "We're not paying."
Why did he add this? I hadn't made a move to look for money in my
pocket, hadn't thought of it. A forgotten gesture. I didn't know I had
any money. I only found out I did in Bordeaux. It was the return
bonus.

"And now I'm going to show you where you pick up your travel
pass. That's free also." And he took me to another counter. People
were waiting. We stood in line.

"Do you have your returnee card?"

When will he stop all these questions . . . He's a good fellow, but
why does he have all this energy?

"A returnee card? What's that?"

"They must have given you one when you got here."

"Then it's in my room."

"Go get it while I wait in line."

I was so frightened at the thought of leaving him, of finding myself alone in the corridors, losing my way in them, that I tried to answer, "I don't want to leave." The comrade was waiting patiently, still friendly. I said, "I don't know where my room is." I must have looked exhausted. The comrade was looking at me. I was perspiring. Drops of sweat fell from my forehead to my eyebrows, stayed there for a moment, then ran down my cheeks, fallin on my dress.

"You're in room 326. Right next to me. If you tell me where your paper might be I'll go get it."

"I don't know."

"All right. Stay right here. I'll look for it."

He left. I felt relieved. He was much too energetic for me. My weakness, my fatigue were so great I could not bear his liveliness. I had the impression he was pushing, hustling, forcing me to do things when in reality he was kind, having become an instant brother. I realize it now. When he came back, it was my turn to act. I was so frantic at the idea of having to talk, give answers, explanations, so stricken with panic at the prospect of devising an ineluctable plan of action, that I wanted to flee. But the comrade from Mauthausen was pressing forward. "Bordeaux, tomorrow morning," and he showed me my papers. I did not budge, making myself inconspicuous behind him for fear of having to answer more questions.

"There you are. This is your travel voucher. Don't lose it. I'm putting it into your pocket together with your returnee card," and he carefully folded all the papers.

"Do you have a handkerchief to wipe your face? You're all per-spired."

"No, I don't have a handkerchief."

"Wait a moment. Mine is clean." He wiped my face with his handkerchief, ever so gently, delicately. I felt utterly stupid, yet I did not mind being stupid with this comrade.

"And now, you should go up and rest before dinner."

"I don't know the way to my room."

"It's on the third floor. I'll take you there."

I had a hard time going up. These flights of stairs covered with a red carpet seemed endless. The comrade from Mauthausen walked ahead. He waited for me at each landing, and when we reached the last floor he helped me by taking my hand. "You're just like me. You can't look at steps any more." He said this with a kind of smile. I didn't understand what he meant. He must have carved the Mauthausen stairs, but at that time I had no idea there were stairs at Mauthausen. In front of my door he said "Here you are. You see: 326." I did not thank him. I was ashamed of acting like a fool. I would have liked to say something nice, show my gratitude. No word came to my mind, and I could not wait to be alone. The moment I stepped through the door, I took my leave of him and threw myself on the bed, drained of every bit of strength.

It was still light when he came for me to take me to dinner. Dinner was served early. It was June and the dining hall was full of light. No so in my room, where I had not opened the curtains. The dining hall was as animated as this morning. The hubbub buzzed in my head. I would have preferred staying in my room, but the comrade had insisted and I didn't have the will to resist.

During dinner, he made the rounds of the dining hall and, when he came back, declared in an encouraging tone: "Other people are taking the same train. There'll be a car to take you to the railway station. You'll have to be in the lobby at seven." I turned this over in my mind, trying to think. Everything was so disconnected in my head that I was unable to formulate a single idea, to put a sentence together. Tomorrow morning, seven o'clock, in the lobby. It seemed as unrealizable as a trip to China. How would I know it was seven? I was wondering whether I should stay all night in the lobby, or remain in my bed and let the time slip by. The comrade from Mauthausen was organized and perspicacious. He added, "I'll tell them to knock on your door. Two of them are on the same floor as you. Had I received

my telegram I would have left with you. I was supposed to get it
today. It's strange . . ."

Was he worried about not having received his telegram? I didn't
concern myself with it. I couldn't pay attention to anything. Everything was happening behind a veil of fog. From there I could hear the
questions of my comrade: "And your mother? You no longer have
your mother?" And I heard myself answer. My own voice also came
from behind a veil of fog:

"My mother died giving birth to my sister."

"So then you have a sister. . ."

"She died in Auschwitz."

"I understand," said the comrade. "Coming back like this will be
quite a blow."

My father was waiting for me at the station. He had not changed.
He was only slightly stooped, weary. He kissed me, not asking any
questions. He had learned through women from Bordeaux who'd
returned before me that Dédée wasn't coming back. I felt faint, and
would have liked the trip to last forever.

At home, everything was as I remembered it. Dédée's things here
and there, her room, were all the same. Gradually, as the fog began to
lift, objects reacquired their contours, usage, the traces of their past.
Everything became sharp, threatening. I didn't know what to do to
avoid contact with these things that encircled me, attacked me,
knocked against me. Where could I run, fade away so as not to be
captured by the past, or go knocking against the walls, things, memories? At the same time, everything was unreal, as though deprived of
consistency. Without consistency, yet cutting. Everything bruised me,
I felt I was covered with black and blue marks with no spot on my
skin free of pain.

Since then . . . How did I manage? I often wonder. I don't know.
My father became sick. I took care of him. He died four years after
my return. Getting married? Yes, I did think of it a little. It would
have been to have a child. But while my father was sick—he needed
constant care—I couldn't think of it. Later I was too old to have a

child. At least, that's how I felt. I had to live elsewhere, leave the house where Dédée was born, where I had brought her up. Everything was wrenching. Settle down somewhere . . . I'm still not settled. Things have been set down here and there, not in their proper place, they're not incorporated in the rest, not connected to one another. They've just been dropped without ever assuming their rightful place. I was too weary.

And then . . . I don't know. I'm not doing anything. If someone were to ask me what happened since I came back, I would answer: nothing. I admire those who had the courage to start life over again. Mado . . . She married, had a son, is useful to her husband and her son. She has a reason for living. For those who rejoined their husbands, their children, like Lulu, it must have been easier. And yet, I wonder . . . Perhaps they are happy. To be happy, is that a question we ever raise? I keep on telling myself, just to make sure of it, that we came back twenty-five years ago, otherwise I wouldn't believe it. I know it as we know the earth is spinning, because we learned it, but you must think to know it.

I cannot look at people without examining their faces. It's been this way since I came back. I peruse their lips, eyes, hands, seeking an answer there. Facing people I meet I wonder, "Would he have helped me walk, that one? Would he have given me a little bit of his water?" I examine all the people I see—passersby, strangers—the mailman, former friends, a saleslady—yes, all of them everywhere, no matter where, those we brush past, those who accompany us part of the way, and those we've known a lifetime. I can't help staring at them, scrutinizing them. This is how I tell people apart since my return. With some, I know from the very first glance they wouldn't have helped me walk, nor have given me a mouthful of water, and I need not hear them speak to know their voices ring false, as do their words. Others I scrutinize a bit longer, though I've read the answer at once. I examine them with desperation since I wish they might be among those who would have helped, since I long to love them—my father when I returned . . . I attempt to discover in a fold of their lips, an involuntary expression in their eyes, the sign of a maybe. I try desperately. Their lips, their eyes remain stingy. These wouldn't have helped either . . . Then who? Who remains? And I continue to seek. Those about whom I know from the very first glance that they would have helped me walk are so few . . . I tell myself I'm stupid. I no longer need to be held up, given a drink of water, I no longer need someone to share her bread ration with me. It's all over now. And yet I can't stop examining faces and hands, hands and faces. It's a miserable quest. This is no longer the way we ought to look at people we meet in life, yet I have nothing to say to those whose lips suddenly tighten, whose eyes grow dim. I tell myself: it's stupid, you must transcend this nonsense. I tell myself it's of no importance today. So what's important today? I'm left with the fact that I know many more human beings than I require to continue living among them, and there will always be between them and me this useless knowledge.

Each one had taken along his or her memories, the whole load of remembrance, the weight of the past. On arrival, we had to unload it. We went in naked. You might say one can take everything away from a human being except this one faculty: memory. Not so. First, human beings are stripped of what makes them human, then their memory leaves them. Memory peels off like tatters, tatters of burned skin. That a human being is able to survive having been stripped in this manner is what you'll never comprehend. And I cannot explain it to you. At least, when it comes to the few survivors. People call the inexplicable a miracle. The survivor must undertake to regain his memory, regain what he possessed before: his knowledge, his experience, his childhood memories, his manual dexterity and his intellectual faculties, sensitivity, the capacity to dream, imagine, laugh. If you're unable to gauge the effort this necessitates, in no way can I attempt to convey it.

Whether you return from war or from elsewhere
when it's an elsewhere
unimaginable to others
it is hard to come back

Whether you return from war or from elsewhere
when it's an elsewhere
which is nowhere
it is hard to come back
for everything in the house
has grown foreign
while we were in the elsewhere

Whether you return from war or from elsewhere
when it's an elsewhere
where you conversed with death
it is hard to come back
and speak again to the living.

Whether you return from war or from elsewhere
when you come back from over there
and must relearn
it is hard to return
having contemplated death
with eyes wide open
it is hard to relearn
looking at the dull eyes
of the living.

Mado

It seems to me I'm not alive. Since all are dead, it seems impossible I shouldn't be also. All dead. Mounette, Viva, Sylviane, Rosie, all the others, all the others. How could those stronger and more determined than I be dead, and I remain alive? Can one come out of there alive? No. It wasn't possible. Mariette with her eyes like quiet water, eyes that did not see because they saw death in the depths of their quiet water. Yvette . . . No, it's not possible. I'm not alive. I see myself from outside this self pretending to be alive. I'm not alive. I know this with an intimate, solitary knowledge. You, you understand what I want to say, what I feel. People don't. How could they understand? They did not see what we saw. They did not count their dead every day at dawn, they did not count their dead every day at dusk. We spent days keeping track of time, we spent time keeping track of the dead. We would have been afraid to keep track of the living. And for each dead person we added on, we had neither regret nor tears. Just a weary pain. We had nothing but fear and anguish: how many days until I'll be on the list? How well we kept track of time. "The time you measure is not the measure of our days." Over there it was. This came from a poem you used to recite. I still remember it. How many days until they add me to the list? Who will remain to take the final count? Don't you see it isn't possible? Our willpower held us in a vise, like a fit of delirium, prompting us to bear, endure, persist, and issue from this place to be the voice returned to tell all, the voice promulgating the ultimate count. But why come back as the sole returnee to a frozen void? Here I am, dead like the others. My voice gets lost. Who hears it? Who knows how to heed it? The women, my companions, also wanted to return to deliver their message. All the deportees wanted a chance to say what they had to say. Am I alive when there is nothing I can say? Alive when my voice is choking? The very fact we're here to speak denies what we have to say.

One morning, when it was still pitch dark, I woke up to the sound of roll call. Next to me, Angèle Mercier did not move. I did not shake her. Did not feel her. Without even looking at her I knew she was dead. She was the first to die next to me. She was dead, and I had to jump down quickly and run outside because of diarrhea. I did not shout. Did not call for help. I felt neither disgust nor surprise. Angèle was there, dead. She died during the night. Lying next to me. Without my hearing anything. So, what about me? It's not possible. I'm living without being alive. I do what I must, because I must, because that's what people do. Because I have a son to raise. Don't think for a moment that I'm tempted to put an end to it all. There's nothing to put an end to. I wonder how the others do it, those who came back. You, for example. Like me I suppose. One pretends. They have the appearance of being alive. They come and go, choose, decide. They make up their mind about where to go on holiday, or the color they want for their bedroom wallpaper. To think people do such things when we had to decide every minute between living and dying. I do what one does in life, but I know very well that this isn't life, because I know the difference between before and after. Over there we had our entire past, all our memories, even memories from long ago passed on by our parents. We armed ourselves with this past for protection, erecting it between horror and us in order to stay whole, keep our true selves, our being. We kept on dipping into our past, our child-hood, into whatever formed our personality, our character, tastes, ideas, so we might recognize ourselves, preserve something of what we were, not letting this situation dent us, annihilate us. We tried to hang on to who we were. Each one of us recounted her life thousands and thousands of times, resurrecting her childhood, the time of freedom and happiness, just to make sure all this had existed, and that the teller was both subject and object. Our past was our lifeline and reassurance. But since I came back, everything I was before, all my memories from that earlier time, have dissolved, come undone. It is as though my past had been used up over there. Nothing remains of what was before. My real sister is you. My true family is you, those who were there with me. Today, my memories, my past are over there. When I project my thoughts backward they never overstep these bounds. They go knocking against this milestone. All the efforts we made to prevent our destruction, preserve our identity, keep our former being, all these efforts could only be put to use over there. When we returned, this hard kernel we had forged at the core of our hearts, believing it to be solid since it had been won through boundless striving, melted, dissolved. Nothing left. My life started over there. Before there was nothing. I no longer have what I had over there, what I had before, what I was before. Everything has been wrenched from me. What's left? Nothing. Death. When I say that I know the difference between before and after, I mean to say that before I was alive and that I have forgotten everything of that life, the life before. Presently, I am no longer alive. I can take full measure of this difference, but neither sentient knowledge, nor lucidity can be of any assistance. Nothing can fill the abyss between other people and myself, between myself and myself. Nothing can bridge this gulf, nor narrow it.

Is it because before I was young, and later I was burdened by an experience beyond my years, a weariness, an erosion? Have I ever been young? When I reached the age of being young we were at war. No, I have never been young. Silly, naive, yes. Impassioned. Impassioned by action, struggle, by the chances we were taking and their mortal stake, by the harshness of an inexorable law based on the fact that the smallest error was irreparable since you paid the price at once. I was impassioned to the point of madness. You remember, don't you? It's a story I told you already. In one of the notes I had thrown onto the tracks as we were being transported in the cattle cars, notes written to inform our parents, and which the railway men kindly mailed when they found them on the ballast, I had written, "I'm being deported. This is the greatest day of my life." I was insane, insane. The heroine crowned with her halo, the martyr going to her death singing. Undoubtedly, we needed this exaltation to maintain our clandestine way of life, pretending all along to be like everyone

else while contantly grazing death. What do I do today? I pretend to
be like everyone else, but have no hold on life. The greatest day of my
life . . . It was the last day of my life. I'm still the same age because I
haven't grown older. It is just that time has stopped moving. Time has
come to a stop. I am not time-worn. Far worse than being care-worn
is to be empty of life. Disillusionized, if one must find a word. I use
"disillusionized" when I am being logical, when I imitate the way
normal people think, those who never went over there. I don't have
the word I need. How can we not be disillusionized when after
having suffered what we suffered, sacrificed so much and held such
high hopes, we see that all of this came to naught, that we continue
waging wars, that we are threatened by still more cruel wars, that
injustice and fanaticism reign and the world must still be altered?
When I make these statements, I am using my reason. This reasoning
self is distinct and alien from my real self. I ought to be affected by the
anguish human beings do not express as they face cataclysms about to
be unleashed upon them, at least in regard to my son, who is starting
out in life and will have to do battle against the very same monsters,
the monsters we failed to destroy. I know all this but it does not touch
my deep self. How can I explain? I can't explain it any other way
except by saying: I am not alive. This superhuman will we summoned
from our depths in order to return abandoned us as soon as we came
back. Our stock was exhausted. We came back, but why? We wanted
this struggle, these deaths not to have been in vain. Isn't it awful to
think that Mounette died for nothing, that Viva died for nothing?
Did they die so that I, you, a few others might return? Our return
must therefore assume some meaning. This is why I keep on ex-
plaining what it was like, around me. I speak to my colleagues, particularly the young ones. I stop when I see they're about to cry. I notice
they're close to tears although I felt I was speaking so calmly, dispas-
sionately, in an almost flat tone. As you can see, I do tell others. Not
my husband, no. So far as he's concerned, I would like to feel he
understands. I do not expect others to understand. I want them to
know, even if they cannot feel what I feel. That's what I mean when I

say they don't understand, no one does. At the very least they must
know.

I'm not alive. I'm imprisoned in memories and repetitions. I sleep
badly but insomnia does not weigh on me. At night I have the right
not to be alive. I have the right not to pretend. I join the others then.
I am among them, one of them. Like me they're dumb and destitute.
I don't believe in life after death, I don't believe they exist in a beyond
where I join them at night. No. I see them again in their agony, as
they were before dying, as they remained within me. And when the
day rises once again, I feel sad. Isn't it awful they died harboring so
many illusions, died believing that those who'd return would burst
with joy, rediscover the taste of life. Isn't it awful they died certain liberty would triumph in the end, and that they were dying just before
witnessing its triumph? It's true liberty was found again, true to some
extent, such a puny, miserable extent. Isn't it terrible they died
believing they were dying just before witnessing the end, dying just
before the birth of a dazzling truth? Isn't it terrible? Everywhere war,
violence, fear.

When I came back—oh! I waited a few years, I was much too
tired when I returned—I wanted to have a child. When my son was
born, I was suffused with joy. I say "suffused" because it was like
being covered with a warm, caressing water rising around me, rising
within me, carrying me and making me light, happy, bathing in happiness. The son I had wished for was there, mine. A calm, benevolent
joy. I would not let myself be carried by this joy, unable to give myself
over to it. At the very same moment as this sweet, enveloping water of
joy was rising around me, my room was invaded by the ghosts of my
companions. The ghost of Mounette was saying, "Mounette died
without ever knowing this joy." Jackie's ghost stretched out useless
hands. These were the ghosts of all the young girls, all the young
women who died without knowing what it meant to be suffused by
this joy. The silky water of my joy changed to sticky mud, sooty snow,
fetid marshes. I saw again this woman—you remember this peasant
woman, lying in the snow, dead, with her dead newborn frozen

between her thighs. My son was also that newborn. I look at my son
and I recognize Jackie's eyes, Yvonne's pout, Mounette's inflection.
My son is their son, he belongs to all of them. He is the child they
will not have had. Their features are etched over his own, or merge
with his. How can one be alive amid these masses of dead women?

I wanted to have a child who would grow fearlessly into manhood.
He is seventeen. Except for some unforeseeable twist of fate, he is
bound to have a frightful future. Nor do I believe any longer in destiny's
boons. What can one do for him, for the other children? I am power-
less, unarmed, as much at a loss as the comrades who died back there.

They say spiritless people, people with no appetite for living, are
not alive. This is not what I mean to say. Obviously, I'm neither opti-
mistic nor joyful—who among us can be? Sometimes, of course, we
still experience a surge of enthusiasm, isn't that so? With all the dead
we bear in our arms, hearts, memories? I'm not despondent, bored,
occasionally I even laugh. No, it isn't that I am given to sadness or
ennui. I just don't feel myself living. My blood circulates as though it
flowed through veins outside my body. All of me is outside of me and
yet escapes from the others. Don't think that I am constantly busy
taking my pulse, observing myself. I do observe myself all the time
but without wanting to, without knowing I do. It's not like merging
from a dream when you wonder whether you're awake. It's something
else. It's as though I were split in two, one part of me is dream, the
other comes from elsewhere. I do what I must because I tell myself it
has to be done, and I look at myself doing it, yet I realize how futile it
is. My reason tells me, "Your son, your husband." If my reason didn't
tell me so, they wouldn't exist. They're not present within me, not
part of me. They're outside of me, as I am outside of myself.

I don't complain. Don't think I do. For so many, coming back was
much harder than for me. Gilberte . . . I wonder how she manages,
how she is now. Is she able to go to sleep without feeling her sister's
body against hers, can she get used to her arms empty of the weight
of the sister she carried pressed to her breast, before embracing her
once more as she lay her dead body down in the snow? And you? And

all of us who found no one when they returned, nothing to help them as they questioned their decision to survive taken over there?

I'm not alive. I look at those who are. They are vain, ignorant. Probably that's the way to be in order to live, to reach the end of one's lifespan. If they had my knowledge they'd be like me. They wouldn't be alive. I'm saying this to you becaue I can do so only to a like, because you understand. I wouldn't even need to tell you. You know. But can you explain to me why I'm not alive, why I do what all the living do withough being one of them, a stranger in their midst, forced to pretend so they'll tolerate my presence. I can't approach them barefacedly. They'd assume I feel nothing but scorn for their humdrum existence, their small worries and plans, their ephemeral passions and fleeting desires. And yet, if we struggled as we did, if we held fast, it was indeed so that human beings might in the future have only insignificant cares, cares on the human level, so they'd never be caught again in history's maelstrom, ground into dust, or borne aloft, high above themselves, so they'd never have to choose between heroism and cowardice, martyrdom and surrender, but could rediscover life with its small and great joys, an existence free of tragedy. The life we wanted to find again when we used to say, "If I return . . ." was to be large, majestic, flavorful. Isn't it our fault that the life we resumed on returning proved to be tasteless, shabby, trivial, thievish, that our hopes were mutilated, our best intentions betrayed. Despite knowing I'm not at fault, I feel guilty. I cheated our dead and betrayed my own self, my ambitions, my fits of enthusiasm. I'm ashamed of putting up with this. If Mounette had come back—and what would it have taken for her to return? She was stronger than I was. Why her and not me?—had Mounette returned, would she have accepted, made do. Would she have returned in order to do boring office work, race in the morning to catch her bus? Mounette, who used to say, "If we return, nothing will be the same"? Everything is the same. It is within us that nothing is the same. I am well aware of what is not the same within me, what is unlike what I was before and thus makes me dif-ferent from the others. This mountain of corpses between them and me. Mounette did not die so that you and I, and perhaps a few others, might preserve her idealized image. She continues to live within me, whereas the people around me today exist marginally, on the periphery of my life. She lives within me, yet I didn't do any of the things we promised each other we'd accomplish, the things we said we'd do so that nothing would ever be the same. She lives within me, but in vain. What can we do to insure Mounette's death was not for naught? Nothing. These ritual commemorations, these reassuring parodies played out for other people, who are thus given the opportunity to grieve once a year in good conscience, are of no use whatsoever. Whatever we do, it is to no avail. To live in the past is not to live. It is to cut oneself off from the living. But what shall we do to cross over to their shore, to stop remaining paralyzed on the other side? We have no way of grasping the present. I try at times to imagine what I'd be like were I like everyone else, that is, if I had not been taken over there. I don't succeed in doing so. I am other. I speak and my voice sounds like something other than a voice. My words come from outside of me. I speak and what I say is not said by me. My words must travel along a narrow path from which they must not stray for fear of reaching spheres where they'd become incomprehensible. Words do not necessarily have the same meaning. You hear them say, "I almost fell. I got scared." Do they know what fear is? Or, "I'm hungry. I must have a chocolate bar in my handbag." They say, I'm frightened, I'm hungry, I'm cold, I'm thirsty, I'm in pain, as though these words were weightless. They say, I'm going to visit friends. Friends . . . People at whose house you have dinner, or with whom you play bridge. What do they know about friendship? All their words are frivolous. All their words are false. How can you be with them when you bear only heavy, heavy words? There are images behind my eyes. When my concentration slackens, they burst forth, occupy the foreground, foist themselves on me, and I no longer see what is before me but images coming from behind my eyes. At every moment I must push them back into the storeroom or they will separate me irretrievably from all that surrounds me. I must exercise a perpetual, exhausting control. At night I'm not free. I allow them to come to the fore. They rush in. They've lost nothing of their sharp outline, their implacable preciseness. These are not nightmares, horrible, terrifying visions. I do not see piles of corpses. No, these are familiar images from daily life, the kind of daily life we had over there. A face, a mouth, eyes. All those eyes growing larger in shrinking faces, all those eyes losing their color and expression, those eyes that defy, beg, grow resigned. Or a landscape emerges, takes shape, a detail I recognize is crudely spotlighted, soon surrounded by the rest of the scene. After so many years, so many changes . . . After all that happened since. After all this I got married, had a son. Read books. I made new acquaintances, formed relationships. All those I met since I came back do not exist. They're not close to those I call mine, the real ones: our comrades. They're peripheral. They belong to another universe and nothing will allow them to enter ours. Sometimes, it seems that they're about to rejoin us. Then they utter one of these superficial words, one of their empty words, and they plunge headlong into their world, that of the living.

I'm not one of the living dead. I'm neither inert nor insensitive. Not inactive. At times I'm weary, mentally rather than physically. I feel this fatigue every instant when I must readjust myself to people, to their frivolous talk. Looking at me one would think I'm alive. I work. I take care of my home. I take an interest in what goes on in the world, what goes on in my neighborhood. I'm interested in my son's studies, in his future. Again one of these mendacious words, the future . . . He enjoys studying. He has good grades at the lycée, in fact very good grades. It's interesting, a boy of seventeen. I'm very pleased with him. I'm glad he's not attracted by money, that his plans are not centered on a brilliant career, that he doesn't care to become rich or important, is not a go-getter. He admires those who do what they do free of charge, because it's a good thing to do, because they feel like doing it. He gives me satisfaction, not joy. Joy . . . Seen from the outside, I'm one of the living among the living. My husband is nice. He's a reliable companion. He is devoted to his son, his wife. I never wonder whether he understands because I know he doesn't and

I also know from the beginning that my explanations are beyond his
ken. Could I even explain? He'd say in a quiet, reassuring voice, "I
know what you lived through. I know one doesn't return from there
without scars that bleed at the lightest touch. That's why I never raise
the subject with you. I want to help you forget. To speak about it
hurts. We must not speak if we wish to forget." You see, it's all wrong.
Those who love us wish us to forget. They don't understand it's
impossible and that, moreover, to forget would be atrocious. Not that
I cling to the past, nor have I made up my mind not to forget. Forgetting or remembering doesn't depend on our willing it, had we the
right to do so. Our loyalty to the comrades we left back there is all we
have. In any event, forgetting is out of the question. Even those of us
who believe they buried the past within their innermost secret depths,
even those who added to that past all kinds of new memories—voyages, adventures, mad flings, all sorts of things—piling them up in
order to cover the past, it will not disappear. Time will not pass. At
any moment, carried by a smell, a day from over there returns . . .
One day I feel I'm walking by the kitchens: it's because I left a potato
rotting at the bottom of my vegetable basket. At once everything sur-
faces again: the mud, the snow, the blows of the truncheons received
because walking in a certain direction was forbidden . . . Memories
borne by a taste, a color, the sound of the wind, the rain. When my
son pulls a sour face in front of his plate of food, I don't say, "If only
we had had this chop over there . . ." It would be odious to say such
things to a child, and I always acted in such a way as to prevent him
from suspecting the extent to which his mother differs from other
women. I never made this kind of remark, nevertheless it runs
through my mind every time, and each time I'm angry at myself for
harboring such thoughts, knowing all along it will always be just like
that. What would I have done had I had a poor eater for a child . . .
When you remember any of those days, don't you think it was only
yesterday, perhaps even today? "I want to help you forget, I'm doing
all I can," yes, that's what my husband thinks. He is tactful because he
thinks he knows. I never tried to make him really understand. Was

I supposed to stop living, never marry because my comrades died
without having had a husband, without having had a child? I have a
husband, I have a son. It's not unfair, it's abnormal. It seems all I've
done since I returned was to insure forgetting, when in fact, as I now
realize, it's impossible to forget. To compel forgetting while doing
what everyone else does in life, what a miscalculation! The instinct or
willpower that allowed me to return must still have had some strength
when I had just come back. Yet it was not powerful enough to give
me back to life. My husband is here. I can do nothing to help him
imagine what it was like. It's impossible, even if it took us a whole
lifetime to talk about it. So I simply don't speak about it. I never dis-
cuss it with him. For him, I'm there, active, orderly, present. He's
wrong. I'm lying to him. I'm not present. Had he been deported too
it would have been easier, I think. He'd see the veil over the pupils of
my eyes. Would we then have talked together like two sightless
people, each one possessing the inner knowledge of the other? It
might have been easier because I wouldn't have had to keep anything
back. You'll ask me why I hold back from speaking, from telling him?
It would hurt him so. He'd realize that all his caring hasn't alleviated
the pain. I'm not alive. People believe memories grow vague, are
erased by time, since nothing endures against the passage of time.
That's the difference; time does not pass over me, over us. It doesn't
erase anything, doesn't undo it. I'm not alive. I died in Auschwitz but
no one knows it.

Perhaps our expectations were enhanced
by expectation
of what we were awaiting.
Every part of us stretched
towards what we were waiting for
our hands
hard
gentle
sensitive
impatient
ready to grasp
our hearts ready to give
impatient
avid
inexhaustible
our hands and hearts
stretched towards what we were awaiting
which was not awaiting us.

Do not say they cannot hear us
they hear us
they want to understand
obstinately
meticulously
the edge of their being wishes to understand
a sensitive border at their edge
but their deepest self
their inner truth
remains remote
flees as we think we're catching it
retracts contracts escapes
do they withdraw and fall back
because they hurt
where we no longer hurt . . .

A poet promised us roses
Our way would be strewn
with roses
on our return
said he.
Roses
the road was rough and dry
when we returned
Did the poet lie?
Certainly not
Poets see the world beyond
This one's vision
was prophetic
if no roses were in sight
it was not because he erred
but on account of our plight
Moreover
why roses
we harbored no such expectations
love was all we needed
had we returned.

Poupette

Returning was hard. We should have expected it. However, least of all did we think of what would follow. From over there, returning seemed incredible, legendary, miraculous. We had held fast to the idea of returning, clutching it so hard it had become our faith. Yes, it was like a religious belief: unaccounted for, inexplicable, yet pure and simple. Our flights of imagination, which soared up to wondrous, supernatural heights whenever we envisioned crossing the barbed-wire fence, stopped right there. Beyond that barbed wire, freedom lay in wait. That was all.

Yes, I believe that coming back was hard for all the returnees. Once we were free and had resumed our daily lives we mourned as we had not done over there. The empty places were noted more keenly, we missed intensely those we lost. Why had their absence seemed less cruel over there, and so unbearable once we were free? Perhaps because over there nothing seemed real, I mean to say that everything was extraneous to our real life. As for myself, it was only when I came back that I lost my dear mother. She died while we were in jail, Mariette and I. And it is also when I returned that I really lost Mariette. I witnessed her death over there, but on returning I no longer had a sister. It was hard for everyone, but for me the return was wretched. Wretched, sordid, a pile of shabby details.

My father had remarried while I was over there. His new wife was much younger than he. They had heard of Mariette's death but had no news of me. They believed I was dead too. My return upset all the plans this woman had made. The property she coveted was a trifle: a small hotel for traveling salesmen, which my parents, starting from nothing, had succeeded in acquiring. A lifetime of work, of depriving themselves, of constant effort. I came back. There was no place for me at home. Literally. My stepmother had turned my room into an extra hotel room. Were I to reclaim my space it would mean that much less

a day, that much less a month in the till. My father was completely
subservient to his new wife. He never raised his voice to speak in my
defense, to back me up. I had to fight to get my room back. I threatened to claim the inheritance owed me from my mother's passing.
Yes, that's how far I had to go. I even consulted the notary to lend
greater weight to my threat. To fight like this when I'd become
anemic, decalcified, when I burned with fever every afternoon. I
reconquered my room but paid a high price for it. My stepmother
made my life intolerable. I didn't yield an inch. Why? I still wonder
sometimes. Over there we used to fight for life, and now I had to
fight for a place to sleep, a portion of food. Was it worth the struggle?
Was it worth it to have to come back for that, to have put so much of
myself into bringing about my return? How many times I almost gave
up, how often I said to myself it would have been better not to have
come back! How disgusted I was! When the former leader of our
Resistance group started to court me, I almost fell into his arms. He'd
give me everything I didn't have: a home, a house, tenderness,
someone to lean on. Alas! Do you have any idea how it turned out.
He was looking for a position. Except for that of hero, which,
granted, he had practiced magnificently from the age of eighteen, he
had no professional skill. To supplant my father, whose young wife
had left him when she realized I was hanging on—and I promise you
that, with my hands grown thin to the point of having become transparent, I desperately held on to life with a strength I never suspected I
could still summon upon returning—to supplant my father and be in
charge of the cash register, that's all my betrothed aspired to. Again
there were niggardly discussions, miserable accounts, expenses and
receipts flung in one another's faces, suspicions. "You're raiding the
cashbox—Where does this coat come from?—And you, this car?"
Low, foul deeds . . . Love, there was no more mention of it. To come
back from Auschwitz only to be taken in by the platitudes of a calculating moral midget, like some simple little goose . . . I was nineteen
when I got married, but that wasn't my real age. My heart was sixteen
the year I was arrested, my character that of a world-weary woman, as

aged as the planet and experienced beyond all measure. To have my husband unfaithful with the hotel help, as in some nineteenth-century novel, you must admit is laughable. It took me years, however, to be able to laugh at it. How long was I blind to these goings-on? A short time if you count in terms of love, of happiness. Time enough to have had two children.

I divorced. We'll skip the details, as shabby and sordid as the rest but with the children at stake in the bidding, the detailed accounts and the sharing out. My father died. I found myself alone in charge of my business. It wasn't what I had been dreaming of, but it was the only thing I could do to earn my living. I was still in school when I was arrested. I didn't have a modest civil service diploma to be a post office employee. Managing a hotel I knew it from birth, so to speak. But I was tired, weary of this life, of this lack of life! Over there I learned from the comrades that so many other things existed, discovered unsuspected perspectives. All those things you talked about: books, theater, painting, music, voyages . . . What schooling it had been! I would drink in your words and promised myself that if I were to return . . . On returning, I would have liked to read everything, see everything. And there I was, tied to my means of subsistence, my provincial town, conversations with traveling salesmen . . . I had no choice, I had to bring up my children. How did I ever survive twenty such years? Thanks to all of you, to books, music, all that you opened my eyes to. My disappointment upon returning was so bitter I couldn't have surmounted it had I not felt this desire to live, to know what you knew, you, the older girls, who had lived and spoken of your lives during roll call, during our long, shuffling walks to the marshes. For twenty years I kept this providential faculty which helped me get out alive from Auschwitz: to split myself in two, not to be there. You know, that's what I used to do in camp. You say it was impossible to achieve this split in two over there. I did. Passing by a pile of corpses, I saw it, of course, but I'd quickly look away; you must not look, must not see. And I succeeded in not seeing. In the same way, when I returned and my father and husband quarreled, fought, when my husband would start one of those squabbles, I'd seek refuge in a world of my making, I escaped. When everything was all set—the divorce, the inheritance—my daughters full grown, I drew up the balance sheet. You see, I still use the language of the business world. Let's see now, you're forty years old; if you want to travel, rather than spend your whole life before the key rack, you've got to make up your mind now. Soon it'll be too late. It appears that at forty you still dare start something new; by the time you're fifty you're resigned. I reached a decision: sell the hotel, leave France, try something elsewhere. I left for Puerto Rico with my daughters. They're big now, they've almost completed their studies. Why Puerto Rico? Truthfully, I don't know. I didn't know anyone there, was not particularly attracted to that island. I had simply decided to settle elsewhere, no matter where so long as it was in a warm, sunny place, by the sea, with light and vivid colors. So, here I am. I feel so good, so healthy since I'm no longer cold! The scenery here is so beautiful! I have my books, my records, but also, right under my balcony, there's this blue, transparent, warm sea . . . I know I should work hard to establish myself again. I'm resolved to do it. Next time back—yes, I plan to go back to France once a year—I hope to be able to tell you my business ventures are in good shape. At the moment, however, my plans are still sketchy. Perhaps I did something crazy . . . At least I'll have done one crazy thing in my life. Does this make sense to you: to have had the luck to survive and return from Auschwitz only to continue living as though nothing had happened?

You'd like to know
ask questions
but you don't know what questions
and don't know how to ask them
so you inquire
about simple things
hunger
fear
death
and we don't know how to answer
not with the words you use
our own words
you can't understand
so you ask simpler things
tell us for example
how a day was spent
a day goes by so slowly
you'd run out of patience listening
but if we gave you an answer
you still don't know how a day was spent
and assume we don't know how to answer.

You don't believe what we say
because
if what we say were true
we wouldn't be here to say it.
We'd have to explain
the inexplicable
explain
why Viva who was so strong
died
and I did not
why Mounette
so passionate and proud
died
and I did not
why Yvonne
the undaunted
and not Lulu
why Rosie
who was innocent and had no idea
why one lived
or died
why Rosie
and not Lucie
why Mariette
and not Poupette
her younger sister
a wisp of a girl
why Madeleine
and not Hélène
who slept by her side
why why
because everything there is inexplicable.

Back to the camp back to the ruck
after history
the everyday
after the maquis
a humdrum life.
We used to say
life will be beautiful when freedom comes
life will be bountiful once we are free
all will be simple
open and frank
we'll get everything back
once we get liberty
beauty love friendship
everything
liberty
is all we need
we'll just have to live
what could be simpler
easier
for those who know
how to suffer how to die?
To return
who among us envisioned more?
To return
is already asking for the impossible
asking for everything
could one expect more?
Returning
means getting it all back.
Returning is not all
it means return to live anew

experience the everyday
work run into debt
save to pay off the debt
sell soap
that's all one knows
go to the office
that's all one knows or does
in daily life
look for a place
that's how one lives
be on time
because at work you're to be punctual.
. . .
Stop grumbling
that's life
what did you dream of over there?
Of eating your fill
sleeping your fill
loving your fill
You dreamt of eating sleeping loving
you've got it
since you returned.
History
is over
be happy like everyone
History
is one moment in time
living
is now
So why on earth did you want to return?

Step out of history
to enter life
just try that all of you
you'll get it then.

Marie-Louise

"As you can see, I've got everything I need. I'm happy." She was
taking me on a tour of the house, pointing out certain features which
eased her household tasks—"because housekeeping must be kept to a
minimum, don't you think?"—a color in harmony with the others, a
piece of furniture she had found in her former attic and which put
the right finishing touch to this corner room. "Isn't our new house
pleasant? In a moment I'll show you the garden. No, better leave that
to Pierre. The garden is his pride and joy. This nook, here, I call my
study. I shut the door when I need to think, read, or write. After-
noons I write. Oh, I'm not a writer, don't take myself for one. I write
for my own enjoyment. You must feel the same; we need to remember,
and Pierre likes to read what I write. I've got all my books here. I read
a lot, just look. I've got to put up another shelf. I have no place for
this pile of books you see on the floor. I can't wait to see them neatly
lined up, one next to the other. Yes, they're all about deportation. I
think I've got everything that's been published. I read and reread them
frequently. There aren't many about Auschwitz. That must be why I
write. Here, you see, I have several notebooks. I pass them on to
readers. Since I can't type, Pierre made some copies. People ask for
them. My daughter's girlfriends. Oh! Pierre could write all this himself, you know. He's read all the books here, and I've told him everything. I also clip articles. There are many interesting ones. If you need
any, I can lend you some. I like being in my study. It's the most tran-
quil room of the house. All I hear is the small stream running at the
back of our garden. D'you hear it? Not that there ever is much noise.
At the end of our pine-lined walk we're at peace. Here, in my study,
no one disturbs me. People know that when I'm here they shouldn't
interfere. Yes, we're happy in our new house. The other one was all
right but it was right in town and I can no longer take any noise.
Here, we're far from the center, a ten-minute walk. Moreover, I don't

go there much. And we have the garden. Come, we're going to sit
down in the living room and have a glass of port while we wait for
Pierre. He won't be long. You'll have lunch with us, I've got a rabbit
stew. Pierre would be horrified if he missed you. He'd be really hurt
to hear you were here and didn't wait to see him. Particularly since
this is your first visit . . . Of course, we're a bit far from Paris. We
hardly ever go there. Pierre and I, we don't like to go too far from
home."

She spoke in a low, soft voice, in perfect harmony with the soft
hues of her draperies, the pale color of her dress, the gentle light
streaming through the shirred tulle of her curtains and, beyond, the
leafy boughs of a tree covering the window.

"It was nice of you to stop here with us. I'm so happy to see you
after all these years." She was pouring the port into pretty glasses.
"Santé! I drink to the joy of seeing more of you now that you know
the way here." She was sitting now, eying me with a smile. "And you,
how are you? Are you working? Did you get your job back when you
returned? I couldn't get back to it at once. You know that I was in
charge of the books of my husband's firm. But I was so weary when I
came back! Mentally more than anything else. I just couldn't keep
things straight in my mind. I kept on wondering whether I'd ever be
able to balance the figures. I did pick it up when I recovered some of
my strength, and went on with it for a few years, but now I've retired.
It's also because Pierre cut back on his work. Age . . . and the garden,
now that he has a garden. He brings the books here and we do the
accounting together. Yes, I was so weak and tired I thought I'd never
bounce back. But, little by little, things improved. I got all my powers
back again. Thanks to Pierre. If he hadn't been here to help me, I
couldn't have made the adjustment. With him by my side it was
smooth sailing but no sooner was I in the presence of other people,
even friends, everything got mixed up in my head. Unable to find the
right words, I'd start trembling, sweating. If Pierre hadn't been here, I
would have gone into hiding, given up all contact with fellow human
beings. I was halfway there already, withdrawn from everything:

people, things, events. Even my own daughter filled me with fear. She was thirteen when I came back. I rediscovered her without recognizing her. Of course she was glad to have her mama back. At her age you understand what it means. It's not like those of us who left small children back home. When they came back, the children didn't know them. With my daughter it was quite different, but she had gotten so thoroughly used to being alone with her father, having the run of the house, that she couldn't speak to me any longer. I felt she was scared of me. Of course, with the way I looked . . . You remember? No one was as scrawny as I was. When she was looking for something, the key to the cellar, or money to buy milk, she'd ask her father. For a long time, Pierre went on taking care of everything that had to do with the house. I can't tell you how he did it: he put me back in this life without my even noticing it. 'It's like teaching children to speak,' he said to me once. 'You speak, you show them how to move their lips, they imitate you, and one day they're talking.' I think it's more like teaching people to walk. I have a very nice husband, you know. Our daughter got married, but the house isn't empty. We're happy together. We're never bored. We spend evenings talking. We never stop talking about Auschwitz. My memories have become his own. So much so I have the distinct impression he was there with me. He remembers everything, better than I do. Here he comes. I can hear his car." She went out to meet him on the front steps. "Pierre, we have a visitor. Guess who. Charlotte."

"Ah! Charlotte! I'm so happy to see you at last. I didn't say 'make your acquaintance'; I've known you a long time."

"You know one another quite well. I also spoke of you to Charlotte, over there, didn't I?"

"Yes, indeed, we know each other."

"Then you must kiss, like old friends."

He was just as I had imagined him from what his wife had said. A bit older, with a melancholy look he probably did not have back then when she spoke of him to me.

"It's nice you've come to see us. You'll stay a few days, won't you? We'd be so happy to chat at leisure."

"I'll leave both of you for a moment. I'm going to set the table. Everything is ready. Toast Charlotte, Pierre. Your glass is over there."

"So Charlotte, how are you? Still a true Parisian, always going to the theater? My wife is very good at portraits. I'd have recognized you right away. Did you resume your former occupations? It wasn't too hard at first? Marie-Louise found it very hard at the beginning. I wondered whether she'd ever find her footing again, particularly one day, when I saw her pick up wilted cabbage leaves which had fallen out of a vegetable hamper at the greengrocer's. I began to doubt she'd ever be normal. She'd wake up in the middle of the night, jump out of bed, thinking it was morning. I'd do the same so she wouldn't feel too lost in the house with everyone asleep. She got over the cabbage leaves bit quite quickly. She just went on staring at them with regret. I watched her take a head of lettuce apart, examining every leaf to make full use of the large outer ones. As to the waking up, that took longer. In fact, we never got back to rising at our former time. It doesn't bother me, quite the reverse. In the summer, there's always something to do in the garden early in the morning. I spray the rose-bushes, water the tomatoes, while she makes coffee. In the winter, I have the cellar. There also there's something to do. As to Marie-Louise, by getting up early she gets rid of all the household chores in the morning and then has the whole afternoon to herself. She reads, writes, answers letters. It's like what happened with coffee. When she came back, she no longer enjoyed coffee. So I began by making her some chicory. Little by little, I mixed chicory with real coffee, always a little more, and she recaptured her love for coffee. It would have been a pity. She'd enjoyed coffee so much before."

Marie-Louise chimed in from the dining room, raising her soft voice ever so slightly: "Don't tell Charlotte I used to eat rotten leaves."

"You didn't eat them, but if I hadn't held you back . . ."

"I was so ravenously hungry when I returned I'd have eaten anything."

"She couldn't bear to see a crumb left by her daughter on the table. The poor little thing was taken aback because here we hadn't suffered that much from rationing during the occupation. We'd been deprived of almost nothing; sugar, but then we had honey. The countryside is rich and we were well known here. Everyone brought us supplies. Nor was I ever short of what to put in the parcels I mailed to the camp."

Marie-Louise came back to join us: "As soon as we were allowed to write, that is, as soon as he had my address, he sent me a parcel each week. A ten-kilo parcel. I could almost have done without the camp soup and the bread ration. Do you remember the taste of that bread? The taste of horse chestnuts, don't you think? I got all the parcels, at least all those he sent to Auschwitz. After that, at Ravensbrück . . . And you can't imagine how he thought of everything. He'd always stick in one or two handkerchiefs to steady a can, wrap up a cookie. He thought of everything, even of writing messages on the bottom part of cardboard containers."

"Yes, I wrote on the container's bottom—with a very fine pencil, holding it lightly, so that one couldn't see it by looking at the outside . . .—and I glued a round piece of paper over the outside which adhered only to the rim."

"When they inspected the parcels, they never thought of turning the cardboard containers upside down and ungluing the round pieces of paper. It was so skillfully done. No puffiness of any sort. I was rather proud of myself for discovering this ruse. But you know what we did with parcels, over there? . . . Nothing escaped us. We'd take a wrapper apart with a clockmaker's precision."

"The last parcel I sent to Auschwitz came back with a large black rubber stamp, 'Return to sender,' in German of course. This is how I learned you had been transferred to another camp."

"You weren't afraid Marie-Louise might have died?"

"No. It crossed my mind, but that's all. At that time we didn't know anything about the camps."

"Pierre, go get a bottle from the cellar. Some Bordeaux. I made a stew from the rabbit Christine brought yesterday."

"My Burgundy wouldn't be bad with the stew. The Chambertin. But if you prefer Bordeaux."

"Just as you say, but I believe in Paris a good Bordeaux is much sought after."

Pierre went out. "What do you think of my husband? Isn't he exactly the way I described him? He had all the patience in the world with me, helping me get back on my feet. When I came back, I couldn't do anything any longer. I was scared of everything, of going to the post office, to market. As soon as I had to speak to someone I'd start shuddering, shaking. Pierre stayed by my side, never left me for a moment. Gradually, he drew back. Just as you act with children who are learning to walk, as I told you earlier. You let them go but squat in front of them, with your arms wide open. Gradually, you take a step back, still keeping your arms wide open. And when you see that they're standing on their own two feet, you wait for them at the other end of the room, letting them come to you by themselves. That's what Pierre did with me. When I'd reach the post office window or stand in front of a shopkeeper, he'd move back just a bit. As soon as he let go of my arm I felt I was drowning, so he'd take a step closer, speak in my place. Later still, he let me manage on my own while standing by, ready if needed. You can't imagine how wonderful he's been."

Pierre came up from the cellar, "Here's your Bordeaux. I hope Charlotte will like it."

The hors d'oeuvres were alluring, the stew delicious.

"If only you had had something like this in Auschwitz! Your health, Charlotte! Come visit us soon."

"Next time, drop me a line. I'll prepare something more delicate, more original, a local specialty."

"One of the recipes you gave her in Auschwitz . . . You could have served your paté."

"I considered it, but then I thought stuffed neck was more exceptional for a Parisian."

"Marie-Louise, I must ask you something. The other day a young woman called on me. I don't know how she got my address, nor who sent her to see me; someone from our group, to be sure. She found out I'd been in the same convoy as her mother and she wanted me to tell her about her mother. Unfortunately I wasn't able to tell her anything. I never knew her mother. At any rate I didn't remember her, not even her name. I asked Mado, who has the best memory of anyone in our group. She doesn't remember either."

"How's Mado?" Pierre inquired. "What became of her?"

"She got married."

"Yes, we know that, and she had only one son? How old is he now?"

"Seventeen."

"Oh, I'm so glad for her."

"What was the name of the young woman's mother?" asked Marie-Louise.

"Mathilde. Did you know her?"

"Mathilde? From Britanny?" Pierre said at once. "That's the one who had a daughter the same age as Christine and whose bed was next to yours at Romainville? It's with her you planned to exchange daughters during the summer holidays. Hers would have come to the country while ours would have visited Paris. She lived near the Place Clichy, I think."

"Yes, that's the one," said Marie-Louise. "What was her daughter's name?"

"Monique," Pierre said. "She was a year older than ours. She must be thirty-eight today. How is she? It must have been dreadful for her not to see her mother again. But why did she wait all this time to seek information? She could have published a message in our bulletin. We'd have written her. Does she still have her father?"

"Yes, he married again," I said.

"Oh!" Pierre exclaimed.

"Pierre wouldn't have remarried if I hadn't come back."

"Darling . . . Since she'd like to have us speak of her mother, you ought to write her. Charlotte, you'll give us her address. Let her come to see us. Unfortunately you won't be able to tell her anything about her mother's disappearance since you lost sight of her in Birkenau."

Marie-Louise was smiling, pleased. "I told you Pierre is informed about everything. He remembers better than I do. You can speak to him about any of the women in the convoy, he'd know who she was."

"Yes, Pierre said, I know all of you. And when I saw Birkenau . . ."

"You went to Birkenau?"

"Certainly, with Marie-Louise, a few years ago. It was one of our first pilgrimages. Marie-Louise had described so well the blocks, the marshes, the place where you lined up for roll call, the sentry box at the entrance, every detail, that I recognized the site at once: the place where you endured the endless roll call in front of block 25, ten days after your arrival, the field where you remained standing in the snow a whole day, the mad race you were made to run in which Madame Brabander and Alice Viterbo were caught. The flower bed at the entrance gate you had to make on a Sunday, your aprons filled with earth scooped out from the ditch by male prisoners positioned between that ditch and the barbed-wire enclosure, has all but disappeared, grown over with weeds. They should have preserved it, kept it up. Marie-Louise could not recall the place of her bunk in block 26."

"You know, the block looks so different empty, and with the roof half caved in there's light inside. Then again, it was summer. With the sunshine . . ."

"She no longer knew whether she was on the right or left side. At any rate, it was in the second bay, since you were able to see the courtyard of block 25 from your spot."

"It was on the right, in the second bay," I said. I happened to remember.

"You see, I was right. When you explained to me you could see the courtyard of block 25 but not the door, I told you it must be on the right. I took photos. If you wish, I'll show them to you after lunch. I also went to the marsh. There's a small bus now that takes visitors there, but I preferred to go on foot. Naturally, it couldn't be the same. The weather was beautiful, and I had good shoes. But as I thought of the snow, your clogs, the dogs, the wind, your state of fatigue, I could almost re-create it in my mind. Marie-Louise still wonders how she was able to drag herself there sick with typhus. Fortunately you were with her, giving her your arm to lean on."

"We all gave an arm to one another," I said.

"Of course. I saw more than you did when you were there: the crematoria, the gas chambers, the wall below against which the men were shot. We visited everything. You didn't go back, did you Charlotte?"

"No. I didn't have the heart to."

"I understand. For me it was different. I was going with Marie-Louise. Charlotte, shall I give you a bit more stew. I believe you liked it. How are Lulu and Carmen? We see the ones from this area whenever there's a commemoration."

"We don't go out much," said Marie-Louise. "We like being home together, the two of us, but we attend all the ceremonies. First because it's a duty, and also because we're always glad to see our comrades again."

"We quite frequently see those from here, but not the ones from Paris or Marseilles . . . We found out that Carmen got married when she came back and had three children. Do you see them often, Lulu and her? We'd love to see them again, receive them here. Tell them to come and bring Cécile. What a trio they made! They had guts, those three. We'd be happy to have them here. Isn't that so, Marie-Louise?"

The meal was about over. "Pierre is going to make us coffee," Marie-Louise said. "He always makes the coffee. Let's go to the living room. We'll be more comfortable to go on chatting. You really don't want to stay, at least overnight? You'd see Christine. She comes every day after school. She's a schoolteacher. Did you know that? She's heard me speak of you so often she's dying to meet you."

"No, not this time. I can't stay. Forgive me."

"You'll come back. Do come back before winter, we'll take you for a walk in the woods. The forest here is very lovely, with the tall beech trees."

We drank the coffee.

"Charlotte can't stay overnight," said Marie-Louise.

"That's a pity," Pierre said. "You'd have taken her for a walk in the woods, shown her where you were arrested. Deep in the forest."

"She'll come back," Marie-Louise said. "It's a promise."

"Charlotte, you know that this is your home, here with us, with your comrades," Pierre said.

I left them standing on the threshold of their pretty house at the end of a cool, shady walk lined with pine trees.

Ida

I didn't know anyone in the train. I'd been in Drancy only three days when we left. I hadn't had time to get to know anyone. They put me in a dormitory for women and children. No one paid the least attention to me. No one spoke to me. No one asked me where I was coming from, who I was, how I got there. People weren't a bit curious, probably because they were too preoccupied, too worried to take the slightest interest in anyone else. I was there all alone. I stayed in my corner without making any noise, careful to be unobtrusive. I heard their conversations, their apprehensions and their appraisals of our situation. I was there in my corner, serious, careful to behave like a grown-up. When they assembled us for inspection, almost the whole dormitory was called. The women were crying, wiping their eyes with the back of their hand before leaning over the children to calm them down, and tell them gently to keep quiet. "Be good, Mama's right here. Stay close to Mama. You mustn't get lost." Their wise counsels were addressed to themselves. They were a bundle of nerves. The children did not seem surprised. They had gotten used to not being at home, to have broken with their habits, with discipline. Some women were bustling about, trying to warn their husbands who were on the men's side of the camp. Was he leaving too? They were afraid of being separated. When they saw their husbands among the men assembled for departure, they felt reassured.

When they ordered us to fall into formation in order to proceed to the train, everyone looked haggard and edgy. The women with children tried to get a grip on themselves. Not one of them said a word to me, or gave me a passing glance. I wasn't a member of their family. They had their hands full taking care of their own, particularly those who had several children. I was alone and almost proud of it; I was considered an adult. My meekness didn't come from fear. I only wished to go unnoticed, and not to attract trouble. I was always in my place at every

given moment, always quickly obeying orders. Forward! Right!
Left!

The cattle cars, their doors wide open, stood on the tracks. Bunches
of people were pushed in together, with the men herded in the head
cars. As they climbed in, they cranked their necks to have one last
look at their wives and children waiting for their turn. The women
and children stayed together. When the car I was in was full, the doors
were pushed shut, sliding shakily in their grooves. The sound of heavy
iron being struck. With the doors tightly sealed, we were in the dark.
The cries on the platform died down. I found myself seated on the
floor, among women I had hardly noticed during the three days I had
spent in the dormitory. The mothers gathered the straw littering the
car to make a bed for their children. The resourceful ones settled in
corners. We let the old women sit against the walls; it was more comfortable. Since I was among the last to climb in, I was stuck with a
place in the middle, next to the corrugated iron bucket which was to
be our toilet. I was bound to be disturbed frequently. I settled myself
down quietly. I folded my coat carefully, spread my old raincoat under
me so as not to get dirty, and I put my small bundle in the raincoat's
collar to make a pillow for my head. Alice had made me take my good
coat, because of the cold, and my old raincoat to make sparing use of
the coat. I had no idea of the length of the trip. Neither did the others.
I settled down for the trip which was bound to be very long, given
the best of conditions. No one bothered with me. I had to look out
for myself by myself.

The cars waited a long time. Gradually our eyes got used to the
semidarkness. I kept wondering how many people were herded
together in our car, but I never succeeded in making an exact count.
On the one hand, it was too dark to make out who was there, and on
the other, many women huddled beneath piles of clothing which I
confused with bundles. We were squeezed tightly together. The
mothers choked back their tears, clearing their throats as though they
were sore; women who had no children cried soundlessly, bitterly.
The aged were silent, dazed. All of them formed groups, sharing their

blankets, rolling up clothing to use as pillows. They had spent weeks together in the dormitory, they knew each other. For me, the trip was not frightening. On the contrary, I was glad not to have wasted time in Drancy. I couldn't wait to be with mama. I was certain of being reunited with her. Consequently, the unpleasantness of the trip, the lack of comfort, was a matter of complete indifference to me.

The train started. Children began to cry. Their mothers rocked them to sleep. The women started to talk, deploring what was happening. All were frightened. And when they expressed their fears as to what was lying in wait, they predicted frightful things without thinking that perhaps all the children might not be asleep, and without sparing me, which strengthened my pride. They did not take me for a child. I was only fourteen but wouldn't admit to this age. I wanted to be considered an adult.

With the train on its way, women drew pads and pencils from their bags. They tore off pages from the pads, gave some to those who didn't have any paper, and most of them scribbled notes, folding them carefully so as to be able to slip them through the cracks in the doors. Some had no one to write to. Others gave them addresses of people they could trust. All of this accompanied by complicated explanations, encouragements and doubts. No one asked me if I wanted a piece of paper. I didn't need it. My father was in hiding. I thought I knew where, but his residence had to remain secret. He would find out soon enough from my nurse that I was gone. I'd left my father behind to join Mama. I was happy. I imagined her joy when she'd see me, the comfort it would bring her. Alice, my nurse, had given me a food parcel for the trip: bacon, a pâté made from the rabbit she cooked on the eve of my departure, a pot of salt butter, the jam we made together the previous fall, the confit. During the three days in Drancy I had not touched these provisions. Nor did I do so in the train. I was keeping it all for Mama. Mama, who had already spent six months there, was bound to need them. Judging by Drancy, the food would be neither good nor plentiful. During the trip, I made do with half a roll of bread and the paper-wrapped salami they distributed before departure.

The train was moving. Around me they were whispering, sobbing, dozing. Children whimpered. I was thinking of Mama. How would I find her there? Her beautiful golden hair, her soft skin. I wanted to kiss her, rub my cheek against hers a long, long time, play with her fingers, her rings. No, they must have taken her rings. I had learned from a letter from father that Mama had been arrested. I never doubted they'd put all of us in the same place. This meant I'd be seeing Mama soon. I couldn't wait to get there. I wasn't so stupid as to believe that Mama was there on holiday. They must have made her work hard. Perhaps she was caring for the sick. Mama could do everything and, brave as she was, she'd endure all of it, so that soon we'd be reunited at home. The war would end soon. Even Alice, who never bought a newspaper nor had a radio in the house, said so. From our village in Poitou, the war seemed very far away. We were far away from the road. I'd never seen any Germans. Working hard, feeling cold and never eating your fill, that's how I imagined Mama's life. My small parcel would cheer her up, and the butter would build up her strength. I had also packed carefully the two thick pullovers I knitted while watching my nurse's goats. Poor Alice, how she wept as she tried to figure out what to put into my parcel. Between sniffles she proferred advice: "Be reasonable, Ida. Take good care of yourself. Try not to catch cold. I'm putting in a warm pair of woolen socks." Tears ran down her wrinkled cheeks onto her old, wrinkled hands. At the time, I hadn't noticed them. Alice wasn't that old. She must have been Mama's age, or, if she was older, it couldn't be much. Mamma was so beautiful, so elegant. "You understand I can't keep you any longer, Ida. You've got to leave. They said they'll take Emile if you don't. Go. You'll be back soon." And she broke into tears again. I listened to her without feeling anger, but I was thinking, "How cowardly you are, Alice. All Emile would have to do is go into hiding too. You know so many farms where he'd find shelter. Vendée would be far enough. You don't know what's going to happen to me where they're sending me. I don't either, but they say it's terrible over there." Then all my fears vanished. I was filled with joy: I'll be with Mama again. I hadn't thought about it earlier. How stupid I was. Alice was sobbing but also trying to talk: "We can't do anything else, Ida. You understand, don't you?" as she took apart tangled bits of string to tie up her parcel. It was finished now, and her sobs grew less frequent. "Fortunately I've kept bits of string. You can't get string now. You see, Ida, you've got to hang on to everything."

When the police forced us to report to them and start wearing the yellow star, my parents sent me to the country. They looked for a place where no one would know who I was, where I could go to school and also have better food than in Paris. They had first investigated the Free Zone but, when they found out that people were being arrested by German patrols as they crossed the demarcation line, they decided it was advisable not to run this risk. They found Alice and Emile in a tiny village in Poitou. Emile worked as a day laborer. They owned a few goats, which grazed along the roads and on the edge of fields. They also cultivated a tiny garden, using every bit of it. They were poor; a lodger whose parents could pay them regularly would help balance their meager budget. My mother took me to Alice. Before parting from me, she instructed me to go to mass like the other children, and study hard in school. She'd come back for me soon, with papa, and we'd go together for a seaside holiday, some pretty beach with fine sand and lovely shells. Mama had left instructions with Alice about church and school. I was sad walking Mama to the motor coach, but I smiled bravely to show I understood the situation. I was barely thirteen, but I believe I did understand.

Alice's house was one of the last at the village edge, together with those of other poor people. I felt at home there. Alice and Emile were basically kind people. They were fond of me. And I, well, I discovered the countryside, flowers, animals. I watched the goats, walking with them along the road, knitting at the same time, like the peasant women. Mama sent me some wool she had kept from before the war. She also sent me pocket money. I didn't spend it, keeping it to send her food parcels: butter, bacon, eggs, all the things one could pick up from the neighboring farms. I used to go regularly to the railway station—it wasn't very far, eight kilometers, and papa bought me a bicycle—to register the parcel for Mama. The two railway employees knew me. "How are you, Ida? You're sure you made a strong package?" They always had a kind word for me. I didn't have papa's address, but in each of her letters Mama wrote he was well and sent me a big hug and kiss.

After the summer holidays I started in school. The teacher was very nice. I liked her a lot. Sometimes she patted my cheek saying, "My little Ida, how reasonable you are for your age! In your situation, I understand, but it's when you're still a child that you must have fun." She looked at me affectionately, but also a bit sadly, I thought. I worked well in school. Each compliment from my teacher filled me with happiness. "You ought to go to the lycée," the teacher said. "If you'd like, I can arrange it with one of my colleagues, at T. You could board with her and go on with your studies. It would be a pity not to go on with them. Here, you're losing a year." I'd been thinking of going to the lycée. Mama and Papa had decided that I should do it after my *certificat d'études*. For the time being, however, it would be unwise to leave the village for town, mother wrote in a letter. In the village I'd become one of them, and the children played with me without inquiring why I was there. I was completely at home with them. My given name sounded foreign. Other girls were called Suzanne, Yvonne, Simone. When I realized this it was too late to change. The whole village knew Ida and liked me. The mayor, an old peasant, was like a grandfather to me. Sometimes he'd stop in the house, and I caught him in conversation with Alice. I heard him say once, "So long as I'm here no one will touch Ida. You don't have any-thing to be afraid of, Alice." It had worried me. I didn't write this to Mama but I spoke to the teacher. "Look out, dear Ida. If you feel the slightest danger, run through the fields to the county seat. Go straight to the school. The headmistress is a friend of mine, she'll hide you. I'll warn her this very evening since, as it happens, we're having dinner together."

One day, I received an unsigned card coming from a city I didn't know. It was Papa's writing. Mama had been taken away, no one knew where. He added, "Be good, go on with your studies in school." There was also a message for Alice, specifying that she would receive a monthly money order for my keep, just as in the past. There was a postscript: "Stop sending parcels since Mama is not there." So, the Germans had taken Mama. I cried. I was crying as I walked with my goats. I told them all my sorrows. I told them how beautiful Mama was, how much she loved me, how sad I was she was gone. Did you ever notice that goats have melancholy eyes? You can really imagine they understand when you're speaking to them.

It was during the summer. Autumn came, then the cold. At long intervals I'd receive a card giving me news of Papa. Why didn't he ever mention Mama? Since her departure—and I was counting the weeks and the months—she could well have written. Then I figured out that Mama didn't write so they wouldn't know where I was. Papa writes but he posts his cards from all kinds of places, and there's never an address.

One day, toward the end of winter, the old mayor dropped by Alice's. I was just coming back from school, and I was scraping my sabots clean on a stone, right under the kitchen window. It had rained all day, a cold day, and my sabots were weighed down by lumps of mud. I was carefully knocking my sabots against the stone, under the kitchen window, when I recognized the mayor's voice. I huddled under the window to hear what he was saying. He spoke loudly because Alice was a bit deaf. Judging by their voices they were discussing something serious. "I could feel safe for Ida so long as we had Bertrand at the gendarmerie, but he's just been transferred. The new captain looks like a double dealer who wants to make sure he's on the good side of the powers that be. I don't know what advice to give you, Alice. Perhaps, if it's not too late, we might send her back to her parents, let them look for a safe place."

"That's impossible. Her mother was arrested and her father sends me money but always without a return address. Where could she go, the poor child?"

The old gentleman was puzzled. I reached a decision. Say good-bye to Alice and, taking shortcuts, run to the headmistress of the district school. The mayor was on his way out. I greeted him as though I had just arrived. He kissed me. My worst fears were confirmed. I had to leave. I began to pack my things. "I'm leaving, Alice. I'm sorry I can't tell you where I'm going. I think I must run without losing an instant. Don't worry about me. I'll manage. I know where I can go." I put my things into a bag as I was speaking.

"Wait, Ida. Don't go yet. You can't go in this kind of weather. The mayor didn't say the hounds are loose yet."

I unpacked my things, scolding myself for losing my head. The following day, at midnight, the whole house was awakened by the gendarmes' arrival. When I heard the car stopping at the door I already knew. Alice, bursting into tears, was standing by my bed telling me that the gendarmes had come to take me away. There were three of them. Three men to arrest a girl of fourteen. It must have been to bolster each other's spirits. I leaped out of bed, ready to jump through a back window into the courtyard or flee through the fruit shed at the back of the garden, cutting through the grove.

"You can't leave, Ida. You can't. The captain said if he couldn't find you he'd take Emile."

I could no longer leave. To have Emile taken in my place was unthinkable. Alice got busy preparing food for my journey, happy of having made a pâté the day before. The three gendarmes were waiting for me, standing in the kitchen. They didn't rush us. I kissed Alice, who got my face wet with her tears, and I also kissed the mustache of Emile, who had also gotten out of bed. I picked up my bundle. On our way. First Drancy, and now this cattle car.

During the trip I had no regrets. I didn't regret having given into Alice's cowardice. I was happy at the prospect of seeing Mama. The others, with their fears and lamentations, irritated me.

On arrival—no one knew that it was Auschwitz we had reached; had we known, it would not have increased our fears since this name didn't mean anything to any of us—on arrival, I was on the lookout, observing everything, trying to grasp the commands that were shouted from every corner, holding myself straight with my small bundle, my scarf neatly tied under my chin, and staying aware of what was happening. I understood some German thanks to Yiddish, which I had learned at home. When an officer—he wore epaulettes and a flat, visored cap—shouted to the women with children to line up in front of him, "All the children, here," I did not move. I stayed at the end of my row. I wasn't a child. Separating women and children from the rest did not inspire confidence in me. Don't ask me why. After all, I didn't know anything. Who did at the time? I was tall, well developed, I could have been taken for a seventeen or eighteen year old, not a girl of fourteen. I found myself in the right column and entered the camp.

I hadn't struck up any friendships during the trip. The other women thought only of themselves or were on their guard. Once in the camp, I found myself utterly isolated. Don't think I felt lost. I was looking for Mama everywhere. I'd find it difficult to explain to you how I managed. I made friends, everyone helped me. As you can imagine, I didn't find Mama. I had to give up Alice's food parcel at the entrance, the one I had kept for Mama. It was intact, and I swallowed back my tears when a German woman tore it out of my hands. At that time I was still hoping to find Mama. What a pity, all these pots of pear jam, from pears I picked myself in the mayor's orchard. He always let me take all I wanted. In the camp, we learned things little by little. And yet, it didn't take long for me to realize I'd never see Mama again.

After a few weeks in Birkenau, I was sent to Buna, the rubber factory. It was painful, we worked long days, but it was still more bearable than Birkenau. We could wash, the soup was better, and roll calls were shorter. We weren't punished too often—I mean major punishments, because when it came to cuffs, they were dealt out all day. One day, in a column of men walking in the direction of the factory, I recognized my father. How he had changed! Old, thin, dressed in tatters. He who had always been well dressed . . . You can imagine, he was a tailor. I shouted, "Papa! Papa! It's Ida! Ida!" The others held me back from running to him. At the sound of my name, he turned around and threw a frightened look in my direction. The column went on walking. My father did not recognize me among the others.

Papa never came back. When I returned I no longer had my camp comrades. Each one had returned to her home. I had no relatives left; everyone had been taken. They all died over there. I was taken in by a friend of the family, who got me to work with her in the garment industry. I would have liked to pursue my studies, but this poor woman didn't have the means to keep me. I learned too late I could have gotten a scholarship from the Jewish community. My parents had never been religious and I never thought of going to see a rabbi. When I think of my teacher, who wanted me to continue! Now it doesn't matter. I'll go back to school with Sophie.

When I met Charles I was twenty. He also worked in the garment trade. He had not been deported, and I thought that it was better this way. He was both deeply moved and horrified at the thought that I had been in Auschwitz. We got married. The beginnings were hard. Neither one of us had anything. You've got to make many coats to earn your food and lodging, to settle in. We didn't want any children before becoming established, having a position, paying off our debts. Friends of Charles helped us find a small place and purchase sewing machines. After a few years, we got a decent apartment. It's not bad here, don't you think? Sophie was born. We were wild with joy. "Isn't she pretty? She's so delicate!" Well, you know, silly like all doting parents. It's true she was cute, our Sophie. She already had her large, dark eyes and finely etched eyebrows. And then I don't know what happened to me. One day, just when everything was going well—Sophie was a beautiful baby, Charles had work—one day I was seized with an insurmountable anguish. My throat was choking, an iron hoop was crushing my chest, my heart was smothering me. I let out shrieks of terror. It was the middle of the night. The doctor tried unsuccessfully to get me to sleep. They took me to a clinic. Charles took care of Sophie. Since we had the workroom in the apartment, he was able to do this without undue complications. He placed the crib in a room that opened onto the workspace, leaving the door ajar so as to keep

an eye out for the baby; he prepared the bottles, changed and dia-
pered Sophie at the regular time. He did it very well. The concierge
came up to watch Sophie when he had to make a delivery or go to
visit me at the clinic. I was given tranquilizers to make me sleep. I'd
fall asleep, wake up, then fall back into a strange kind of sleep. I felt I
was two people. When I came to my senses, I was amazed; "Why am
I here? What am I doing here? I'm locked in. I'm being kept in con-
finement, shut up." I was scared. Could I wait and not seize the opportunity? No! I had to flee. Quickly. My mind was made up in the blink
of an eye. I slipped into my robe and jumped out the window. It's a
miracle I didn't kill myself. You can kill yourself even jumping from
the second floor. A small glass roof deadened my fall. I got away with
five fractures, the pelvis being the worst one, and a year in the hospital.
The doctors thought I'd tried to commit suicide. I didn't succeed in
persuading them they were wrong. All I had wanted was to run away.
Anyway, it's difficult to explain. I was double and unable to meld the
two parts of me into one. There was a ghost inside me wanting to adhere
to its double yet unable to do so. I could see it approach like some soft
shape which I recognized as being me, but no sooner was it next to
me than it came apart in shreds if I tried touching it. They cured me.

When I came back home, Sophie was toddling through the apartment. She was already a little girl and Charles dressed her as such.
He was so happy to make his daughter's clothes. A real doll! She was
growing prettier, cuter all the time. I resumed my activities at home. I
was cured. I assumed I was, but probably I wasn't. There are times
when I feel fine, very very well. I'm happy. And all of a sudden, without knowing why and how, why at that moment rather than another,
without the least forewarning, I feel the same anxiety rise in me, the
one I experienced shortly after Sophie's birth. I try to fight it off. In
vain. Everything becomes a burden, the least bit of work, the least
thing I must do, washing the dishes, making the bed, sewing on a
button. I'm drained. It's as though, suddenly, a spring broke within
me. Charles calls the doctor and I have to go back to the clinic. I stay
there a few days, sometimes longer, a week, two weeks. Oh, it doesn't

happen too often. Hardly more than once a year. I don't understand. You know, I don't often think of the camp. When I came back, I was afraid of having nightmares. I had some at first, now never. I often see friends from the camp. We have so much to say to one another . . . Children, plans. Imagine, some of them are about to give their children in marriage. Time passes so quickly, it's incredible. Happily, time passes. It seems to me that I've forgotten all of it. I've only kept very tender memories of Mama: her voice, her hair, her skin. Today, Mama is younger than I am. It's extraordinary when you think of it: to have a mother younger than yourself. My father . . . He's disappeared. So then, these feeling of anxiety that assail me when I least expect it, this ghost which detaches itself from me and wants to assume its place . . . I don't understand.

When I came back, I went to see Alice. I didn't hold what she had done against her, poor soul. She was happy to see me. "I knew you'd come back, Ida. I prayed for you, you know." Emile had died. "He did see the end of the war, poor man." If he had run off with me, gone into hiding . . . I went back again with Charles after our marriage, and also several times for holidays with Sophie. I showed Sophie the places where I used to take my goats. Alice no longer had goats, she wasn't up to taking care of them—you've got to do a lot of walking with goats, and her legs were bad. She did some day labor for some neighboring farmers. Sophie marveled at the thought that each of my goats had a name, and that they came when I called them. I showed her my school. My nice teacher was no longer in the area. She's headmistress of the Saint-Loup lycée. Her husband was killed in the Resistance. He was in the maquis, but no one suspected it in the village. That's why she could easily have found a hiding place for Emile and me. Now we won't be going to Alice for the holidays any longer. Last year, one winter evening, she hanged herself in her kitchen. Winters are sad in the country.

A Year and a Day

How long this first year lasted. It seemed endless, the first year of our return. How restlessly I awaited its conclusion . . . I thought it would never end. I wanted to reach the day on which I'd no longer say, A year ago, at this time. A year ago, at this hour, we were lined up for roll call. A year ago, at this hour, we were on our way to the kitchen to fetch the jerrycans of soup. A year ago, at this time, how cold it was, how cold I felt. A year ago, at this time, we were digging coal. Tears and sweat ran black down my cheeks, yet I didn't have the tiniest piece of rag to use as a handkerchief. I couldn't wash, change my underwear, make my bed, eat, make the smallest gesture, without finding its counterpart in something I'd been doing the previous year. I envisioned my life as nothing more than a filigreed design or a watermark. I could not tell whether I was the etching on the paper or the pale design you see under it when you raise it to the light. I'd say to myself, When a year will have passed, I shall no longer say, Last year at this time . . . Finally it happened on the day when I was able to state, A year ago, at this very hour, we arrived at the Bourget. I felt at that moment I had reentered my true life.

Loulou

Loulou's been found. Yes, found. Where? You'll never guess. To think we found him eight days before the day we set for our reunion, it's extraordinary. No, he wasn't in jail. Let me tell you. I'll make it short, because I'd never finish if I were to give you a detailed account—the steps, the inquiries, the investigations, even announcements in the "Personals" columns. We began by questioning all the tenants in the building, then the local tradespeople, because I remembered the number of his apartment house on the rue Rambuteau. All in vain. No one knew anything. We'll tell you all next week, point by point, when there'll be seven of us at the table for the choucroute. To feel like having a choucroute on a Third of July, that's a craving of the starving, a desire of twenty years ago. And then we'll set up our next reunion in twenty years' time, before parting, each one going his way . . . You'll never guess where we found him. I say "we" because Lucien tried even harder than I did. He's stubborn, Lucien. You won't guess. In an insane asylum. In a psychiatric hospital, if you prefer. Don't worry, he's not crazy. He has all his wits about him. A little strange, perhaps . . . Of course, after twenty years with the crazies he's a bit peculiar. He never stepped outside for twenty years, not even for a little walk. Strange, it's not quite that, but I should say outside the ordinary, outside the present, outside life. He knows very well how he got to this establishment, this asylum. It's in the suburbs. He told us very clearly, without any gaps. He remembers everything. The only thing he doesn't know is how long it's been.

When we returned on June 3, 1945, once the formal procedures were over, the checking, the papers, each one went his way. No one was waiting for Loulou. He went straight to the rue Rambuteau. Nobody. He asked the neighbors. His father, mother, sister had been taken away. Their apartment had been assigned to people he did not know, people who had lost everything in the Brest air raids and been moved at the time of the Liberation to this requisitioned lodging. Naturally, the furniture, the clothing had been carried off. Poor kid. Eighteen, no, nineteen when he came back. He made the rounds of the neighborhood, looking for relatives, friends. Nobody. They had either moved so as not to be caught, or had been deported. Poor Loulou found himself all alone, with his gratuity, a cake of soap, and the civilian suit he was given as a discharged serviceman. He took a hotel room near his home to wait, and went every day to the rest center. He stayed there, leaning on the fences from morning till evening, looking at those who were coming back, asking questions, hoping to recognize one of his own, or at least to have news. After July 3, after we got back, the arrivals became scarce. He had left his particulars with his neighbors on the rue Rambuteau so they'd be able to send word in case someone returned home. He waited and waited. Nothing. Nobody. After a while he ran out of money to pay for his room. He found himself out on the street. He was exhausted, had no idea of what to do next. He slept on benches, and one morning—he remembers clearly it was the Place de la République—he was roused by two policemen. He jumped up, showed his camp number tattooed on his arm, his returnee card. The policemen were understanding. They took him to the police station, but without manhandling him. Seeing Loulou in that state—unshaven, unwashed, with the way he looked coming back . . . you remember? He was the one who looked like a living skeleton; now he's fat; it's a shock to recognize a kid of nineteen year old in a man of forty—the chief of police had him escorted to a hospital. What hospital? Loulou doesn't know. When he saw himself there he got scared. He can't say why. Perhaps thinking he was locked in. He got scared and ran away. Since he wore a robe, it didn't take long for him to be arrested again. This time he was taken for an anmesiac. He was so tired he could no longer find words. The doctors of the psychiatric ward behaved very well. They healed him, that is, they plied him with food, reassured him, and let him rest . . . By that time, he was at the end of his rope and no longer afraid of being locked up. He was a wet rag. The nurses spoiled him. He became their pet. After five or six months, he was back on his feet. There was nothing left for him to do but leave. He was fearful, embarrassed. One of the nurses went on a reconnaissance mission to the rue Rambuteau. Nothing new, no one had come. Loulou didn't know where to go. He was out of money. He asked if he could stay. He felt safe with the nurses and the patients. And they kept him. The hospital administrator told us that after a while this cured patient became a problem—his accounts, his paperwork—but since Loulou didn't wish to leave, he had managed. You can do anything with papers if you're willing to go out of your way. So there you are. Twenty years.

If you could only have been there! You should have been! First, we were received by the director. He showed us his account book. Surname, first name, age, profession—you know that Loulou worked with his father in the fur business—it was all there, it was definitely our Loulou. This was followed by the usual wiles. The sick person is made to go down into the garden so we can observe him. We had a hard time recognizing him. He's got a belly now, and this lovely, girlish skin . . . With all that so calm looking, so—how shall I put it?—removed. Then the director summoned him to his office. If you could only have witnessed this scene! No! You should have! He recognized us right away, he did. As though we hadn't changed at all, Lucien and me. As for myself, my hair . . . With my shaved head when I came back, and my bald spot today . . . As though we had left him yesterday. We both started to cry, Lucien and me, crying like two fools. As to Loulou, he was beaming, no more amazed than if this reunion in a madhouse, twenty years later, were the most ordinary occurrence in the world. We all sat down together. "Come on. Take your valise. You're going with us." Poor Loulou, he had no valise, only the hospice handouts. "Come as you are." But he didn't want to leave without making the rounds of the establishment, without bidding farewell to everyone there. Of course, twenty years in a place, you become attached. He came back with his hands and pockets full. Candy, cookies, knick-knacks, all kinds of nonsense. He would have liked to wait for the evening shift. But at that point we pushed him a bit. "Come on. Let's go. You'll come back to see them." We took him away, still wearing his dressing gown, his creased nankeen trousers. Between the two of us, Lucien and I dressed him from head to toe. For the time being he lives with us. Soon we're going to find a place for him, help him move in. My wife has already heard of a small two-room apartment nearby. It won't be hard to furnish, with Marcel's help. We'll take what's needed in his store. As to finding work, that'll be more difficult. Loulou has no profession. The work he did with his father did not teach him a trade. At the asylum, he used to unwind wool, help with the housework, carry trays, assist with gardening. At any rate, he must begin by getting used to things. My wife, or son, or myself will accompany him till he's able to go out on his own. You can't imagine how he reacts to things. It was amazing when we bought him a pair of shoes. He understands nothing about money, does not recall the pre-war prices, so today's prices do not surprise him. What surprises him is that I should have a son of eighteen, that Lucien is married and the head of a family. Think of it, to keep a kid of nineteen . . . Even though it was out of humane feelings . . . To have kept him like this for twenty years . . . We're somewhat at fault. And to think he never thought of coming to see one of us, of writing . . . That was the first thing I asked him, as you can well imagine. He had a simple explanation. At first, he knew our addresses by heart, but he was hoping to find his relatives. He looked for them stubbornly. Later, when he was at the end of his rope, he forgot all the addresses he used to know. Once he entered the asylum, he let himself go. From time to time, he thought of our scheduled reunion. Yes, yes, he told me he had. But, as he lost all notion of time, it didn't help. Otherwise, he remembers everything. He may even have better recall than you and I—for him the past is closer than it is for us—except that he feels it didn't happen to him. He has a past that is not his, so to speak. It won't be easy to reinsert him in everyday life. We'll all have to take care of it. At any rate, we couldn't have left him there, with the insane. Lucien shall take him in his leather workroom, to begin with.

He's not stupid, Loulou. And when he gets used to things again . . . Remember how skillful he used to be. He was the only one able to make four matches from one matchstick when Valdi, the Pole, passed us a cigarette and a match and we wanted to keep a bit of fire handy for the next stroke of good luck. Four matches from a single matchstick; they were as thin as us. And he always succeeded in lighting them without breaking them. After that, we'll have to take care of his papers. Anyway, he'll be at our reunion next week. If you want to see him before, come up to the house. He's as happy as a kid at the prospect of seeing all his pals. Jacques will come from Charente, Simon from Marseilles. We'll all be there, all seven of us.

"Seven. Out of how many . . ."

Poupette

That a superhuman will was needed to hold fast and return, everyone understands this. But no one has the slightest idea of the will we had to have, once we were back, to start living again. All the time we were over there, we strained our whole being toward a goal, a single goal: to return. The return, we did not see beyond that point. First return, after that everything else would be easy. What could life's difficulties be in comparison with what we had endured and surmounted? And this is just where we were mistaken, taken unawares. We had to face all the ordinary problems of daily life—work, lodging, making one's way, carving out a place for oneself. The return had not solved everything. We had to embark on all these endeavors with diminished physical resources, our health impaired, our willpower dented. No one realizes the courage required of us at that time. And moreover, I believe that there lies within each one of us a deposit of ideas received since childhood, a kind of faith in the immanence of justice. Within each one of us there is a double-columned register wherein a balance must exist between debits and credits. In the debit column we list the total of our misfortunes from which no one escapes, the sum total of our whole life. In the credit column, we have that part of happiness to which every human being is entitled, one that serves as a counterbalance. The returnee tells himself that he's had his entire quota of misfortune at a stroke. And that's where he's caught off guard. As for myself, when I returned I got married and was happy. My happiness was due me, I had earned it. And so, when my marriage soured, I was filled with the spirit of revolt. It was unfair. You can't imagine how hateful my husband became, to the point of wanting to take my daughters away from me. He claimed I was too sick to take care of them, that I was abnormal, mad. Yes, since our return we had to learn that you don't pay off your debt all at once. Have we been seasoned by the camp experience? . . . Just the opposite. We have been sorely wounded in our flayed sensitivity. People will say, "Poor soul, what a monster he must be to have treated her so cruelly after all she suffered." No, I've no wish to inspire pity. But to fail taking Auschwitz into account, to fail entering it in the ledger of debits and credits, one would have to be utterly insensitive.

The Death of Germaine

Her husband stepped out through the French window opening onto the terrace where we were waiting and, with an almost imperceptible blink of his eyelids, indicated it was all over and we could come in. He held open one of the door's glass leaves, stepping back to let us pass. All three of us entered the room where Germaine was laid to rest. Maurice had closed her eyes, yet the memory I kept of those luminous eyes, eyes the blue of light, full of kindness itself, were it possible to separate kindness from all support, confining it to a pure look, my recollection of these eyes was so precise that I felt their look and saw their light shining from under the eyelids Germaine's husband had lowered a moment ago, making his rough workman's hand as light and gentle as he could.

Germaine was laid out on the bed, her face pale against the white pillow. In death she had become herself again. Her features, which I had seen distorted by pain only a few days earlier, had regained their symmetry, together with their former nobility and beauty. Someone, the nurse or perhaps Germaine's daughter, had plaited her hair into a silver crown. Once again we could see the pre-camp Germaine, Germaine as when she had first arrived at the fort of Romainville with her neat, hieratic hairdo. Her hair was not gray then, but I no longer took notice of such details. For me, it was Germaine as she had been before, which seemed like yesterday.

Maurice left us alone with our comrade. He remained standing on the threshold of the French window, facing a horizon of hills framed by potted geraniums glowing in the light of an autumn day. We were looking at Germaine and felt comforted by the beauty of her face whose gaze was not extinguished since we had known this face illuminated by eyes so blue that, for us, their blueness continued to shine from under the eyelids. We looked at her and our looks spoke to one another. They said, "She's not suffering any longer." A week ago we'd been unable to bear her expression of intense pain and had averted our eyes. The alteration of her features tormented us and we wished that her suffering might cease, quickly. What could we do to put an end to this pain and see Germaine finally at rest? Now it was over. "We should have come yesterday," said one of the three of us. "We would still have seen her . . ."

"Oh! last week she no longer recognized us, or hardly at all. She doesn't suffer any longer. How beautiful she is."

Even as we knew this beauty to be a lie, realizing it was doomed to disintegrate in a few hours, we found solace in the contemplation of eternal beauty.

Resting on the hem of the sheet, Germaine's hands still possessed the litheness of life. I took one of them in mine and kept on holding it.

"Do you recall when you used to say, in Auschwitz, 'Let me hold your hand so I'll fall asleep. You have my mother's hands.' Do you remember saying that, Charlotte? You promised to come to see me if we ever returned. How long have we been back . . . And you're coming to see me only now." Germaine said this to me in her tender voice, devoid of rancor or reproach, tinged only with regret. Now I was the one full of regret. Why hadn't I come to see her earlier, why had I waited for her to get ill, to be in a clinic, rather than visit her at home, where she went about her tasks, performing them with her firm hands so much like those of my mother. Yes, I used to say this in Auschwitz. I'd forgotten, but no sooner had I touched her hand than I recaptured the warmth and sweetness Germaine imparted to me whenever she let me take her hand in mine to fall asleep. I held on to her hand now. It's true, these hands looked just like my mother's— the shape, the feel, the tender dryness of the skin.

"Forgive me, Germaine. Did you hold this against me?"

"No, my sweet friend. But you should have come. You'd have seen my house and its surroundings, which I described so often over there. We'd have taken you for a walk. It's pretty around here. I often think of you. I often thought of you all these years, since we returned. I was happy to learn that you had found your mother again. How old is she now?"

"Much older than you are, Germaine, but her hands are still young, like yours."

"You will have kept your mother longer than my children theirs."

"How old are the youngest, those who were born after you came back?"

"My daughter is seventeen, my son fifteen. That's early to lose one's mother."

"Don't say that, Germaine. You'll get well."

"No. You see, people always believe they have time. You never came to see me and yet it's only a matter of a few hours on the train between you and me, you never came because you always intended to come and thought you had time to postpone it. One shouldn't do that. Things must be done in their time."

"Germaine, don't fill me with remorse. Get well so I may come back to see you, and be forgiven by you."

"I've forgiven you, but you won't come back to see me. I'm on my way."

"Yes, yes, I'll come back. I won't delay coming back again."

I had come back today, together with two comrades, and when we arrived at the clinic the nurse took us out to the terrace aflame with red geraniums and told us to wait there. "It won't be long now. Her husband is with her." That's how nurses speak: It won't be long now. Last week was the last time I saw Germaine, the first time I saw her after our return. She tried to give me a tender smile, but her lips found it hard to shape a real smile, effacing the expression set upon them by pain.

I held her stiffening hand in mine, and was overcome by remorse. Dear Germaine, you helped me so much, warmed me when I was chilled to the bone, let me hold your hand so it might carry me off to sleep, fill me with the taste of something sweet, yet I hadn't taken the time to visit you, speak with you, behold how you had resumed living —of course you know it took me a long time, and afterwards . . . yes, afterwards I should have found time—I didn't return to let you know just how much I owed you, to tell you all these things we never said over there.

I leaned forward over Germaine's hand resting on the white sheet and kissed it. I would have liked to give her back all the sweetness she had given me. At that moment, when I touched her hand with my lips, I was seized with terror. I could see Carmen and Lulu on the other side of the bed, and wondered whether I'd get a grip on myself. It was no longer Germaine laid out upon a white bed but Sylviane lying on rotting boards. The three of us stood at the foot of those boards, Lulu, Carmen, and myself. We had come to see Sylviane. Why her and not the other two skeletons on each side of her, for nothing distinguished Sylviane from those dark-skinned bags of bones, and how had we managed to identify Sylviane among the surrounding skeletons, skeletons that filled three levels of the block, how did we know it was she, Sylviane, and not the one next to her, or that other, all of them alike, all prostrate on the rotting planks, unable to stir. It was Sylviane we'd come to see, no one else, Sylviane, becaues she was one of us and might recognize us, deriving perhaps some comfort from our presence, or at least the courage to die since nothing could be done, since she was dying.

"This is she, I see her. I recognized her eyes," Carmen said, stopping at a bay just like the other bays after looking searchingly through all the bays where skeletons lay one against the other, a thousand Sylvanies, squeezed together so tightly that one imagined a swarming mass of skeletons whereas not one of them stirred, because skeletons do not have the strength to move.

"On the left, the fifth one, in the middle level. Don't you recognize her eyes? She still has her blue eyes."

As soon as we had located the landmark of her blue eyes shining from the jumble of skeletons, we recognized Sylviane. Carmen wasn't wrong. These burning eyes belonged to Sylviane.

We drew near the boards on which she lay, and saw nothing but Sylviane's flaming blue eyes. So far as we were concerned, everyone else had vanished the moment we identified Sylviane. We stood close to her, as though alone with her, like those people who have come to call on their sick and stand by their beds, ignoring everyone else. Carmen called softly, "Sylviane? Sylviane?" An expression rose in our friend's feverish blue eyes. "She saw us," said Lulu.

"How do you feel, darling Sylviane?" Carmen asked, and this nonsensical question sounded right. Does one inquire of the dying how they feel? However, the tenderness in Carmen's voice was real. Sylviane had recognized us, but she no longer had the strength to speak. Her burning blue eyes were directed at us, yet we couldn't decipher the burning blueness of her eyes which shone brilliant and clear in her face, its skin turned purple, striated with brown, like marble; it was the face of a Sylviane about to die.

"Don't tire yourself, don't speak yet," Carmen said tenderly. Neither did we have anything to say to Sylviane. What can one say to a twenty-year-old girl who's dying when you cannot even ask her if she'd like to have something since there's nothing to bring? Sylviane was dying and her eyes, the blue of precious stones, would be extinguished, turn the dull brown of her face. We stood there in front of her and just looked at her, since she didn't have the strength to tell us anything and we had nothing to say. A motionless Sylviane looked at us, and we read nothing in her eyes except solitude and anguish. She did not move. Her look did not move. One might have assumed she was already dead when she was suddenly shaken by a coughing fit that rattled her ribs, their frail arches clearly outlined under the blanket teeming with lice. Sylviane drew her gaunt hand from under the blanket—it was nothing but the transparency of a hand, one that might have just as easily belonged to the skeleton next to her—and raised it to her lips. She was trying to suppress her cough with a hand so utterly fleshless that one expected to see the bones come apart, fall in pieces upon the lice-covered blanket. The strangled coughing fit became a death rattle which shook once more the ribs' outline under the tattered blanket. Sylviane took her hand away. A pink drool foamed on her lips. Exhausted by her cough, Sylviane let her head roll on the boards, a head connected to the torso only by knotty cartilage and seemingly on the verge of becoming detached—just like that, gently, without a crack or a tear—rolling on the lice-infested blanket to knock against the ribs of the nearby skeleton where, stopped on its course by the other skeleton's protruding ribs, it would come to a standstill. Leaning over the unfamiliar skeleton lying on the outer edge of the rotting boards, Lulu inclined her body over that of Sylviane, delicately straightening her friend's head so it might remain fastened to the rest of her body a while longer, lying in her torso's axis as it did before. Putting her hand down the top of her dress, Lulu extracted a piece of rag to wipe off the pink foam upon Sylviane's lips. However, she failed in this attempt, afraid to rub too hard a trail of dried blood which earlier had flowed out into the corners of the dying woman's lips. Taking the rag from Lulu's hands, Carmen leaned over the skeleton next to her friend, to pad Sylviane's eyelids. "I've never seen eyes so blue. Look how beautiful they are still. And her hair . . . Do you recall the hair she had, Charlotte, a golden blond that went so well with her eyes?" Then she leaned closer to Sylviane and kissed her. "Sleep, my darling. Sleep now. We have to leave. We can't stay any longer. But we'll come back. Sleep." Carmen knew we wouldn't come back. She said this in case Sylviane could still hear, and caressed her forehead tenderly to accompany the rocking of her words. "Sleep, my little one," and she kissed Sylviane's shorn head, its eyes burning within gaping brown holes. Straightening up, and drawing aside to let me take her place, Carmen said, "Kiss her too." Just like that. "Kiss her," as though it were the most natural thing in the world to kiss a dying woman whose mouth is covered with mortal dribble. I leaned over Sylviane's face. Her burning blue eyes looked at me, becoming larger and larger, more and more blue, deeper and deeper as I leaned over them. I wanted to flee, run far away from this bay of skeletons, these tiers covered by skeletons, far from the stench of death and rot. I leaned over Sylviane's burning blue stare, wishing I had the nerve to cheat in the presence of Carmen and Lulu. But since I didn't, I kissed Sylviane with my mouth almost closed, wondering, as I felt my whole being contract with revulsion, if this was satisfactory in my comrades' eyes. Mara, is this how you kissed your sister Violaine, or did you find within yourself a surge of love powerful enough to allow you to forget her face, eaten away by leprosy, a face in which you remembered seeing her blue eyes? Have you ever felt deeply ashamed in your life?

One mustn't feel shame, nor have regrets, for these are useless feelings. Now it was Germaine who was here, not Sylviane, Germaine who had returned with us—was it yesterday or the day before?—in any case not too long ago, since Sylviane was dead already, not too long, since her appearance had not altered, Germaine's still endowed with her forgiving mouth, her luminous blue gaze, the kindness and tenderness reflected in her eyes. I kept Germaine's hand in mind, holding on to that hand, soft and full since she had not grown gaunt during her illness, had merely become transparent without losing her richness of form. I held on to Germaine's hand, reluctant to be separated from it, just as over there, when I could not bear separation from my mother's hand in the evening, before falling asleep.

"I believe we ought to leave her now to her husband," said Lulu—no, that day it wasn't Lulu, I'm getting mixed up—as we stepped out on the terrace. Maurice had remained standing there, not moving, standing before the hilly landscape, framed by flaming geraniums, not moving since he had yielded us his place in Germaine's room. We shook his hand. He went back to be near Germaine. We lingered a while on the terrace illumined by the last rays of the setting sun. One of us three said, "We ought to ask whether we could do something." "At least tell him we'll be back the day after tomorrow for the funeral," added the other. I know that the two others who were with me on that day, the day Germaine died, were neither Carmen nor Lulu. It's only because Lulu, Carmen, and I were together to bid farewell to Sylviane that I confuse them with those who were really with me when Germaine died. One of them, who was neither Carmen nor Lulu but another, waved to Maurice through the French window to let him know we had to catch a train. Maurice

came out on the terrace to thank us, saying that he didn't need anything since their eldest son would take care of all the arrangements
and that, were we unable to return the day after tomorrow, he'd
understand. He was glad to have seen Germaine's comrades on that
day.

Jacques

I was the only one returning to A. that day. No one was waiting for me at the station. The greater part of our contingent had returned earlier, in two or three groups greeted by the entire city, together with the civil authorities, the police force, and the party comrades. They had been warmly welcomed. There were still some flags on the station platform. No one would expect me, I arrived too late. My group—there were seven of us, the seven survivors of the convoy—had been delayed on account of Marcel, who got sick. We waited for him to be up to the return trip. All of us had agreed long ago that we'd never separate before reaching Paris. All seven of us had arrived the day before. I was the only one to go back to the Charente region. I had been alone since Paris. In the train, people were very attentive to me. They offered me food and drink, asked me questions. I was so tired I could hardly answer. Someone from A. who had traveled in my compartment later stated that it had seemed strange, and that I did not look at ease. I found this out much later. At the time, it seemed to me that people resented my answering only by agreeing with them. You must have been hungry, you must have been cold. Perhaps they were wondering whether I was a real deportee. And yet, you just had to look at me . . . I wanted to be left alone, but people wanted answers to their questions. I don't know if it was so for other deportees, but I at first did not feel like speaking to people. It was hard, after having spoken for days and days with comrades. With people, you always had to start by giving explanations. To answer the most insignificant questions, you had to introduce the subject, describe the places, name the time of day, say something about the weather at that time, and give detailed accounts of this or that. Endless. With the comrades you didn't need any points of reference. When you'd say, "The day the fat one ran after Simon," everyone knew what it was about and why Simon had to run to retrieve the bread the fat kapo had stolen from him. I pretended I was asleep. I would have liked to look at the landscape, recognize the bell towers, read the stations' names. People didn't understand I wanted to stay quietly in my corner and recognize things, the switchings, the transformers we blew up, the curves of the tracks where two years ago we had brought about derailments. People spoke to one another. They were happy to talk. They hadn't yet exhausted the joy of speaking freely, asking direct questions. A woman said to me, "It must feel strange to come back." Yes, it did feel strange. She expected me to answer something. That's when I pretended to be asleep. A man, who thought I was sleeping, said, "Poor man, he must be so tired. Never saw anyone so thin . . ." In the corridor there were prisoners of war returning home. They were eager to talk, and people were glad to listen to their stories. I could hear them without following their conversation, but enough to realize that for them their captivity would become part of their war memories; I envied them this.

Coming out of the station, I recognized one or two employees, particularly the one who checked the tickets. They were still here? That seemed strange indeed. It's difficult to express what I felt. I had hoped to find things and people as they'd been before my departure, and yet I was surprised because everything was the same. Surprised and off balance. It was strange to be the only one to have changed.

The travelers scattered in different directions in front of the station. Some gave me a hard look. I waited a moment as people do taking their bearings, not quite sure yet where to go. I had to regain a foothold. I knew where to go: home. It was ten minutes away. I believed, because I had found the station and avenue the same, that I would find my former alert gait. How many times had I walked along the avenue to the station . . . But as I was setting out my legs grew heavy, my shoes acquired cast-iron soles. I was so disheartened that I went back into the station—how hard it was! I was reeling—to sit on a bench. I knew that no one was meeting the train since I had not announced my return. I hadn't expected anyone to welcome me, yet I was disappointed. As if everyone was supposed to know I was coming back. So that's how it was, the return? I remained on my bench a long time, telling myself, "You've got to set out, don't wait for nightfall," yet I didn't make a move. Undoubtedly no other train was expected because the station emptied out. I was there, all alone in the waiting room, alone on my bench, telling myself that I had to go home. I'd get there in time for supper. A railway employee passed two or three times in front of me, looked at me. I turned away so as not to have to speak to him. I felt that another employee was looking at me from his window. He closed it and disappeared. Then another approached me and asked whether I was catching a connection: "We don't have one today," he said.

"No, I'm not changing trains. I got where I was going." He was waiting, favorably disposed. I added, "I'm coming back home."

"Yes, I can see that you've returned," the employee said. "Where are you from? D'you need anything?"

There was warmth in his voice, and at last I felt like hearing people talk and like talking myself. I told him where I lived. "Are you certain your house is still there? There were heavy air raids in that neighborhood." I was taken aback. I had not foreseen such a possibility. Yes, I knew about the air raids, the bombing, and that was all to the good, but in my neighborhood . . . No, I had not foreseen that. I forced myself to inquire whether there had been victims. "Some twenty or so," answered the employee.

In the camp, there were hundreds of dead every day. But I never thought of people dying outside the camp. What could one die of when one was free? In the camp, we thought of our relatives and friends as people to whom nothing could happen, except if they were in the maquis. So one also died on the outside? The obvious is always disconcerting.

"My working day is over," said the employee. "If you wish, I'll accompany you."

I got up. He stretched out his arm to help me. "No, no, I'm fine." I tried to hold myself straight. I didn't speak to him on the way because I was both worried and out of breath. He also wanted to ask me questions. Long before we reached the spot where our house used to stand, I saw. I stopped and said, "It was there."

"You're the son of the Dumont family? Forgive me, I didn't recognize you. Your parents were killed in the bombing."

"I knew it," I said. In a flash, I realized I ought to have known. Had my parents been there, they'd have gone to the station to meet every train. I remained standing in the middle of the street, my head swimming. My knees buckled under me. The employee took me by the elbow. He was waiting respectfully, with the respectful air one assumes at funerals, when one approaches the grieving family to extend one's condolences. Then he suggested, "Come. We'll make up a bed for you at home. Tomorrow, when you're rested, you'll go to the town hall to make inquiries." At first I thought it might be better to go to the house of a comrade rather than to that of a stranger. He said he knew me, but I couldn't remember him at all. He'd known my parents. I accepted when he told me it was very close.

The following day I went into town. I didn't know where to begin. My comrades might have been arrested after me, shot, deported. Now I could imagine all kinds of misfortunes. I weighed in my mind who from our group had the greatest chance of escaping. Vincent? Albert? Louis? Which one might have survived?

Vincent was home. It was he who opened the door. I went toward him, trembling with joy. My chin trembled, my lips too, and I would have liked to shout with joy. Vincent stood by the door, his arms hanging down close by his body. I was taken aback, wondering whether I was hallucinating. No, it was indeed Vincent. At last I got my voice back: "Vincent! It's me, Jacques. I know I've changed, but it's me, Jacques." He kept on standing there, in front of his door, utterly silent, and I stood before him not understanding anything. I couldn't say today whether he was troubled, embarrassed, or angry, I was too shaken to notice anything. All kinds of conjectures were racing through my mind, too quickly for me to formulate anything clearly. Vincent had been arrested and had squealed. Or else, Vincent was not one of us and had joined the other side. Perhaps Vincent had gone mad. Or perhaps it was I. Not one of these suppositions seemed believable, and I stayed there looking at Vincent, who avoided looking at me. Still not looking he stepped back, starting to close the door. I was wretched, ashamed, stupefied. The shaking that a moment before had seized my whole body, legs included, yielded now to a feeling of numbness. My blood ran cold. I left, not knowing where I was, where I was at. I couldn't figure it out. My head ached. My heart ached. Utterly baffled, I made my way through the streets without recognizing anything I saw. Something that might have yielded a key kept on eluding me. What? Something had to be cleared up. What? It was all inextricably mixed up, the access blocked. I remained a long time sitting in a café, unable even to formulate the kind of questions I should have asked myself. I just had to know.

When I rang Louis's bell he wasn't there. It was Aline who opened the door. The sight of me made her draw back. She said breathlessly, "Louis isn't here." She wasn't moving, didn't open the door wide. I didn't move either. Then she said, "You've returned?" She was using the formal "you," *vous*. My first reaction when she opened the door was one of relief: she hadn't been arrested, apparently neither had Louis, so why the *vous*? My mind was becoming more and more confused. I was seized with vertigo and had to lean against the doorpost. Aline was waiting, looking down. "I'm sorry, I was on my way out." She closed the door behind her and started down the avenue, walking briskly, her back very stiff. I couldn't understand what was going on. What I did understand was the uselessness of going to see the others. I went in the direction of the railway station, walking along the rails. Had I heard a train coming, I'd have summoned the strength needed for hoisting myself onto the ballast and lie down across the tracks. I kept on pricking up my ears.

At the station I looked for the railway employee who housed me. He obviously wasn't on duty at that time, I didn't see him. I let myself fall on a chair in the buffet. I wasn't hungry. I wasn't thirsty. I felt cold. I would have liked to put my ideas in order, to unravel the tangled threads. Nothing was working right in my head. The more I tried to understand, the more it was getting mixed up. That's how you lose your mind or feel when struck with amnesia. I became mad. I thought of the hospital as a refuge. I'm crazy, and at the hospital they'll take care of me. The waiter asked me whether I wanted lunch. I ordered something and ate while trying to puzzle things out. I kept on returning to the same questions. Why? Why was everything blocked on my first visit? What should I do? Nothing to be done. Where should I go? No place to go. The buffet was filling up, and a crowd milled on the platform on the other side of the windowpanes. I can't stay here indefinitely. It seemed to me that people were looking at me with Vincent's empty stare, or Aline's shifty eyes. Where could I go? Except for the hospital I didn't know where to turn.

It took me a long time to remember my aunt, one of my mother's sisters, who lived a few kilometers out of town. I left the buffet without a glance. Going there took hours. At closer and closer intervals I'd have to sit by the roadside. Each time it seemed to me I wouldn't get back on my feet.

My aunt burst out crying when she recognized me. I hadn't seen her in years. When I was arrested I hadn't kept up family connections. The comrades were my family. My aunt hoped I'd return, but she was so afraid of having to inform me of my parents' death that she hadn't gone to meet any of the trains. She also wanted to ask me questions. "You're tired, my poor darling." Some of the expressions she used annoyed me. "You're exhausted. It's quite normal after what you had to bear. We'll get you back on your feet." Now you couldn't stop her—the bombing, my parents' funeral, their plot in the cemetery and what she had done for the interment. "I waited for you for the monument. It's up to you now. Your brother was buried in the plot reserved for the executed partisans. You may want to transfer his body to the family plot. What do you think? Well, you'll decide." I let weeks pass before seeing the other deportees, those who had come back before me. There were some I knew, they had not been arrested for the same thing, nor transported in the same convoy, but they were party members. As soon as they returned they had been warned against me by Vincent. They had never imagined, over there, that I was the one who betrayed our resistance group, and they resented now my hypocrisy. It was lucky I had been separated from them when I was sent to the commando of Lucien's group; they'd have regretted sharing their food parcels with me. That's what I gathered later. When I saw them again they didn't say anything, so I kept on wondering about their stony looks. And during all that time, in the background, in an obscure region where I dared not venture, there was Denise. I did not utter her name, even in my mind. I feared meeting her. I was afraid of meeting anyone. I thought sometimes of going to see my parents' friends. I thought of it for a few days, always postponing doing so. When by chance I'd run into acquaintances, I'd greet them briefly and hurry by. For a long time I didn't have the courage to write to the comrades of my group, those with whom I returned: Lucien, Marcel, Henri. Later, when Denise insisted I do so, she succeeded in having me write Lucien. But I never told him what had happened. When I told them the full story twenty years later, at the reunion planned upon parting in Paris, they reproached me for my lack of trust. By that time, I no longer trusted anyone. If I hadn't had Denise, I'd have blown my brains out. Fortunately, that evening, at the Third of July dinner, they paid attention only to Loulou. I'd have much preferred to be in Loulou's place. Even after careful deliberation.

Denise came to me first. She likewise had been warned against me, as soon as she came back from Ravensbrück, but she refused to believe the accusations piled upon me. She enlightened me about the whole thing. "You understrand that, after the dismantling of the resistance group, the comrades who had not been arrested—Vincent, Louis, Aline—tried to figure out why almost all of us were caught. The only explanation they came up with was that the group had been denounced by an informer. After cross-checking and deductions, they concluded there must have been a traitor among us, and that the traitor was you." I felt like running to them to shout it wasn't me, prove it wasn't so. Prove. Isn't sincerity obvious, readily seen and felt? "No," Denise said. "They won't believe you."

From that day on, I tried to think of who might be able to back up my statements, prove my good faith. Not one of those who could have testified in my favor was alive. All had been shot or deported. To be the sole survivor didn't argue in my favor. It even seemed to be a proof of guilt. Only Denise had kept an unwavering trust. With her it wasn't the same. The comrades ordered her to break with me. she refused and was excluded from the group. We got married. It was a sad wedding. I wanted to leave town, put roots down somewhere else. Denise thought this would be viewed as an admission of guilt. We had to stay there, hold out and hold our heads up, in order to prove I was innocent. Years passed, and I kept on looking. Denise also looked obstinately. We thought of nothing else. Many a time I wanted out. Why didn't I die over there? To have struggled so hard to survive and return, and for what?

One day, Denise, who had gone out to the market—I'll always remember it, it was a Sunday morning—Denise saw Vincent walking straight in her direction. He walked straight toward her but approached her indirectly, not daring to look her in the face. Imagine, they had just arrested one of the police inspectors who put all of us in jail, the one we nicknamed Don Carlos because he looked Spanish. He'd been laying low for years. Vincent was summoned as a witness to the examining magistrate's chambers—it was Vincent who brought charges against the police immediately following the Liberation. He wanted to let Denise know I would be summoned too. Denise listened carefully, still distrustful: "So, you don't want Jacques to testify?" "I do, on the contrary. But I wanted to tell you"—he used the familiar *tu*, but was obviously ill at ease—"I wanted to let you know that the judge read me the reports on the shadowings. It all started with me. What a misfortune. I'd been identified on a train. You remember that it was I who was responsible for liaison operations along the Paris-Bayonne line? A cop who had arrested me in 1939, when the party was declared illegal, recognized me. At the time I'd given them the slip, run off from the police station. Imagine a cop who arrested me in 1939 recognizing me in 1943 despite my bleached moustache and hair. We were a bit unwashed behind the ears with all our Resistance stuff. You can alter anything except the way you walk. They identify you by your walk. When he saw me walk in front of him as I was leaving the station, he knew me at once. He said to himself that a guy like me hadn't fallen into line. So he had me shadowed. As they went step by step, from one to the other, they reconstituted the entire web. Once they had all the threads in hand—it took them over three weeks to pull them together, and during that whole time we went about as cautious as Sioux Indians, certain of foiling any possible shadowing, and sure of ourselves—held the threads, all they had to do was pull in the net. Once again I had a narrow escape, you remember, don't you? After that I changed my center of operation. Tell Jacques he'll be called. And if he wants to come and see me . . ."

I was rehabilitated. Although I realize that in their place I'd have done the same thing—because I'm also a diehard—I can't feel the same about the comrades, not the way I felt before.

Denise

I had such a hard time bringing Jacques back ashore
I did all I could to bring him back, back to life.
Not a moment left to think of myself.
His house
his father and mother
his brother executed, shot
what a hard homecoming
the comrades' cold stare,
backs turned,
comrades who wanted nothing to do with him
everything lost
loss of a whole life.
I'd say to myself now I've got to be everything to him
everything isn't much it's nothing
it's nothing and I'll never be everything to him
I count for nothing
I'll only make a difference if I can give him back the courage to live.
I'd say to myself: Don't try to balance accounts
Jacques I'd say
you can rely on nothing but your guts
we've got to face up to it
Denise Jacques would say
what's to be done against suspicion
Jacques I'd say
suspicion isn't betrayal
Denise he'd say
to face up to it you can't lose face
I've looked death in the eye
but I can't look into my comrades' eyes
to see suspicion

Jacques I'd say
to die now would be cowardly
Denise he'd say
better to die than be unable to look people straight in the eye
Jacques
I'd say
Jacques hold fast
And every morning he'd say
Denise
humbly as when you ask permission
And every morning
I'd say No Jacques
No Jacques you mustn't you've got to hold fast
take all the time you need
I had such a hard time giving him back the will
to live
there was no chance to think of me
all those years

Gaby

I don't go out because I feel cold. When I do go out, even muffling up as I do, even wearing a warm coat and fur-lined boots, I catch cold. If my feet get cold I get diarrhea right away. I couldn't reach the end of the street. In the summer, when the weather is really lovely, I take a short walk in our garden. Here, the summers . . . Even in summer I feel cold. We heat the house almost all year. Just to go to the door to open it, look, my fingers turn white. How I envy Poupette! How right she was to leave for a warm country! She told me she was leaving because she couldn't stand the cold any longer, couldn't take the interminable winters. In the Caribbean she's in good health, she's come back to life. I haven't heard from her for some time now. What's happening to her, do you know? In the final instance, she had the intention of opening a store, I believe. As for myself, with Jean's situation, and my son, I've got to stay put. We'll go to the Midi when Jean retires. What's more, I'm happy in my house—My fingers are coming back to normal. Shall I make you some coffee? I'm always rubbing my hands. It might be taken for a mental condition. I don't get out of my sheepskin slippers from one end of the year to the other, but after all I can't go about the house wearing gloves . . . When I returned I had to spend two years at Plateau-d'Assy. There was a spot on my lung. At night we had to keep the window open. Neither the nurses nor the doctors wanted to admit that cold air made me winded. "You've got to get used to it. You'll get used to it." Making her rounds, the nurse always checked, making sure the window was still open. To think they told someone coming back from Auschwitz that he or she must get used to the cold . . . However, I had a measure of luck when I finally came back. Yes, after my father's execution, after seeing both my mother and aunt die over there, it was indeed fortunate to find Jean again. So many never found their fiancés again. Jean had returned before I did. He was coming back from Germany and knew nothing about Auschwitz. He hadn't been too worried. If all those waiting for us could have imagined what we had had to bear, and how few survivors there would be, we wouldn't have found them when we returned. Jean, had he known . . . We got married and started settling down. That's when I had to go to Plateau-d'Assy. At the time, there was no home care as there is today. Jean came to visit me very frequently, every second Sunday, and he spent his whole vacation time with me. He'd preach to me, encourage me, and keep on saying that after a separation of five years—he was made prisoner in June 1940, you see—two years were nothing. For me, on the contrary, after Auschwitz two years seemed even longer. Without Jean's encouragement I'd never have stayed to complete the cure. The mountains were covered with snow. To return from there and see snow . . . Jean did all he could to convince me it wasn't the same. With all my sweaters—that's when I took up knitting—with my three or four sweaters one on top of another, I looked like a baby bear. He used to call me: "My sweet little bear cub, you'll be all well soon. You'll come back home. You'll see how nice it is." It's true. The house is easy to heat. Do you remember when Germaine used to say, "If I ever come back, I'll live in a warm house"? And her question-riddle, "If you were given a choice between—now, at this very moment (it was during roll call when we were standing with our feet in the snow)—if you had to choose between a big bowl of boiling hot, foamy chocolate, or a hot bath with a cake of fine lavender soap, or a cozy, warm bed, with a hot-water bottle, covered by a plump eiderdown comforter as round as a balloon, which of these would you take first? I'd take the warm bed. Oh, to slip into a cozy, warm bed!" We always thought of things warm. It was also Germaine who used to say, "If I ever come back, I won't wash lettuce under cold water in winter. I'll use lukewarm water instead." Well, imagine, that's exactly what I do: I take the chill off the water before rinsing the lettuce. Yes, there's nothing like a nice, warm house . . . That's why I don't go out, not even to run to the corner bakery when I run out of bread. I prefer to do without. I very rarely have to, almost never. It would take an unforeseen event, such as one of my son's buddies staying to dinner. On Sunday, Jean does the shopping for the whole week. I no longer have to give him a list, except if I need something special. With my large refrigerator I've got everything right there. Go to market? Not me . . . We have a drafty, open-air market, where we shake with cold. I feel sorry for the merchants. As soon as I feel cold, I imagine myself over there. Frozen roads, frozen mud, wind, snow, snow squalls at roll call. And with the rags on our backs! . . . How did we ever survive, I often wonder. Just talking about it, as I do now, I start shivering, crawl into my armchair all wrapped up in a warm shawl. At home I feel good. I'm never bored, although I see no one during the day. Taking care of the house, a bit of sewing, knitting, it keeps me busy. Jean comes back at seven. The first thing he does is go down to check the boiler. We have dinner, we talk, listen to a record, to the radio. We don't have television. One sees too many horrors. We used to have it, but when it broke down Jean didn't have it fixed. It was during the war in Algeria. Uniforms, soldiers, machine guns . . . We prefer to read. Most of the time we're alone, the two of us. Evenings, Jean-Paul isn't here much, now that he has his little fiancée—he's twenty years old, can you imagine? Twenty years old . . . They're getting married once he's done with his military service. The girl's very sweet. She often calls on us. On Sundays. We never go out on Sunday. I'm much too cold, in a car. We always have people at home, friends, family. In the summer, the men play a game of lawn bowling in the garden, in the winter, a game of cards, while the women chat and fix the evening meal. It's restful. Of course I have to go into town from time to time, when I need an item of clothing, a pair of shoes. Rarely. My things don't wear out. And I knit. I've even knitted myself a coat. I'll show it to you. You'll tell me what you think. Jean takes care of everything that has to do with the house. Before leaving in the morning, he takes a good look at what's in the kitchen. If we're out of butter or coffee, he brings it in the evening together with the bread which he picks up on the way. I purchase large items—sheets, blankets—through catalogs. Even knitting wool. I adore looking at catalogs. I receive whole piles of them. I'm so cozy here, in my warm house, leafing through catalogs, daydreaming. It's lucky I didn't have to go out to work, out in all kinds of weather . . .

Louise

I don't know why Mado took it into her head that things would have been easier had she married a deportee. Look at me and my husband. We met two years after our return. He was twenty-nine, I was twenty-six. He came back from Buchenwald, and I from Auschwitz. Without having the same memories, we had the same frame of reference, the same code, spoke the same language. Can you guess what happened then? After twenty years of marriage there's only one deportee in this couple. He's the deportee. He was deported and so he gets tired immediately. He was deported so he can't stay up; he goes to bed right after dinner. He was deported, so he's frail, sick, nervous, sensitive to the cold. His head hurts, or his stomach, back, legs. He must take care of himself, monitor his strength, spare himself any undue effort. He goes to the dispensary at least once a week. If you could only see the pile of pharmaceuticals . . . Powders, ampules, pills, phials all over the place. In the summer, we don't leave on holiday. He goes for his cure in a rest home. I try to suggest a cruise, the beach, the country. He tells me, "As for us, deportees, we don't make old bones. I'm doing all I can to last a bit longer . . ." He was deported, so he must keep a strict diet. Two yogurts every morning because he had typhus. I too had typhus, but just watching him eat his two yogurts . . . At least with him you hear talk about deportation. He goes to the office, but as soon as he gets home don't bother asking him anything. It's housecoat and television time. The house is a regular infirmary. You know that typical smell of sickness, the odor of antirheumatic liniments. Before going to bed, he wants me to rub his back or his leg. Granted, he doesn't enjoy foolproof health. Not one of us returned whole. But he's the only one who's entitled to getting ill. At any rate, we couldn't both be sick at the same time. So, you know, being married to a deportee . . .

Marceline

She's lucky, Gaby, to be able to coddle herself. I couldn't do it. I never could. When I came back my father hadn't returned from Buchenwald. My mother was alone. She had never worked, didn't know how. Our savings had melted away. What working people save in their lifetime is never a fortune, and since money wasn't worth the same thing, even if Mama had succeeded in keeping what she had—it was impossible, how would she have nourished herself during the three years my father and I were deported?—even had she been able to keep her savings, the amount would be a ridiculously small sum of money. One more surprise upon returning . . . When I received the demobilization bonus, I thought I was rich and could wait to go back to work. But with a sum that equaled three months of my pre-war salary I could barely live fifteen days. But believe me, mother had worked miracles. She had stocked soap, sugar, rice, even coffee. I don't know how she had lived in our absence. It didn't look like she had touched anything. She'd kept it all for our return. I realized right away that my father wouldn't come back. At his age . . . But mother didn't want to believe this. For a long, long time she went on hoping she'd see him again. And even afterward, for a long time, when she'd say she no longer had hope, when her lips said she no longer hoped, her eyes kept a glimmer of hope. I'd tell her, "Think, Mama. If Papa had survived, he'd have sent us news when the camps were liberated. He'd have entrusted a returnee with a message for us." Hope can be tenacious! Hope can be desperate! There were stories about prisoners and deportees taken to Russia, stuck in Odessa waiting for a ship, or hospitalized, or wandering over there . . . In Poland, Hungary, Romania . . . You remember all those legends in the making? Until one of my father's comrades, who hadn't been able to come earlier because he was sick and no doubt also because he didn't have the courage to be the bearer of tragic news, until his visit my mother per-

sisted in keeping up her hopes. How many times she repeated the
same question: "You saw him dead? With your own eyes?" The poor
man was on tenterhooks. As for me, I didn't have a chance to rest
when I returned. I might have been able to take advantage of one of
the rest homes created for returning prisoners in hotels requisitioned
at various spas; they were free of charge, but wouldn't have brought
money into our home. There wasn't one sou left. It was amazing that
my mother had been able to hold fast until the end without getting
into debt. I was tired, tired! The smallest gesture made me perspire:
brushing my hair . . . My hand would drop down as though made of
lead, with the brush falling out of it. How exhausted I was! I was
there, sprawled out on the dining room couch, and I felt I'd never be
able to stand up again. Yet it had to be done. For a short time I received
help from an organization. A small sum. It was barely enough. My
mother did not yet receive her pension. So long as she'd kept hoping
to see my father return she hadn't made her claim. I rested six weeks
and then went back to work. It wasn't easy, you know, real toil. Even
the morning trip . . . I'd arrive at the office utterly exhausted. Fortunately, the people I was working with were nice. My colleagues
helped me. I took tonic, calcium, vitamins, yes—but no rest. If I'm
not very well today it must be the reason. We should all have had two
years of complete rest. But even if I'd been taken care of for two
years, what would my mother have done? I confess that when we
returned—except for those stricken with tuberculosis, who had no
choice in the matter—not one of us felt like withdrawing to the
country and remaining there without moving. All of us were eager to
live, to get back to a full life. Some threw themselves into militant
action, others got married and had children as quickly as possible—as
though to recapture the time they had lost. As for myself, I waited
four years before marrying. And I didn't want to have children. My
husband didn't particularly care. He had two already from his first
marriage, it was enough for him. I can tell you I wouldn't have had
the needed strength. I was also terrified of giving birth to a defective
baby. No, I didn't have enough health to give any to a child.

After my marriage I went on working for some time. I'd always worked, so I couldn't face the idea of being a housewife dependent on her husband. I stopped only when it became impossible. Besides, my husband preferred to have his wife at home. I stay home, but don't coddle myself. Oh no. I've got a lot to do. The house is a big responsibility and we receive a lot. With the situation he has, my husband has to entertain. We give dinner parties two or three times a week. We also go out a lot. My husband has to go out and he wants me to accompany him. There are days when I'd prefer to stay in bed. My husband is a very energetic man. Winter sports, tennis . . . He doesn't understand what it means to feel tired. You mustn't let yourself go—that's the motto he lives by. The way I describe him you'll assume he's a tyrant. No, no, he's not an executioner. Deportation was a terribly trying experience, he knows it, but he believes that human nature is endowed with an extraordinary plasticity which allows individuals to adapt and readapt themselves to everything, without even the use of willpower. "The proof of what I'm saying is that you've returned," he says. (I could easily prove the opposite by counting the few who survived. Better to drop it. I avoid discussing this point with him.) He admits that bad memories tend to linger, awful memories, but one should not be their prisoner, ought not to be obsessed. "You must not let them crush you. It's a matter of making up your mind. What's over is over." There you are. One should not let oneself go. He's built a whole theory on this principle. You can tell his field is science. Unfortunately—I say "unfortunately" because if he were right I'd be in better health—his theory is defeated each time I run a fever. Every year, at approximately the same time, I have an attack of very high fever which lasts for days. No medicine seems to help. Laboratory analyses and X-rays do not show anything. My doctor can't make heads or tails of it. My sickness has no name. I call it the anniversary of my typhus. After each bout it takes weeks to replenish myself. I tried to find the cause, to know what provokes the attack—is it the result of some kind of shock, fatigue, nervous exhaustion? No, not at all. It's inexplicable. It always starts in the same way: a violent migraine, stomach cramps, and temperature suddenly climbing madly. And so suddenly, without any warning, without my feeling prostrate, or even sad the day before . . . Despite all this, I still don't coddle myself, you know. As soon as I'm back on my feet I resume all my activities. My nerves are solid. My husband must be right after all. I don't want to give in, lead the life of a sick person. Never.

The Funeral

We were supposed to meet at the train. When I got to the station, three women from our group were there already, purchasing tickets. We kissed. "How many of us d'you think there'll be?"

"I don't know if there'll be many. For those who live in provincial towns it'll be tight. I sent a message to all those whose addresses I have. Marie-Louise called me up. She'll go there directly by car, with her husband."

The four of us lived in Paris and saw each other quite often, so we engaged in small talk. We waited for a moment near the kitchen window, then casting a look backward we walked in the direction of the platform, where we had told everyone to meet us. No one yet. We remained standing near the car marked with the name of the town where we were going. Meanwhile we went on with our small talk—"How are you? And your husband? Your son?"—while on the lookout for our comrades.

"Who's that one over there, in gray? Seems to be looking for something."

"Who?"

"The tall woman in gray. It might be one of us, but I don't recognize her."

"Neither do I."

The woman in gray was drawing closer to us, but she passed us and went on. "No, she's not one of us. I don't recognize her walk."

The woman had walked by us. She turned around, hesitating, then with a smile came back toward us.

"Looks like Jeanne. I think I recognize her."

"Jeanne? How she's changed. . . ."

She was near us. "You don't recognize me? Jeanne." She no longer seemed changed. As soon as we recognized her, it was she. As soon as we recognized her, without a moment of hesitation we erased her wrinkles and faded skin, the circles under her eyes, a bitter fold near the corner of her lips, and all at once she became the one she'd been. Retouched, washed clean by our memories, she was again the Jeanne we knew. I thought: How strange . . . Do I also have several faces? It seems that each one of us has one face—weary, worn down, frozen— and under that ruined face another—full of light, mobile, the one in our memories—and, covering both of these, a latchkey mask, the one we put on to go out, move through life, approach people, a polite mask like the one salesladies assume when they slip into their uniforms. No doubt we're the only ones to see the truth of our comrades, no doubt we alone see the naked face below.

Jeanne recognized us and kissed us. "How did you hear? I didn't send you a message. I never had your address."

"I met Mimi yesterday, by chance. It was strange. It was in a place where I never go. I was taking my daughter to a new dentist. Ours . . ."

"You have a daughter? How old is she?"

"Nineteen soon."

"Nineteen and she doesn't go to the dentist alone?"

"I was going with her because he's a friend . . ."

"Nineteen . . . that means you got married as soon as you returned?"

"Almost . . ."

"You have only one child?"

"I also have a son."

"How come we didn't see you all these years?"

"I don't know. Days fly by. Then years. We never have enough time for anything. A husband, children, the house, work."

"You work? What do you do?"

"I'm a chemist, like before."

"So Mimi got my note. Did she say she'd come?"

"I wouldn't have recognized Mimi. And yet she hasn't changed. It's hard to say what it is. She seems so weary. She's the one who recognized me. No, she won't come. She went to see Germaine two days ago and was there for the last moments. So the funeral . . ."

"You haven't changed either."

For Jeanne it was also both true and false. Looking at her carefully, one could see everything had changed—the expression, the bitter fold at the corner of her mouth, her hair, her silhouette. Actually, she wasn't as gaunt as she'd been over there. She was dried out now rather than thin. And yet she hadn't changed—the expression in her eyes, her voice, the gestures of her precise, skillful hands.

"We all have our home, our work . . ."

"Then I don't know. Days go by, years . . ."

"Do you feel the years are slipping by? I don't. I know I've aged, and even that isn't quite true. I grew old all at once, when I returned, and since that time I've been old but stopped aging. I haven't moved."

"It's a good thing you make an effort to attend funerals," said another one of us, who had come to join us in our compartment and walked over to give Jeanne a kiss. "We'd start hoping there'd be more of them."

"As for you, you haven't changed one bit," said Jeanne. "Still the same biting sense of humor."

"Well, someone has to be dead for you to think you may be needed!"

Jeanne smiled. Her smile brought her totally back to us, despite two capped teeth.

"Don't be mean now!"

"You're quite right to go out of your way for the dead since it gives you the chance to catch a glimpse of the living again. We need more such occasions."

"Enough! Be quiet!" said one of our comrades who had not yet joined in the conversation. Spiteful remarks may be funny as long as you know when to stop.

"Well, what about funerals? Our comrades aren't the only mortal creatures in the world?"

"Does that mean you run to other funerals as well?"

"Sometimes. It doesn't affect me that much. I go but it doesn't take that much out of me. After Auschwitz, I no longer cry at funerals

. . . People are lucky to have a funeral. When I think of Viva, Mounette, Claudine . . ."

"I often think of Mariette."

"There goes the whole litany!"

"What about Gaby? Was she informed?"

"Of course. But you can't count on her presence. You know she never leaves her house."

"Here comes another one! Here, this way!" shouted the one posted at the window. She beckoned to the new arrival, who was running, waving her hands. She jumped into the train and appeared at the threshold of our compartment, where she was greeted with laughter.

"Still the same. Afraid of being late. Why are you afraid of missing a train? There's one you ought to have missed, but you certainly made that one."

"Well, this is how I had the pleasure of making your acquaintance. How are you?" She offered her cheek to be kissed.

"She certainly hasn't changed. Still harebrained. Do you remember the day she lost her shoes?"

"I didn't lose my shoes. They were stolen."

"Same thing. Here, sit down. Don't just stand there. Here we're allowed to sit down. If Carmen hadn't stolen another pair from the Gypsies . . ."

"You stole shoes?" Jeanne questioned her in a reproachful tone.

"Didn't you ever steal?"

"From the SS, when it was possible, yes—never from other prisoners."

"You and your virtue. It's a miracle you ever returned. Fortunately we were there. And what could we do? Go to roll call barefoot? We wanted to bring that silly goose back."

"Yes, to drive me up the wall."

"The gypsies stole everything they could from us. They had loads of shoes. It shows that you never went through Birkenau, Jeanne."

"If you hadn't been so harebrained, you'd have kept a close watch on your puddlejumpers. All the time we were in block 26, I'd stick them under my head at night, instead of a pillow."

"You know I lose things. You're not going to scold me for misplacing my clodhoppers every time I see you?"

"Lucky we brought you back. Losing everything the way you do, you'd certainly have gotten lost yourself."

"Everyone of us who returned was lucky," Jeanne said. "Lucky to have had the others."

"I see you insist on it—virtue, morality, justice, everyone getting their just deserts."

The train started. "No one else is going to come." We folded our coats, placed them in the rack, made ourselves comfortable. Jeanne sat down next to me.

"How happy I am to see you. You haven't changed, you know. Not one bit. How did it go for you? What did you do? Did you marry again?"

"No."

"Why not? It's not good to live alone."

"I can't imagine living with anyone else."

"After all this time?"

"After all this time."

"You never considered it?"

"I never intended to, never had the opportunity. I don't know. Never thought of it. At first, it was too soon, later too late."

Answering Jeanne's questions, I was able to gauge the degree of closeness between myself and my camp comrades. Only one of them could allow herself such a direct question and expect a straight answer without my considering it indiscreet. Jeanne went on, "You're not bored, all alone?"

"I've got a lot of friends, a lot of work."

"You're happy?" She was looking straight into my eyes. "That's not what I meant to say. I know. Are you happy with what you're doing?"

Jeanne was as natural with me as if we'd seen one another quite recently. That's what my comrades mean when they say they feel good among themselves. Between us, there's no effort to be made, no constraints, not even that of common politeness. Between us, it's us. I had no idea what Jeanne had done these twenty years, how she had lived, but it didn't matter. It was as though we'd never lost sight of one another. And yet, Jeanne hadn't been on our convoy. We met her at Raisko—by "we" I mean those survivors who had the good fortune of being sent to the Raisko laboratory commando. Today she was just as she was then, straight-shouldered and serious in her white lab coat, attentive, coming and going, handling the instruments with a sure, light touch, serious and impenetrable before Herr Doktor, loyal and generous toward her comrades, and bold to the point of recklessness when it came to improving our daily fare.

"Jeanne, do you remember the tomatoes?" The question came from the end of the bench. "The tomatoes we stole from the hothouse? What an adventure! You came close to getting caught that time."

"Tomatoes? There were tomatoes at Raisko? It's the first time I've heard that."

"Yes, in the hothouse. Do you remember where it was?"

"I do, but I don't remember any tomatoes."

"Of course they were there. Jeanne had seen tomato plants growing in boxes. They were almost buried in the compost."

"They had acquired a strange taste."

"No, I can't recall any tomatoes. I wasn't part of that expedition."

"Of course you were. Everyone of us was there. You'd even picked more than anyone else, letting a few drop on the way back. I was behind you, picking them up."

"You're sure Charlotte was there the day of the tomatoes? Wasn't it after her departure for Ravensbrück?"

"Sure I'm sure. They—all eight—left Raisko for Ravensbrück at the beginning of January. It was after our performance of *Le Malade imaginaire*, and we gave *Le Malade imaginaire* around Christmastime. The tomatoes were during the preceding summer."

"Tomatoes . . . And we ate them?" I was perplexed. No, I couldn't recall the taste of tomatoes.

"We certainly ate them, believe me!"

"I can't remember ever eating a tomato all the time I was there."

"They certainly tasted like tomatoes, didn't they Jeanne? Funny you don't remember. It was on the day Germaine was caught with a cucumber."

"To hear you talk we spent our days carousing. Cucumbers, tomatoes . . ."

"Germaine hid a large cucumber under her dress. She was caught by the chief garden kapo. The following day, they punished her by sending her back to Birkenau."

"Do you recall how scared we were for Germaine?"

"Yes, I do. That's what must have erased the memory of tomatoes."

"Germaine spent the night in solitary. We were terrified for her."

"Can't you tell a funnier story? It's still curious that you don't remember the tomatoes."

"I know why she doesn't remember. It was the time she was in a daze. She was off her head."

There must have been many times like these, times when I was off my head. How come I feel so lucid now, so much in control? What should we remember and what must we forget in order to keep clear-headed? Stupid to forget those tomatoes. Tomatoes don't constitute a weighty memory. Why not rather forget the smell and color of smoke, the red and sooty flames rising from the smokestacks, twisted by the wind, sending the stench in our direction? Why not rather forget all the morning dead and the evening dead, why not forget the hollow-eyed corpses, their hands twisted like the feet of birds dead from the freezing cold. Why not rather forget thirst, hunger, fatigue, since it does no good to remember all this, and since I'm unable to impart this knowledge? Why not rather forget how time dragged on and on since everyone today firmly believes that twenty-seven months in a lifetime isn't that long, and since I can't explain the difference between our time here and time over there, this one being empty yet heavy with

all the dead, heavy with individually weightless corpses that nevertheless crush you when thousands of skeletons are piled up, let me say
that at least that time over there was empty, while time here is hollow.

"As for me, I remember nothing. (Who was the one who said
this?) Actually, I remember nothing. When people ask me something
about over there, I feel a kind of void opening before me and instead
of being seized by vertigo and stepping back, I run and fall in headlong, plunging into the emptiness under my feet in order to escape.
Only when I'm with all of you do I remember, or perhaps I ought to
say recognize your own remembrances. Generally speaking, you often
evoke them, don't you? I mean, when we're not all of us together?"

"I never do."

"I do. I think people should know. They've got to know. Why
would we have made this great effort to return if it's all for nothing, if
we remain silent, if we don't say what it was like?"

"What good does it do to say it?"

Jeanne kept on questioning me. "How're you keeping? Are you
well? In good health?"

"All right. Some problems of the digestive tract, like almost all the
others."

"You look fine. I'm happy to find you in such good shape."

She was looking at me with the eyes people from over there have,
eyes that see.

"And you?" I hardly dared ask this question. Although I'd found
her former face again, under the wrinkles and faded skin, there was
something about her skin color and her gums that was sickly, even
morbid.

"No, I'm not well. I can't sleep. Since I've come back I hardly
sleep at all. No sleeping pill is able to put me to sleep. I've tried them
all. I fall asleep in the morning, for a couple of hours, and not even
every day. And when I get up in the morning I always have a head-
ache, horrible headaches. I can't wait for my children to grow up,
finish their studies. I'd like to last long enough to see them through. I
manage to live, but is it living? I have to go to bed very early, often

before dinner, because I'm so tired, and yet once I'm in bed I can't sleep. That's why you haven't seen me all these years. I'm always waiting to be in better spirits, more lively, and so I postpone. I know what it comes from. When I came back I had nightmares. I was so terrified of having them that I invented all kinds of excuses to postpone going to sleep. Finally, I lost the ability to fall asleep. Don't you have nightmares?"

"Rarely. I have only one, always the same. It returns once a year, without my noticing whether it follows a conversation or a reminiscence. It's always the same theme: I'm in jail. They let me out on parole, and in the evening I come back, as I promised to do, having had the temptation all day of running away, having tried to lose my way. I never succeed in that; the road always leads to the jail. Always the same theme, though the decor changes: sometimes it's the Santé, other times it's Romainville, or a building I've never seen before, or the concentration camp. The most terrible is the camp. Can you imagine leaving Auschwitz and then returning there in a dream, on one's own initiative? That moment, when I go through the barbed-wire enclosure realizing I'll never have the opportunity to leave again, is so horrible, so oppressive, that I want to cry out, and yet I cannot shout because of the pain in my chest. At last I cry out, and this wakes me up. I see the barbed wire, the miradors, the profile of the smokestacks. I never see anything else. I always cry out before I might see more. It's inexplicable. If I'd tried to escape once and been captured and brought back. But no."

"Has anyone heard from Marceline?"

"Why? Is she sick?"

"They don't know what's the matter with her. Fever. She gets it quite often."

"Every year, she has a kind of fever. It's the anniversary of her typhus attack."

"As for myself (the one speaking sat opposite us), in my nightmares I see all those who died. They beg and call. I hear them but I don't make a move. I'm unable to move. My feet are caught in something. It's atrocious."

"Say, you there at the end of the bench, won't you join the general conversation? If Jeanne came back, it's not so you'll keep her to yourself."

"And what was said in the general conversation?"

The dining-car waiter was ringing his bell in the corridor. We bought some meal tickets from him. "At what time do you have your first seating?"

"Eleven."

"Very good. We'll have plenty of time for lunch. We'll get there at one and the funeral procession is at three. We mustn't miss the transfer bus at the station."

"You hear? We mustn't miss the bus."

"I never miss anything when I'm with you." Everybody laughed.

"Did anyone think of the flowers?"

"Yes, I wired an order. They'll be delivered directly."

And now, shall we go from dream to reality? Reality, what's that?

The stranger walking toward me
was
after so many years
the first man I wanted to kiss.
The city was full
of men I did not see
the stranger coming closer
was the first man I looked at
He was speaking to me
I was not listening
just looking at his lips
feeling like kissing him.
At the moment of separation
I had seen only his mouth
armed with this fragile clue
I leave in search of him
through the city
the city of mornings
the blue city of nights
always another city
eluding me.
I seek and know
we won't be reunited
The whole empty city is mine.

Françoise

To start life over again, what an expression . . . If there is a thing you can't do over again, a thing you can't start over again, it is your life. You could erase and begin anew . . . Erase and cover with writing the words that were there before . . . It doesn't seem possible. How did they do it, those who did it? Graft a new heart upon a bloodless one . . . Where do you find the blood you need to have that patched heart beat again? Lend warmth and movement to that dried up heart . . . Where will the heat come from? The pulse?

When Paul . . . Do you remember that morning in May, the morning when you were called the same time I was? When I was taken to him, walked through the jail's long, echoing corridors to bid him a last farewell, I knew my heart would beat only at my command, pulsating with the life I'd give it to carry on the fight to which we were committed, Paul and I. Why struggle now . . . now that we know, now that the scandal has surfaced, the lie been unveiled? My heart beats only under duress. It will never again find the rhythm of love, love's living palpitation.

When I was called that morning, something in me stopped, and nothing can set it off again, like the watch that stops when the wearer stops living.

When I was summoned that morning, I knew when they called my name that it was to bid Paul farewell. Why call me at five in the morning? Why did they call a woman in jail at five in the morning in the month of May 1942?

When I was called that morning, I knew I'd have to choose, choose right away between living and dying. I chose to live because a soldier was standing there, on my cell's threshold, as I was dressing. Paul had risked his life in fighting this soldier of death, and today, when Paul was losing his life, I could not yield before this death-carrying soldier. I had to hold fast till the end, and die of living.

When I was summoned that morning, I wasn't asleep. One sleeps badly in jail. Because of the lack of air, the lack of motion, because the bed is made of ill-joined, lice-infested boards, because you're hungry and cold, even in May. All of this would not keep you awake. You sleep badly because you think. You think against the wall. I haven't been questioned yet. I'll have to hold out, to resist. I'll have the strength. Yes, I'll be strong. Paul had the strength not to speak when tortured. What is he doing now? Where is he? In this prison or another?

When I was summoned that morning, I knew at least the answer to that last question. Paul was in the same prison as I. Would they have called me for a last farewell had he been in another jail?

In prison, you think against the walls. I thought of Paul. I thought of nothing but Paul. How many walls between him and me? What are they doing to him? They're torturing him. Paul will hold out, but his body will be covered with bruises, his gums stripped bare, his head pounded, his limbs broken, and I hurt where the blows fell on Paul's body, joints, lips, the lips I used to touch so gently so as not to wake him, let him rest, yet unable to resist against the desire to caress them. He was fast asleep, having come back late, exhausted by the long errands in town, all the detours he had to make in order to shake off his shadows before rejoining his fellow fighters. I thought of Paul, trying to recall his smile. His smile would quiver, become a grimace as they tortured him. He'd hold his lips tight. Never again would I see his smile.

My thoughts broke against the walls I wanted to break down in order to make way for hope. A glimmer of hope dimly shining through the cracks in these walls . . . But these were walls without fissures. Will they try him? If there is a judgment, will it result in a death sentence? You stop thinking when your heart has stopped. Is there a possibility, a ray of hope that he might not be sentenced to die? Not a glimmer of hope. He was caught, tortured, and if he didn't die under torture he will surely be dealt a death sentence. The trial might be postponed . . . If it didn't take place at once . . . A miracle could happen, a bomb could fall on the prison, demolishing a section of one of these walls, and Paul could flee; the partisans might dynamite the prison and Paul would be snatched from behind these impregnable walls. You're not thinking anymore, you're delirious. There will be no miracle. Paul is going to die.

When I was summoned that morning, I knew at once that Paul would be shot, shot without a trial, and that he knew it. He knew that his heart would be blown to smithereens by bullets that very morning—for how many days, how many nights did he know this?—he knew his heart would burst and mine beat only enough to endure, to hold fast, that my heart would have just enough strength for that, but no more.

I had to hold fast a long time, much longer than I knew on the morning of our ultimate farewell. I was brought back to my cell. My thoughts no longer collided against the walls, my thoughts had died in that collision. I had to hold fast much longer than I had imagined. Time in Auschwitz was drawn out. I held fast because I had to, and it was hard and long. But hard as it was and protracted, I didn't want it to end. While I was in Auschwitz I had no decisions to make. I preferred not to envision the moment of returning, because I couldn't imagine living without Paul. I was afraid of being free again. Free for what? How would I live without him? I still can't imagine life without him. I've been living so many years in a state of suspension, and had Paul not made me swear, at the moment I was bidding him adieu, that I'd continue living, my heart would have stopped because I'd no longer have ordered it to continue beating.

Make one's life over again . . . When Paul is nothing but a shadow in my memory. When I'll be dead, who will remember the fire he wanted to set to the world so that a new dawn might rise from the ashes? I've lost my taste for that new dawn. What's the good of it without him? And now, the lie has been unmasked.

To make one's life over, what an expression . . . I returned. I resumed my professional life. I have a noble profession; I'm a nurse. Those I care for need me. It is not that I live without Paul, but that I live with the sick. Nothing forces me to leave them when my turn of duty is over. All of me belongs to them. The part of me that knows how to care for the sick is wholly theirs. I go back to our apartment to sleep. I still say "our place." I've never succeeded in saying "my place." After all these years, I sometimes still pretend that Paul left on a trip and will be coming back. It's such a taxing trick, I try not to resort to it. Paul is dead. I keep on repeating it to myself as one must when the person one lived for is no longer there. I'm a sleepwalker that nothing will awaken.

Make one's life over, what an expression . . .

I do not know
if you can still
make something of me
If you have the courage to try . . .

When the revolution comes
I'll draw my brain
from my cranium
and I'll shake it over the city
snow will fall out from it
a snow of dust
of dirty dust
the color of the present time
which will tarnish the flag's scarlet hue

And if it takes too long in coming
I won't even have the strength for that much.

Envoi

A man ready to die for another
that's something to look for
don't say this any longer Beggar
don't say it
there are thousands
who stepped forward for all the others
for you too
Beggar
so that you can salute the dawn
the livid dawn
of all the Mont Valériens
and now
it is called break of day
Beggar
this dawn stained by their blood.

Notes

p. 8: Blockhova (Pol. *blokowa*), the woman in charge of a barrack. Although prisoners themselves, blockhovas had no reputation for kindness toward the inmates.

p. 17: Stubhova (Pol. *sztubowa*), the room senior or orderly.

p. 148: A French spelling and plural of the German *Trage*, meaning hod or barrow.

p. 223: Lottas were a corps of medical assistants who drove ambulances, bandaged wounds, and otherwise aided doctors and nurses in emergency relief. The name derives from Lotta Svard, the heroine of a poem by Johan Ludwig Runeberg about the war between Russia and Sweden over Finland in 1809.

p. 354: The poem "Envoi" is a salute to Delbo's great friend Louis Jouvet, who played the role of the Beggar in his own staging of Jean Giraudoux's *Electra* (1937). In the trilogy Delbo often refer to plays staged by Jouvet, and she may well have identified with the Electra of Giraudoux's play.